Voices of Resistance and Renewal

Voices of Resistance and Renewal

Indigenous Leadership in Education

Edited by

DOROTHY AGUILERA–BLACK BEAR

and JOHN W. TIPPECONNIC III

UNIVERSITY OF OKLAHOMA PRESS : NORMAN

The Raven and the Sun, by Opie Oppenheim of the Nlaka'pamux First Nations of British Columbia, is the logo for the Native Indian Teacher Education Program (NITEP) at the Faculty of Education, University of British Columbia, Vancouver, and is used in chapter 4 of this volume with permission.

Ray Barnhardt's essay in chapter 5 of this volume was originally published in July 2009 as "Theory Z + N: The Role of Alaska Natives in Administration," in *Democracy and Education*, 17(2), and is reprinted here by permission.

Library of Congress Cataloging-in-Publication Data
Voices of resistance and renewal : indigenous leadership in education / edited by Dorothy Aguilera–Black Bear and John W. Tippeconnic III.
    pages cm
    Includes index.
    ISBN 978-0-8061-4867-0 (pbk. : alk. paper)
    1. Indians of North America—Education—United States. 2. Educational leadership—United States. I. Aguilera–Black Bear, Dorothy, 1951– editor, author.
II. Tippeconnic, John, editor, author.
    E97.V66 2015
    371.2'011—dc23
                            2015012858

The paper in this book meets the guidelines for permanence and durability of the Committee on Production Guidelines for Book Longevity of the Council on Library Resources, Inc. ∞

Contents

List of Illustrations   vii

Acknowledgments   ix

Contributors   xi

Introduction, *Dorothy Aguilera–Black Bear and
John W. Tippeconnic III*   3

**Part I: Leadership Informed by Indigenous Epistemologies
within Community Contexts**   **13**

1. Sacred Places: Indigenous Perspectives of Leadership,
   Linda Sue Warner and Keith Grint   15

2. Wóksape: The Identity of Tribal Colleges and Universities,
   Cheryl Crazy Bull   35

3. Guiding Principles of Indigenous Leadership from a Hawaiian
   Perspective, *Alohalani Housman*   49

4. A Raven's Story: Leadership Teachings for an Indigenous Teacher
   Education Program, *Jo-ann Archibald*   76

**Part II: The Way Forward: Preparing Indigenous Leaders
for the Future**   **99**

5. Theory Z + N: The Role of Alaska Natives in Administration,
   Ray Barnhardt   103

6. Native American Doctoral Students: Establishing Legitimacy
   in Higher Education, *Dana E. Christman, Donald Pepion,
   Colleen Bowman, and Brian Dixon*   116

7. Getting the Right Leadership: Ten Things We Learned about
   Being a First-Year Principal, *Joseph Martin*   142

8. Native American Innovative Leadership: Motivations and
   Perspectives on Educational Change, *Linda R. Vogel and
   Harvey A. Rude*   161

9. Indigenous Knowldege and Culture-Based Pedagogy: What Educators Serving Native Children in Mainstream Educational Institutions Must Know, *Lisa Grayshield, Denny Hurtado, and Amileah Davis*   179

10. Concluding Remarks: Exploring Indigenous Leadership in the Journey to Self-Determination, *Dorothy Aguilera–Black Bear*   193

Index   205

Illustrations

FIGURES

4.1. NITEP logo, *The Raven and the Sun*   79

4.2. NITEP Holistic Model   80

TABLE

3.1. The Guiding Principles of Indigenous Leadership through the Lens of the Kumu Honua Mauli Ola Philosophy   58–60

4.1. NITEP Graduates' Levels of Education   89

5.1. Contrasting Tendencies of Type A and Type Z Management   107

Acknowledgments

While this book is not intended to be one voice or authoritative statement about leadership or Indigenous epistemologies, the compilation of this body of research, its theoretical and conceptual ideas, and its theory-to-practice examples are meant to stimulate dialogue and action among educators. The book is filled with stories that represent the imaginations, the visions, and the concentrated efforts of but a few Indigenous communities out of many who have shaped the journey to self-determination. Additional and significant contributions on this journey not mentioned in this book have been made by many other communities. We honor all of you and your commitments and efforts as leaders in this journey to self-determination. We thank all our relations, whose knowledge, wisdom, and strength for survival and leadership continue to impact our personal lives and our communities in positive ways. We also want to give recognition to the many scholars previous to this research volume who contributed to the creation of the critical lenses, theoretical frameworks and tenets of Indigenous paradigms and methodologies used by the authors in this book to define, describe, explain and expand theories about community-based Indigenous leadership and leadership in education institutions. We honor our ancestors who teach us to be strong and proud, to learn our knowledge, language, and traditions, and to keep these forever.

Contributors

ABOUT THE EDITORS

Dorothy Aguilera–Black Bear, Choctaw, is currently a research consultant. She is the former vice president of the Office of Research and Sponsored Programs at the American Indian College Fund. Before joining the College Fund, Dorothy was the director of the Office of Institutional Research at Northwest Indian College providing support for the strategic plan, institutional reports, and evaluation of sponsored programs. Prior to working at a tribal college, she held faculty positions in educational leadership programs and provided mentoring, advising, and academic support to Native graduate students at several universities. In 2003, Dorothy earned her Ph.D. at the University of Colorado–Boulder in Educational Foundations, Policy, and Practice. She has twenty-plus years of experience teaching in the fields of educational leadership, multicultural foundations of education, ethnic studies, and research and evaluation methodology. Her dissertation was a comparison of fourteen case studies of school reform models including Indigenously controlled reforms in schools serving Native American populations. Dorothy developed a rigorous measurement to assess culturally responsive education (CRE) at the classroom level (curriculum, pedagogy, assessment) as a way to understand how CRE impacted student success outcomes. As a research consultant, Dorothy has conducted national, state, and local research and evaluation on innovative program development projects with preK–12 and higher education serving Native communities in rural and urban areas since 1993.

John W. Tippeconnic III, a member of the Comanche Tribe and part Cherokee, is professor and director of American Indian studies at Arizona State University. He was a professor of educational leadership and policy studies at Pennsylvania State University, where he directed an American Indian leadership program. John is the former director of the Office of Indian Education Programs for the Bureau of Indian Affairs (BIA). He also was the director of the Office of Indian Education (OIE) located in the U.S. Department of Education and served as vice president of Navajo Community College (now Diné College). His publications include the coedited book *Next Steps: Research and Practice to Advance Indian Education* and the study *The Dropout/Graduation Crisis among American Indian and Alaska Native Students*. He coedited a special issue of the *Journal of American Indian Education* on *Culturally Responsive Education for American Indian, Alaskan Native and Native Hawaiian Students*. He currently serves on the editorial boards of the *Journal of Diversity in Higher Education* and the *Journal of American Indian Education*. He served two terms as president of the National Indian Education Association and chair of the American Educational Research Association American Indian Education Special Interest Group. He was a founding member of the Governing Board of Comanche Nation College, the first tribal college in Oklahoma. In 2011 he was named a fellow by the American Educational Research Association. In 2012 the National Indian Education Association awarded him a Lifetime Achievement Award for his work in the education of American Indians and Alaska Natives.

ABOUT THE AUTHORS

Jo-ann Archibald, Q'um Q'um Xiiem, associate dean of Indigenous Education and Native Indian Teacher Education Program (NITEP) director, is from the Sto:lo-River People and the Xaxli'p First Nation (Lillooet). In 2011, Jo-ann returned to NITEP as its director and began her second term as associate dean for Indigenous Education in the University of British Columbia's Faculty of Education. Her journey with NITEP began in 1981 when she was a sessional lecturer at the various field centers in British Columbia. From 1983 to 1985, she was the Chilliwack Field Centre coordinator and then went to Vancouver to become the NITEP director and has been in and out of that role since 1992. Jo-ann has worked in education for more than forty years.

Raymond Barnhardt is a professor emeritus of cross-cultural studies at the University of Alaska–Fairbanks, where he was involved in teaching and research related to Native education issues since 1970. Over the past thirty-five years, Ray served as the director of the Cross-Cultural Education Development (X-CED) Program, the Small High Schools Project, the Center for Cross-Cultural Studies, the Alaska Rural Systemic Initiative, and the Alaska Native Knowledge Network. His experiences in education beyond Alaska ranged from teaching mathematics in Baltimore, Maryland, to research in Canada, Iceland, India, Malawi, Zimbabwe, and New Zealand.

Colleen Bowman, Navajo, received her doctorate in educational leadership at New Mexico State University. She is the human resources manager at Navajo Nation Head Start. She previously was the principal at Navajo Middle School and before that was the Student Success coordinator at Central Consolidated School District.

Cheryl Crazy Bull, Wacinyanpi Win (They Depend on Her), is Sicangu Lakota from the Rosebud Reservation in South Dakota. Cheryl has served as the president/CEO of the American Indian College Fund since September 2012. Previously, she served as president of Northwest Indian College for ten years. Cheryl was also the chair of the American Indian Higher Education Consortium (AIHEC) for four years as well as serving four years as member-at-large of the AIHEC Executive Committee. Her work experience includes seventeen years at Sinte Gleska University and more than four years as chief educational officer at Saint Francis Indian School, both on the Rosebud Reservation.

Dana E. Christman, Cherokee, is an associate professor of educational management and development at New Mexico State University. Dr. Christman has strong research interests in women's leadership in education as well as Indigenous, American Indian, and social justice leadership issues.

Amileah Davis, Métis and African American, is a doctoral student at New Mexico State University and has studied several disciplines within the field of mental health, including behavioral science and human factors, generalist social work practice, and psychology. She has conducted research within each field. As a counseling psychologist in training, she has clinical and scientific experience obtained by participating in a Native American Research Centers for Health Mentoring Internship.

Brian Dixon, Navajo, is the principal at the Whitehorse High School, San Juan School District in Utah. He is working on his doctoral degree at New Mexico State University.

Alohalani Housman, Native Hawaiian, is an associate professor of Indigenous education at the University of Hawai'i at Hilo. She currently serves as division chair and director of Hale Kuamoʻo Hawaiian Language Curriculum Center, a division of UH Hilo's Ka Haka 'Ula O Keʻelikōlani College of Hawaiian Language. She specializes in language arts, and her research focuses primarily on the literacy curriculum used in Hawaiian language immersion schools statewide.

Denny Hurtado (TacH-Mi-acH-t3n), Skokomish, spent the past forty years advocating for American Indian rights, especially for issues related to the education of Native children. He received a master's degree in school administration from the California State University at Humboldt, a bachelor's degree in social science, and a lifetime secondary teaching credential from the California State University at Sacramento. Denny was the Indian Education director for Washington State's Office of the Superintendent of Public Instruction for seventeen years before retiring in 2013. In this position, he worked with all twenty-nine tribes in Washington State. He helped develop Washington State's groundbreaking online curriculum for kindergarten through high school students, "Since Time Immemorial: Tribal Sovereignty," and the Northwest Native American Reading curriculum (kindergarten through third grade) that focuses on Native lifeways and traditions. Denny also served on the Skokomish Tribal Council for seventeen years, holding the positions of chair, vice-chair, and general council president.

Lisa Grayshield, a member of the Washoe Tribe of Nevada and California, is an associate professor in counseling and educational psychology at New Mexico State University (NMSU). Her research interests include Indigenous ways of knowing (IWOK) in counseling and psychology, which incorporates Indigenous knowledge forms as viable options for the way counseling and psychology is conceptualized, taught, practiced, and researched. She has served the NMSU community as a board member for the Teaching Academy and as an active member of the NMSU Tribal Voice Group. Lisa previously served on the Diversity Committee and the College of Education's Sustainability Committee and worked with the local community as a board member for Indigenous Nations for Community Action (INCA). She was recently elected as the vice president of the Native Concerns Group for the American Multicultural Counseling Division (AMCD).

Keith Grint, professor of public leadership and management, University of Warwick, U.K., spent ten years in industry before switching to an academic career. He previously taught at Brunel University and Oxford University and held chairs at Lancaster and Cranfield Universities. Keith is a member of the Sunningdale Institute, National School of Government.

Joseph Martin, Diné, is special adviser to the president of Northern Arizona University. Joe formerly worked as a leadership coach serving superintendents for the Wallace Leadership Project in the northern portion of Arizona. He served as superintendent in the Kayenta Unified District for twelve years prior to becoming professor at Northern Arizona University (NAU). Dr. Martin has more than twenty-five years of school administration experience, including an extensive background consulting with schools serving American Indian students, school board training, and tribal education departments; and he worked with the U.S. Department of Education. While serving as superintendent, he developed a strong partnership with NAU and the University of Colorado, focusing on special education and teacher training initiatives.

Donald Pepion, Blackfeet, is currently an associate professor at New Mexico State University–Las Cruces in the Anthropology Department. Don was the former director of NMSU's American Indian Program and has been at NMSU since 2007. He also was a former president of the Blackfeet Community College, the tribal health director, and the housing authority director in Montana. He earned both a master's and doctoral degree in education at Montana State University.

Harvey A. Rude is professor and director of the School of Special Education and the director of the Bresnahan-Halstead Center on Disabilities at University of Northern Colorado (UNC). He has a thirty-seven-year career in education, with thirty of those at UNC. His areas of expertise and experience are in teacher quality, special education leadership/management effectiveness, systems of accountability, teacher leadership, policy studies, consensus and negotiation skills, professional development systems, strategic thinking and planning, Native American education, systems change, and adoption of innovations.

Linda R. Vogel is a professor of educational leadership and policy studies at the University of Northern Colorado, where she has taught for seven years. Her areas of expertise and experience are state and local education (preK–12) leadership, assessment, teacher and administrator evaluation, standards-based curricular implementation, school improvement, professional development, school reform policy and finance, leadership for the development of assessment literacy, and development of educational policy.

Linda Sue Warner, a member of the Comanche Tribe of Oklahoma, completed her Ph.D. at the University of Oklahoma in 1989. She earned a master's degree in education administration at Penn State in 1978 and a bachelor of arts in language arts and education from Northeastern State University in 1970. Warner began teaching in 1970 and has worked in various teaching and administrative positions across the United States. Warner's various honors include being appointed, by the White House, to the National Advisory Council of American Indian Education, appointment to the Board of the Foundation for Excellence in American Indian Education in the U.S. Department of Interior, and appointment to the Negotiated Rule-Making Committee for Highly Qualified Teachers in the U.S. Department of Education.

Voices of Resistance and Renewal

Introduction

DOROTHY AGUILERA–BLACK BEAR
AND JOHN W. TIPPECONNIC III

This book introduces a new body of research literature that examines the application of principles of leadership for the purposes of self-determination and educational sovereignty. In particular, it examines Indigenous epistemologies and the principles and practices of leadership within localized contexts, including the function of education in Indigenous societies. Often constrained by the hegemonic tensions of mainstream[1] educational institutions and leadership theories primarily framed by Western paradigms and business models, leadership for the purposes of self-determination and educational sovereignty must be framed within Indigenous paradigms and examined through Indigenous lenses. This volume discusses perspectives on self-determination and sovereignty in education in two sections, respectively, addressing theoretical foundations in Indigenous leadership within community contexts and the knowledge and pedagogy for preparing leaders for decolonizing education. While each section provides knowledge and practice useful for educators who are administrators and teachers, the book's intention is to describe contemporary Indigenous leadership that focuses more pointedly on developing educational sovereignty through action-oriented leadership for self-determination. The contexts of the discourses in this book are varied; however, they are geographically and politically grounded in the work of American Indian Nations in the U.S. and Canadian First Nations communities.[2]

To politicize the discourse around, and the processes of, taking control of educational systems is to make visible the ongoing struggles Indigenous people undergo in moving toward decolonization, especially developing resistance to the colonizing of Indigenous minds through formal education. Developing sovereignty in education has been a slow process because leadership in schools serving Indigenous populations has historically been held by nonlocal administrators who, at best, have limited knowledge about the community and at worst, either intentionally or blindly, fulfill a hegemonic agenda (policy and practice) of state and federal systems that undermines the

Indigenous community's right to self-determination and cultural sovereignty in education.[3] Below, we offer some definitions for terms used in this book.

Education, in the broad sense, refers to the process of acquiring knowledge and life skills, including values and attitudes to prepare individuals to be valued members of societies; education is about the transmission of culture from one generation to the next. Cajete refers to education as the complex nature of activities that form human learning. In essence, education is "learning about life through participation and relationship in community, including not only people, but plants, animals, the whole of Nature." Teaching and learning are integral elements of this complexity, as is the ecology of Indigenous education. The context in how education is used often defines its meaning. "Culturally based forms of education that are not rooted in modern Western educational philosophy and methodology" represent the Indigenous context.[4]

*Formal and informal education*s are concepts that overlap and are not mutually exclusive in their meaning. Lomawaima and McCarty note that "in the American imagination of education, we often refer to everything within schools as formal education and everything outside of school walls as informal" education. *Schools* are considered institutions, most often physical structures where instruction takes place. Schools that ignore or resist the ecology of Indigenous education and emphasize integration and assimilation into mainstream society at the expense of Indigenous languages and cultures fail to provide students a culturally responsive education. Lomawaima and McCarty point out that this "artificial dichotomy" between formal and informal fails to describe the complex nature of education inside and outside of schools and devalues, labels and marginalizes Native education as "accidental" or "unplanned." In reality, all education uses both formal and informal learning, including Indigenous or Native education. Lomawaima and McCarty further note that Indigenous systems of education are formal, organized, and intentionally designed to achieve pedagogical goals, in other words, traditional Indigenous education is highly sophisticated in its teaching and learning.[5] Deloria, in noting the relationship between Western and Indigenous people, states the education "journey spans two distinct value systems and world views . . . in that meeting ground lies the opportunity for the two cultures to both teach and learn from one another.[6]

Self-determination in education involves controlling one's destiny and having access to an education embedded in one's community values, cultural traditions, and knowledge systems (also termed culturally responsive education). Its purpose is developing children into healthy

Native adults who will actively participate in leadership for community development and citizenship for tribal nation building.

While self-determination and control of a culturally responsive education (CRE) was provided to Euro-Americans with the settler colonial system of education in the United States, Indigenous communities were denied this same right—because all schools available to them were run by Euro-Americans—until the Indian Self-Determination and Education Assistance Act Public Law No. 93–638, 88 Stat. 2203 (1975) provided the legal authority for tribal control of education.[7] However, despite this act, the extent to which tribal or Indigenous control of education has been limited cannot be ignored, especially when examining how leadership and CRE—as guiding principles of education—factor into the goals and implementation of self-determination. Tenorio writes, "The privileging of education models based on Western norms and power structures has denied the validity of tribal sovereignty and the rights of tribal communities to fulfill their legal rights to participate as legitimate partners in [the] design and management of their future generations' education."[8]

Educational sovereignty involves decolonizing the systems of a solely Western worldview education and specifically developing culturally responsive education systems to replace assimilationist models of education. It is considered imperative to the cultural sovereignty and survival of Indigenous communities.

Lyons provides a broader definition of sovereignty as "a people's right to rebuild its demand to exist and present its gifts to the world . . . an adamant refusal to dissociate culture, identity, and power from the land."[9] Educational sovereignty occurs when Indigenous communities confront and decolonize hegemonic structures by establishing schools that embrace Indigenous values and beliefs and teach their cultural and traditional knowledge (especially through Indigenous languages) as decided locally by their cultural bearers and realized with the establishment of tribal departments and committees. Thus educational sovereignty addresses Native students' rights to their Indigenous knowledge, including languages, in schools; culturally specific education can facilitate the journey of decolonization from oppression into the freedom of cultural sovereignty. Moll argues that "educational sovereignty must attend to the larger historical structures and ideologies of schooling with the goal of making educational constraints, especially those related to social class, visible and unstable for all in the school; and educational sovereignty must include developing social agency that situates teaching and learning as part of a broader education ecology that taps into existing social and cultural resources in schools, households, and communities in promoting change."[10]

> *Indigenous epistemologies* are bodies of knowledge described as world-views—value and belief systems—ways of knowing the world and relationships with ancestors, other humans, animals, universal life, spirit beings, and all objects in the universe.

Ways of knowing are contextualized vast bodies of knowledge that exist and coexist within a place, a people, their cultural norms and mores, and all that exists in their physical and spiritual worlds. It should be noted that all peoples have such epistemologies; it is only when hegemonic forces enforce one group's epistemology onto another group and deny the legitimacy of the latter's that epistemologies become colonial. Unfortunately, since epistemologies usually define how the world is "supposed to be," colonial epistemologies seek to normalize the "other" by enforcing their own worldview upon a group for whom it is alien.

Contemporary perspectives and ways of knowing and living are informed by reiterative cycles of past, present, and future; relationships are framed by worldviews of ancient origin and ancestors with roles for sustaining Indigenous knowledge.

> Aboriginal epistemology is grounded in the self, the spirit, the unknown. Understanding of the universe must be grounded in the spirit. Knowledge must be sought through the stream of the inner space in unison with all instruments of knowing and conditions that make individuals receptive to knowing. Ultimately it was in the self that Aboriginal people discovered great resources for coming to grips with life's mysteries. It was in the self that the richest source of information could be found by delving into the metaphysical and the nature and origin of knowledge. Aboriginal epistemology speaks of pondering great mysteries that lie no further than the self.[11]

> *Indigenous worldviews* have been described as personal, oral, experiential, local, holistic, and conveyed in narrative or metaphorical language; knowledge is holistic, cyclic, and dependent upon relationships and connections to living and nonliving beings and entities; there are many truths, and these truths are dependent upon individual experiences; everything is alive; all things are equal; the land is sacred; the relationship between people and the spiritual world is important; and, human beings as relationally par with that world.[12]

In terms of better understanding these conceptual ideas, we suggest attention be given to the process of understanding, which requires the inquirer to be open to accepting different realities, regardless of how one uses this term.[13]

OVERVIEW OF BOOK

This book represents research that examines and expands conceptual ideas and perspectives about leadership for a people or group, and leadership for self-determination and educational sovereignty within the contexts of Indigenous communities and higher education institutions. Other topics include political influences and paradigms that either mitigate or impede effective leadership in schools serving Indigenous populations and that affect community control of schools serving predominately Native students, including the standards for success, language used to deliver content, the curriculum, pedagogy, and assessments. Reclaiming self-determination in education and the rights to a culturally relevant education in schools is an ongoing struggle among Indigenous peoples around the world. The longevity and intensity of hegemonic education systems imposed on Native children has undermined tribal nations' powers for self-governance and self-determination in all facets of life and society.[14]

A premise of this work is that educators must have sufficient "intellectual capital" of Indigenous knowledge and leadership skills to facilitate the attainment of self-determination and an educational sovereignty that is shaped and informed within the localized community context. In *Decolonizing Methodologies*, Linda T. Smith states, "The idea of community is defined or imagined in multiple ways as social, psychological, physical, political, historical, linguistic, economic, cultural, and spiritual spaces."[15] The concept of community is also shared among Indigenous peoples based on similar epistemological ideas about the world, relationships and kinship. Denzin, Lincoln, and Smith write, "Indigenous notions of power are defined as being rooted in concepts of respect, balance, reciprocity, and peaceful coexistence."[16] In this book, conceptual ideas of leadership and educational sovereignty are described within a variety of contexts—Indigenous and mainstream communities and tribal, state and federal institutions—and the intersections and relationships among these entities.

Conceptualized as a product from the National Indian Education Association (NIEA) Leadership Research Forums, this book emerged from a dialogic process that brought together community leaders, activists, educators, and researchers to share their views and experiences regarding the evolving roles of leaders in Indigenous communities. The forum was designed as two sessions, including (1) examining the community-based knowledge and the research literature around Indigenous epistemologies and theoretical ideas about leadership, and (2) leaders' perspectives and reflections about their own practices as these are grounded in theoretical ideas and occur within their communities. We began this self-determination dialogue first at NIEA in 2008 and then again in 2009 in an open forum where authors and attendees, many of whom were community leaders, shared their visions, experiences, traditional knowledge, concerns, and relevant ideas as leaders in preK–12 and higher education institutions, tribal governance, and federal programs administration. Invited scholars were asked to join in exploring thematic questions emerging from conference dialogues about how leadership practice and experience were fundamental to Native people as they participate in educational leadership and teacher education programs in mainstream universities. What was glaringly clear from these dialogues was the need for ongoing collaboration and conversations among Native community leaders and educational leaders about self-determination and educational sovereignty. Forum participants told us they want conversations that will lead to action at national, state, and local levels. They also want to see educational leadership and teacher education programs that directly support community goals to revitalize and preserve language and cultural knowledge through educational systems serving Indigenous populations. Much of the dialogue centered on how tribes that control schools serving Native children should operate and how Native educators and leaders can create education systems embedded in Indigenous languages and cultures. A conclusion shared by many forum participants was that Native leadership in education is essential to self-determination because of the miseducation of Native children in schools and consequent colonization across generations of Indigenous peoples. Because resistance to historically anti-Indigenous education was deemed vital to tribal sovereignty, community leadership for improving schools was framed by forum attendees as a vital component of achieving self-determination in education. By revitalizing language and culture and preserving Indigenous knowledge systems, educational institutions actually will begin to function to serve tribal nations. Educational sovereignty at the local level has been driven by both the strong desire to reclaim Indigenous knowledge and by the extremes of postcolonial practice that continue to impact Indigenous communities around the globe.

This volume also explores educational leadership programs to better understand which approaches and processes these programs use to build on the knowledge, experience, and ability that Native students have so as to provide an education that serves their community's self-determination and sovereignty goals. These authors illustrate the principles and leadership practice of Indigenous education and explain why education in Indigenous communities must be understood within the epistemologies that inform both their value and belief systems and knowledge about how the world works. Cajete writes that, quite differently from Western notions of education, "What is called education today was, for American Indians, a journey for learning to be fully human. Learning about the nature of the spirit in relationship to community and the environment was considered central to learning the full meaning of life."[17]

This book provides examples of educational programs that were established through a process of collaboration among leaders in Indigenous communities and faculty in mainstream education institutions. These partnerships contribute to the decolonizing of educational systems, which have historically underserved Indigenous communities and undermined their self-determination and sovereignty.[18] Working toward self-determination through effective leadership practices and political positioning of sovereignty in local education policies can establish local control and resources to support Indigenous knowledge systems in schools; these, in turn, can support healthy child development. Having Native leadership and teachers in schools serving Indigenous populations is an initial step that many see as imperative to educational sovereignty. We recognize the importance of having Native leadership and governance of schools; we also recognize particularly that the existence of Native teachers solidifies children's cultural identity, an essential component of their healthy development. We acknowledge that teacher/leaders and community leadership are lifelines to development and achievement of the vision of Indigenous education that exists in our communities.

The book represents current empirical research grounded in Indigenous epistemology and conceptual ideas about community-based leadership and the perspectives of Native scholars about leadership. These articles contribute to the limited literature in the field of Indigenous education, especially about leadership available to educators, administrators, scholars, and general audiences interested in contemporary perspectives and issues regarding educational sovereignty. This body of research literature provides interdisciplinary content for culturally relevant professional development programs in preK–12 and higher education, and informs leadership about Indigenous perspectives in tribal governance, administration, health and human development, and community and economic development.[19] The scholars whose works are included in this volume provide a variety of philosophical lenses and guiding principles with which leaders at all levels of education and tribal governing systems can support and can use to address self-determination and educational sovereignty issues.

NOTES

1. Mainstream and Western education and worldviews are used interchangeably in this book by numerous authors.

2. Indigenous, native, tribe, Native American, American Indian, First Nations are used interchangeably in this book to describe Indigenous people. American Indian/Alaska Native is abbreviated as AI/AN throughout this volume.

3. Aguilera, D. E., and LeCompte, M. D. (2009). Restore my language and treat me justly: Indigenous students' rights to their Tribal languages. In J. C. Scott, D. Y.

Straker, and L. Katz (Eds.), *Affirming students' right to their own language: Bridging educational policies to language/language arts teaching practices* (pp. 130–72). London: Routledge.

4. Cajete, G. (1994). *Look to the mountain: An ecology of Indigenous education* (pp. 26, 15). Skyland, NC: Kivaki Press.

5. Lomawaima, K. T., and McCarty, T. L. (2006). *To remain an Indian: Lessons in democracy from a century of Native American education.* New York: Teachers College Press.

6. Deloria, V., and Wildcat, D. R. (2001). *Power and place: Indian education in America* (back cover of book). Golden, CO: Fulcrum Resources.

7. The Indian Self-Determination and Education Assistance Act, Pub. L. 93–638, encompasses two acts. Title I is typically referred to as the Indian Self-Determination Act and appears generally at 25 U.S.C. §§ 450f–450n. Title II is known as the Indian Education Assistance Act and appears generally at 25 U.S.C. §§ 455–458e. For full classification of these Acts, consult the tables volumes of the U.S. Code, U.S.C.A., or U.S.C.S. URL address is: Pub. L. No. 93–638, 88 Stat. 2203 (1975).

8. Tenorio, M. (2011). Community-based leadership and the exercise of tribal sovereignty in public school education (Doctoral dissertation). Lewis and Clark College, Portland, Oregon.

9. Lyons, S. R. (2000). Rhetorical sovereignty: What do American Indians want from writing? *College, Composition and Communication, 51,* 457, 447–468.

10. Moll, L. (Fall 2002). Keynote Address at the University of Pennsylvania: The concept of educational sovereignty. *Penn GSE Perspectives on Urban Education, 1*(2), 1–11.

11. Ermine, W. (1999). Aboriginal epistemology. In M. Battiste and J. Barman (Eds.), *First Nations education in Canada: The circle unfolds* (p. 108). Vancouver: University of British Columbia Press.

12. Castellano, M. B. (2000). Updating Aboriginal traditions of knowledge, in G. J. S. Dei, B. L. Hall, and D. G. Rosenburg (Eds.), *Indigenous knowledges in global contexts* (pp. 21–36). Toronto: University of Toronto Press; Maurial, M. (1999). Indigenous knowledge and schooling: A continuum between conflict and dialogue. In L. M. Semali and J. L. Kincheloe (Eds.), *What is Indigenous knowledge: Voices from the academy* (pp. 59–77). New York: Falmer Press; Simpson, L. (2000). Anishinaabe ways of knowing. In J. Oakes, R. Riew, S. Koolage, L. Simpson, and N. Schuster (Eds.), *Aboriginal health, identity and resources* (pp. 165–85). Winnipeg: Native Studies Press.

13. Battiste, M., and Henderson, J. S. Y. (2000). *Protecting Indigenous knowledge and heritage.* Saskatoon: Purich.

14. Swisher, K. C., and Tippeconnic, J. W., III, (Eds.) (1999). *Next steps: Research and practice to advance Indian education.* Charleston, WV: Clearinghouse on Rural Education and Small Schools.

15. Smith, L. T. (1999). *Decolonizing methodologies* (p. 125). Dunedin, New Zealand: Zed Books Ltd., University of Otago Press.

16. Denzin, N. K., Lincoln, Y. S., and Smith, L. T. (2008). *Handbook of critical Indigenous methodology* (p. 252). Thousand Oaks, CA: Sage.

17. Cajete, G. (1994). *Look to the mountain: An ecology of Indigenous education* (p. 223). Skyland, NC: Kivaki Press.

18. Deloria, V., and Wildcat, D. R. (2001). *Power and place: Indian education in America*. Golden, CO: Fulcrum Resources.

19. To examine the historical information on legislation for Indigenous education we suggest Hale, L. (2002). *Native American education: A reference handbook*. Santa Barbara: ABC-CLIO.

PART I

LEADERSHIP INFORMED BY INDIGENOUS EPISTEMOLOGIES WITHIN COMMUNITY CONTEXTS

Community-based leadership is fundamental to achieving self-determination in education. It is within the structures of Indigenous self-determination in local schools that culturally responsive education is possible. Indigenous leadership addresses the processes of self-determination by which tribal members become key players in local schools, including deciding what knowledge is taught, how it is taught, by whom, and to whom. We maintain that establishing teacher and educational leader preparation programs within Indigenous communities is central to achieving the joint goals of self-determination and educational sovereignty. Localized leadership that is consistent in advocating for and providing culturally responsive education is key to achieving educational sovereignty. Cajete (1994) argues that Indigenous leaders "need to advocate [for] culture-based education to achieve the foundational goals of self-determination, self-governance, and Tribal sovereignty" (p. 18). This suggests that community-based leadership must be localized (culturally informed), proactive, productive, inclusive, and consistent in schools to attain the desired outcomes of tribal communities. Community-based leadership is essential to developing institutions of education that serve the goals of tribal nation communities and especially with issues concerning sovereignty and self-determination (Tenorio, 2011). While Indigenous leadership has increased in the governance of schools on reservation lands, particularly tribally controlled colleges and schools, public school districts remain ignorant of the legal foundations of tribal governance and self-determination in the local K–12 schools attended by 90 percent of tribal children.

The chapters in this section provide insights into how leadership is shaped by Indigenous knowledge specific to a place and a people. Authors share stories that help the reader understand how leadership for Indigenous peoples is very much situated within a historically and culturally informed context known as community that is distinct ecologically—in a place, with a people, and based on a distinctive knowledge base. These leadership stories are historically grounded in place and time and create a better understanding of leadership within a community context. Respect for the local community is a key to such leadership, along with knowing the historical, spiritual, and cultural context of the community. Non-Native educators must learn these teachings from within the community not outside the Indigenous communities they serve. Educational leaders typically begin their careers as teachers, and after several years or more decide to earn an administrator degree and license so as to step into a principal position in their school. However, Native leadership often begins from within the community context rather than within the educational institution and context. This section of the book provides some guidance for educators aspiring to become culturally responsive leaders and discusses place-based identity and leadership. Questions that guided this research include: How does local knowledge inform community based leadership practice? What Indigenous epistemologies inform the practice of Native and non-Native leaders?

REFERENCES

Cajete, G. (1994). *Look to the mountain: An ecology of Indigenous education.* Skyland, NC: Kivaki Press.

Tenorio, M. (2011). Community-based leadership and the exercise of tribal sovereignty in public school education (Doctoral dissertation). Lewis and Clark College, Portland, Oregon.

1

Sacred Places

Indigenous Perspectives of Leadership

LINDA SUE WARNER AND KEITH GRINT

OUR PLACE

For many Indigenous peoples in the United States, a sense of place represents who you are and where you come from as well as where you will go. Recognizing that "sense of place" has different meanings for different people, we describe "place" as a dynamic of indigeneity because it is actualized as honoring relatives, those who came before and those who will come after, and because it links the individual with his/her community. This chapter includes a focus on the geographic place that fosters Indigenous perspectives of leadership as well as the philosophical understanding that each individual holds to legitimize a place within a tribal community. We offer perspectives informed by Indigenous epistemologies as described by Native scholars. A sense of place is at the heart of our cultural identity, traditions, and practices. Our lands are the place of our ancestors and carry the spirits of our ancestors. According to traditions, the land lives just as humans do and that the land holds the spirits of our ancestors. We trace our lands and ancestors in the same lineage and traditional way that can be passed down over many generations. Our elders and spiritual leaders teach the traditional ways of living collectively with the land.

From a political stance, we argue that in this country, the sociohistorical impact of the federal government's land policies on the sovereign rights and lives of Indigenous peoples includes (1) denial of rights to land and use of and access to natural resources, (2) disruption of ties to the environment, and (3) loss or weakening of cultural knowledge, language, and identity.

In each of these three areas, we find that leadership systems have been destroyed. For example, a community leader who accepts the mainstream policies or laws that govern the land (perhaps even relocation) can be accused of betraying his/her people. Stories of "fort" Indians are examples of such characterizations. If leaders resisted mainstream policies or laws, then historically the government forced them to acquiesce. Leaders became powerless or martyred in these conflicts. The United States has a well-documented history of attempted separation of Native people from their traditional homelands. This separation from traditional homelands contributes to the designation of "sacred." We propose that what counts as sacred has been diluted through translation into the English language and within the legal parameters of the social institutions of invading governments.[1] The loss of traditional lands and the establishment of reservation lands by the federal government with tribal nations through treaties is linked to that which has been profaned (i.e., the killing of local inhabitants by invaders); these barbaric acts of war transform the "traditional homelands," which held sacred status with ceremonial traditions for time immemorial, into places that have been profaned by the colonizing power—for example, when a place that is considered sacred by the local inhabitants is destroyed, such as an ancient burial site or other ceremonial site when there is construction over their sites' sacred edifices.

LEADERSHIP AND SURVIVAL

The history of the oppression of Indigenous people in the United States is marked by significant incidents of forced removal, specifically removal from places attached to sacred ceremonies and also to leadership or survival. The result of these geographic displacements requires rethinking and expansion of the idea of "place" from one defined solely by legal boundaries to one that includes finding a "space" for the sacred especially informed by Indigenous paradigms. This newer conceptualization moves place and leadership into a situational context. The link to sacred becomes more individualized and allows for the merger of leadership and place. While recorded history is more often than not written from the perspective of the oppressor, the result still matches Indigenous oral histories of removal and the ongoing attempts to recover tribal homelands and to maintain sacred sites. Of course, many of the Indigenous populations were not Indigenous to the land they were displaced from but had already been displaced by previous populations.

Our place, today known as the United States, represents a wide diversity of Native peoples. This diversity of Indigenous nations was thriving in 1491. Henrietta (Mann) Whiteman (1978) supports the perspective that Indigenous peoples have always provided a culturally rich education grounded in traditions. These traditions and education are also linked to geographical and spiritually sacred places. Whiteman articulates, "Contrary to popular belief, education—the transmission and acquisition of knowledge and skills—did not come to the North American continent on the *Nina, Pinta* and *Santa Maria.* . . . We Native Americans have educated our youth through a rich and oral tradition, which was—and is today—transmitted by the elders of the tribe" (p. 105).

In the United States, the disregard for sacredness of the land to Indigenous peoples is linked particularly to Locke's (1960, p. 329) proselytizing that allowed Europeans to displace Indigenous people by deceiving themselves into thinking that the land was "empty" or that ownership of land was derived from "working the land." Hämäläinen's (2008) book describes the Comanche empire, which surpassed the European rivals in military strategy and in political, economic, and cultural force from 1750 to 1850, and challenges historical perspectives. He tells the story of an Indigenous nation's people who "expand, dictate, and prosper, and European colonists resist, retreat, and struggle to survive" (p. 1). Pekka Hämäläinen states:

> Herein lay the ultimate paradox. While initially Comanche adjusted their traditions, behaviors, and even beliefs to accommodate the arrival of Europeans and their technologies, they later turned the tables on Europe's colonial expansion by simply refusing to change. By preserving the essentials of their traditional ways—by expecting others to conform to their cultural order—they forced the colonists to adjust to a world that was foreign, uncontrollable, and increasingly, unlivable. (p. 16)

As one piece of evidence for his theory, Hämäläinen reviewed the replication of Stephen Austin's map of the American Southwest in which Austin depicted a Eurocentric bias about the era and "diminished and delegitimized the power and territorial claims of Indigenous inhabitants" (p. 195).[2] The erroneous idea that Indigenous people were not using the land properly allowed widespread theft, legalized by white man's laws, but nonetheless constituting human rights violations by most societal standards.

Leadership in these diverse communities can be found in just as many diverse contexts. American Indian, Alaska Native, and Native Hawaiian tribal leadership models range from elected, regional representatives—a governance model attributed to Native people and described as the template used by American revolutionaries to create the U.S. Congress—to traditional hereditary chiefs. Leadership models in those communities, like any large, contemporary organizations mirror appointed and elected leadership activities. Culturally, there is evidence of traditional patriarchal societies among Native peoples, as well as traditional matriarchal societies (Terrell and Terrell, 1974, p. 28). There is further evidence to suggest that diverse leadership models flourished prior to white contact. The Iroquois Confederacy has been described as the purest form of matriarchy ever to have existed in modern or ancient times (Anderson, 1981).

Each of these models, however, is culturally based and as a result is "place based" to the traditional geography of these diverse nations. In many traditional tribal communities, each band was considered autonomous and determined its own social, governance, and ceremonial structures according to its own interpretation of tribal histories. These histories are the intellectual property of the spiritual leaders of a tribal community and this, again, reinforces the connection between "sacred" and "leadership" in the context of place.

As we define "sacred" and connect it to place, we begin with a fundamental acknowledgment that in North America today, Indigenous people consider certain places or homelands to be sacred and as integral to the practice of ceremonies connected to their spirituality. The land or Mother Earth constitutes a significant component of Native spirituality. The recognition that all things have a spirit and that all these living spirits are connected and sustained by Mother Earth allows us to postulate that these sacred places are relevant to Indigenous peoples' fundamental philosophical belief in how the world operates.

We cannot enter a discussion about sacred places and American Indians without first having an understanding of the policies that have historically affected the identification of "place" within tribal communities. In some communities, Native people refer to this land as Turtle Island (Snyder, 1999) and use it as a reference to oral histories that link the beginnings of the people to native spirituality, essentially a creation story. Each Indigenous society has an oral history that defines a creation story, which identifies a geographical location and connection to Mother Earth. The historical link to spirituality and the context of sacredness in leadership may not be as clear today as it was in early documentation and the original context, which did not distinguish the two as separate.

Early in the nineteenth century, the federal government's "civilization" policies attempted to Christianize American Indians. In part, this included fiscal support of over two hundred mission schools. The Dawes Act of 1887 specifically prohibited the practice of American Indian religious traditions, a policy and practice that remained intact and unwavering for over fifty years (Friends Committee, 2005). This early assimilation practice sought to replace Indigenous religions and conceptual ideas about spirituality with Christian values. Christianity as a religious ideology has established its own sacred place as a church, whereby individuals collectively conduct ceremonies that spiritually connect them to a higher power; however, most Christians would agree the realm of spirituality does not reside within a building but rather inside the person. The ceremonies are conducted by religious leaders and religious organizations informed by Western rational paradigms that frame U.S. mainstream social systems (i.e., business models for leadership, capitalism) and shaped the Euro-American worldview. Captain Richard H. Pratt (1892), perhaps the country's best-known assimilationist, acknowledged the "pretense" of the anti-Indigenous practices and linked it to place by describing Jefferson's advocacy for removing Indigenous peoples from their lands.[3] His advocacy of boarding schools as places to assimilate Native Americans created a legacy that today is a cornerstone for conscience dialogue, including the Gulag Museum in Russia[4] and the District Six Museum in South Africa among the 183 member museums around the globe. These contemporary sites of conscience dialogue represent the shared work among member museums to commemorate past struggles for democracy through programs that stimulated civic participation and dialogue on current social issues.[5] An example of a current social issue is the hope for the U.S. government's true commitment to protect the religious freedom of all people which arguably extends to American Indians; however, protection for sacred sites or places is uncertain and intermittent at best. For example, the federal courts do not apply either the First Amendment or the American Indian Religious Freedom Act of 1978, PL 95–341 (42 USC 1996)[6] in the safeguarding of or access to sacred sites for tribal people. Despite recognizing that certain activities, for example building a road through a cemetery, would "destroy the . . . Indians' ability to practice their religion," the Supreme Court has consistently failed to protect religious freedoms for American Indians (*Lyng*, 1988). On November 16, 1990, the U.S. Congress passed the Native American Graves Protection and Repatriation Act (NAGPRA), Public Law 101–601[7] with the intention of ensuring that ancestral remains and sacred objects will be returned to tribes. In spite of both of these laws, there is little current legal protection for certain categories of sacred places and there is no specific cause of action to defend sacred places against desecration or destruction. Examples that we cite later in this section have these limitations.

Homelands of tribes today for the most part are not the same as their traditional homelands prior to white contact. The cultural resiliency of tribes, who were forcibly removed to make way for white settlement with the advent of Manifest Destiny,[8] can be gauged by the extent to which tribal languages and religions exist today. Tribal territories, languages, and religions are components of the culture of the tribe. If one removes the components, as Pratt attempted to do with assimilation policies and practices that realistically spanned approximately seventy-five years in the United States, the culture changes. Land, or place, is not an artifact of Indian culture, but rather of the history and evolution of a people and their cultural identity—knowledge of which is connected to land. This sense of place is embodied within Indigenous peoples. Much of the research literature describes the generational loss of cultural knowledge, particularly within the context of Indigenous nations/peoples who have been dispossessed of their homelands. Land, language, and culture are all relevant to sustaining a people's collective citizenship and identity, as are the social systems that establish structures and processes to reinforce culture-based education across generations that effectively support and protect these inherent rights of Indigenous communities.

RESISTANCE AND EDUCATIONAL SOVEREIGNTY

In this section, we present examples of Indigenous nation communities and their leaders who have led the organized resistance to anti-Indigenous policies by federal and state governments.

The Iroquois Confederacy

Some tribes, like the Iroquois Confederacy in upper New York State, remain in the vicinity of their traditional homelands. Other descendants of this tribe were removed to Indian Territory in Oklahoma and occupy the northeastern part of that state. Additional relatives moved out ahead of the removal to regions around the Great Lakes, regions whose ecology was similar to their own homelands and whose people had similar lifestyles. Traditional languages and governance, and even resistance, can still be found in the Iroquois Confederacy. The people of the Six Nations call themselves the *Hau de no sau nee,* meaning People Building a Long House. Originally the Six Nations was five and included the Mohawk, Oneida, Onondaga, Cayuga, and Seneca. The sixth nation, the Tuscarora, migrated into Iroquois country in the early eighteenth century. Today, these peoples comprise the oldest living *participatory* democracy on earth, a recorded eight hundred years. This system provided the model that Benjamin Franklin and Thomas Jefferson used in the conception of the federal system that would become the United States. Onondaga was the Iroquois Confederacy capital because of its central location that made it equidistant for all tribes to travel. The leadership of the confederacy established in this place also was equally accessible to all. To link "the sacred" to this place, it is only necessary to equate all tribal governance (and leadership) to the language, to ceremony, and to the culture. It is essentially equivalent to stating (or restating the obvious) that the pope practices leadership with a spiritual connection in a designated place. Other nations link tribal governance and leadership to place as well.

The Comanche

The Comanche Tribe of Oklahoma's government headquarters is in Lawton, Oklahoma, near the base of Mount Scott. This landmark, particularly Medicine Bluffs, has served as the base of tribal tradition since the tribe's forced removal to western Oklahoma in the late 1880s. Prior to forced reservation life, the Comanche roamed north into Canada and south into Mexico. In this place, Medicine Bluffs has historically been the focus of sacred Comanche traditional religious practices and still continues to have significant religious importance, including performing ceremonies, praying, and gathering plants for traditional use. The Medicine Bluffs are four adjoining bluffs that are about one mile in length on the south side of Medicine Bluff Creek. From the south, the landscape rises to the top of the bluffs. From the north, the bluffs become a vertical cliff of approximately 310 feet high. The south side of Medicine Bluffs is the only side from which one can gain access to the peaks of Medicine Bluffs. It is historically recorded that Medicine Bluffs was used by the Comanche Nation and other tribes prior to the establishment of Fort Sill in 1869.

On September 23, 2008, the Comanche Nation won a preliminary injunction against Fort Sill's planned construction at the base of the southern access to Medicine Bluffs.[9] To obtain a preliminary injunction, the tribe needed to show:

- a substantial likelihood of success on the merits
- irreparable harm to the Tribe if the injunction was denied
- that the threatened harm to the Tribe outweighed any harm to the U.S. Army
- that issuance of the injunction would not be adverse to the public interest (*Comanche Nation v. United States of America*, 2008)

The military had proposed the construction of a forty-three-thousand-square-foot Training Support Center which the tribe maintained violated the Religious Freedom Restoration Act of 1993.[10] Central to the arguments in this landmark decision was testimony from current leaders in the tribe that Medicine Bluffs had remained a sacred site for the Comanche people and still is used today for religious practices for hundreds of tribal members. They also agreed in their testimonies that the south side of the Medicine Bluffs is the traditional way to enter the bluffs, and the entryway's name translates to "Sweet Medicine." Sweat lodges were put up along the south side and herbs and plants were gathered on the south side as well. The unobstructed view of the bluffs plays an important part of the traditions of the Comanche Nation. Wallace Coffey, current chair of the Comanche Nation, testified to the centrality of the use of Medicine Bluffs and its connection to the place. His testimony and his understanding of the traditions surrounding the use of Medicine Bluffs connected this sacred place to the ceremonies and traditions of leadership within the tribe. Jimmy Arterberry noted, "As a Comanche man, Medicine Bluffs is a spiritual center of my religious beliefs and the heart of the current Comanche Nation" (Schonchin, 2008). As a member of the Comanche Nation, Warner and Sevcenko (2008), add their observations of tribal leadership with regards to Medicine Bluffs, "I am sure of the connection to this place and the tribal leadership of the Comanche Nation." Tribal communities, in seeking to reestablish their separate identities through self-determination, look to traditional leaders to create the balance of governance in contemporary interactions with other nations, specifically the U.S. federal bureaucracy. Coffey characterizes this historic win through less than optimistic words by noting "our culture has no life expectancy" in 2008 (personal communication). This understanding united traditional tribal leaders who advocated for the continued use and access to this *place*.

This injunctive relief provided in the U.S. District Court for the Western District of Oklahoma (NO.CIVV-08-849-D) was the first significant case law to establish the rights of tribes; it will have a major impact on future cases involving questions about NAGPRA and Religious Freedom and Restoration Act of 1993 (RFRA). The following description of Native American sacred lands is taken from the president's "Report to Congress of American Indian Religious Freedom," August 1979, pursuant to the American Indian Religious Freedom Act (P.L. 95–341).

> The Native peoples of this country believe that certain areas of land are holy. These lands may be sacred, for example, because of the religious events which occurred there, because they contain specific natural products, because they are the dwelling place or embodiment of spiritual beings, because they surround or contain burial grounds or because they are sites conducive to communicating with spiritual beings. There are specific religious beliefs regarding each sacred site which form the basis for religious laws governing the site. These laws may prescribe, for example, when and for what purposes the site may or must be visited, what ceremonies or rituals may or must take place at the site, and what manner of conduct must or must not be observed at the site, who may or may not go to the site and consequences to the individual, group, clan or tribe if the laws are not observed. The ceremonies may also require preparatory rituals, purification rites or stages of preparation. Both active participants and observers may need to be readied. Natural substances may need to be gathered. Those who are unprepared or whose behavior or condition may alter the ceremony are often not permitted to attend. (p. 52)

For our purposes, it is important to note that the leadership of the tribe, in this specific example Wallace Coffey, is expected to protect the sacred ceremonies of the group and this would be difficult, if not impossible, if Coffey were unaware of the significance of Medicine Bluffs or did not practice traditional ceremonies. Place designates the specific geography linked to sacred ceremonies, but Coffey's leadership embedded with tribal policies and governance practices reinforces the historical and cultural contexts that defines this place as sacred.

THE LANGUAGE OF LEADERSHIP AND PLACE

Connection to place is vital to our identity, personal and communal. In her book, Davianna Pomaika'i McGregor (2007) talks about the life ways of the *kua'āina*, who are the keepers of Hawai'i's sacred lands who are living Hawaiian culture. She tells their stories, their history *mo'olelo*, a succession of knowledge to be passed on one generation to the next. Davianna shares the concepts of "place," a knowledge passed down by elders and spiritual teachers (*kūpuna*). She writes:

"Ke hāʻawi nei au iā ʻoe. Mālama ʻoe i kēia mau mea. ʻAʻohe mālama, pau ka pono o ka Hawaiʻi" (I pass on to you. Take care of these things. If you don't take care, the well-being of the Hawaiian people will end): these words were used by kūpuna to pass on knowledge and stewardship of their lands to a chosen successor of the next generation. Gifted with this stewardship responsibility, the successors held their ancestral lands and knowledge sacred in their memories and passed it on in custom and practice from generation to generation up through the twenty-first century. (p. 5)

The physical location of this sacred place, in the geographical sense, is that group of islands in the South Pacific known as Hawaiʻi. The sense that place is the community and that it is situational permeates each of these site-specific locations. Turner (1997) suggests that a Pacific perspective of place "is rooted in contested views of the past and in claims to separate and distinctive identities, understood to be derived from the past." This assertion parallels many Indigenous perspectives of leadership in the continental United States and provides a framework for our link to sacred place and leadership. The discourse on place and leadership lead us to questions of "home" and "identity" for Indigenous people and the ability to maintain both in the twenty-first century.

Current research on American Indian leadership is often linked to identity. Michael D. Wilson's recent publication "Writing Home: Narratives of Resistance" is a critique of American Indian writers. It highlights well-known American Indian writers such as N. Scott Momaday, Leslie Marmon Silko, Mourning Dove, Gerald Vizenor, and Ray Young Bear. Wilson's critique focuses on how these authors situate their plots in resistance to white colonization narratives by connecting their characters to *home*. Again, we find the connection made between sacred and home (or place). By interweaving empirical research with accessible composite narratives like the following vignettes portraying school leaders—Harbuck and Bull—we breach the gap between solid leadership research and the on-the-ground reality of American Indian leaders who are located in "a sacred place" by the connecting of place and identity. These stories connect leadership theory and practice in the context of school leaders serving Native children and families.

Vignette #1: *Supporting strong cultural identity through language programs and sense of place with a community of Native students as a school leader*
In 2001, LaGaylis Harbuck became principal at Calcedeaver Elementary School, which was ranked in the lowest tier in the state of Alabama when she began to reestablish a sense of place and identity for this reservation school. In 2007, the school ranked number one in the state. Harbuck's leadership, characterized by Cherrington (2007) as a cross between Andy Griffith and

Attila the Hun, initiated a cultural and political connection to return the school to its MOWA Choctaw identity.[11] The connection to place, in spite of overwhelming odds, and the efforts to maintain a traditional homeland presence where the federal government refuses to acknowledge one, is difficult. Alabama, a race conscious southern state, historically defines everyone as black or white. The state (politicians) believes that all Indians were removed in the 1930s during the Indian Removal Act, which forced most southern Choctaws into the Oklahoma Territory. Despite being recognized as a distinct tribal government by the state of Alabama in 1980, the traditional land base, Nanih Chaha, is now owned by non-Indians. Harbuck's initiative to support cultural identity and reintroduce the language is another example of the strength and resiliency of tribal peoples. Her leadership and its foundation in a belief that language and culture will sustain her people lie in an understanding that Indian people are successful when *they know who they are and where they come from* (adapted from quote by Nicole Williams, teacher) (Cherrington, 2007, p. 33).

Vignette #2: *Connecting students to "place" as a school leader*
Adam B. Bull, Jr., served as principal of Wingate High School for fourteen years, retiring in 2005. He moved to Wingate in a supervisory (leadership) position in 1979. Mr. Bull is Oklahoma Choctaw[12] and moved to the Navajo reservation, where he began his administrative and coaching career in August 1977. Highly regarded and widely recognized as a dedicated teacher, coach, and community leader for many years, Mr. Bull's leadership was accepted by the reservation community even though New Mexico is not the traditional homeland for members of the Choctaw Nation of Oklahoma. His own tribal roots lie in the forced removal to Indian Territory in the late 1880s. He was transplanted, in a sense, to a community of Navajo people, who, by accepting his presence and guidance, began to situate his place. When I asked Mr. Bull how long he was on the reservation before Navajo people trusted him, he responded that it took about eleven years, until around 1986 or so. As the discussion moved to place and leadership, he indicated that he felt the place "allowed" him to exercise leadership skills and if they (i.e., the Navajo tribal members in this place) had not accepted his leadership, he would not have been successful. We spoke about his participation in traditions distinctly Navajo and how he became part of that community; again he reminded me that it took him nearly a dozen years to achieve this status.

Finally, Mr. Bull offered some hesitation about introducing some values, specifically personal competition, in a culture and community that does not value that. Even in athletic competition, he was successful, and athletics provided him with access to students and parents on another level (Bull, 2008). His experiences provide an example of how a place can influence the individual, but it also emphasizes how important it is to connect to the centrality of that place through the traditions of the people who occupy it. When asked a different way, Mr. Bull agreed that it was likely that he would have been a teacher, coach, principal (leader) wherever he chose to establish a professional career, but if the parents and students at Wingate High School had not allowed him to be part of their place, he would not have been successful there. From his leadership experiences, we conclude that the sacred is not the place itself but the connection to place as identified by the people in the place. In other words, it is the place that matters. His experiences with place, identity, and leadership parallel those of Harbuck in most instances; the primary difference is that she chose to work in her own culture, in her own place, and Bull chose to become an integral part of the culture where he had relocated.

In examining the practice of leadership and its connection to place, we found Reyhner's (2006) essay "Creating Sacred Places for Children," which emphasizes Indigenous leadership values and research models informing school improvement initiatives for schools serving Native children.[13] He points to honesty, generosity, respect, spirituality, courage, humility, and compassion—traditional leadership values considered important in creating a sense of place with children and family. We reiterate the importance of educational leaders in schools serving Indigenous communities to adopt core Indigenous values that are localized.

Reyhner (2006) elaborates, "Research indicates that strong leaders listen to and involve the people they lead in school improvement. School principals must listen and respond to what parents, teachers, and students have to say. Experts in leadership emphasize that it requires competence, vision, enthusiasm, and trust" (pp. 19–21).

The National Advisory Council on American Indian Education, the National Indian Education Association, and the National Indian School Board Association's work with instructional leadership acknowledges the challenges faced when working with American Indian children. This is particularly true when Native children have no place or community with which to be connected. Deloria and Wildcat (2001) argue that education for Native students is about more than learning skills and facts; instead, they need to develop a positive identity that includes having a sense of place (socially and physically), noting that the word "Indigenous" means to be of a place (p. 31).

Both Harbuck's and Bull's leadership practices targeted the goals of connecting students to a "sense of place" and developing a strong identity as belonging in an Indigenous community and as a people. We follow these K–12 educational leadership vignettes with a vignette that illustrates the perspective of leadership and sense of place by an author on this chapter who was a former tribal college president.

HASKELL INDIAN NATIONS UNIVERSITY

Linda Sue Warner, former president at Haskell Indian Nations University recollects:

> In April 2008, when I was president of Haskell Indian Nations University in the state of Kansas, Haskell's community had a tree-planting ceremony. The ceremony started with the planting of an Oklahoma redbud at a location where I would see the tree every day when I went to work. Seeing this tree reminded me of Oklahoma, the place where I got the strength to do the work on this campus. The tree connected me to my home. Planting the tree and connecting it by ceremony from one place to another merged both places. Ceremony to create and sustain one's sense of place across these landscapes can best be understood in the context of Indigenous worldviews in which relationships with all living things on Mother Earth are of particular import as well as understanding and valuing of the interdependence of these fragile and essential connections. Watching this tree grow reminded me of how important Haskell is to the leadership in this country. The year 2009 commemorated 125 years of leadership. The tree is sacred, the place is sacred, and the work is sacred. (March 2010)

THE POWER OF PLACE

Around the world, Indigenous people instinctively turn to places of memory to come to term with the past and to chart a course for the future. Sevcenko (2004) characterizes "memory" as a critical language and supports an International Coalition of Sites of Conscience.[14] Led by human rights organizations and established to "inspire citizen participation in current struggles for truth and justice," the coalition recently began to study American Indian boarding schools. In our discussion of the federal government's educational experiment proposed by William Pratt—whose intent was to change the traditions, customs, and languages of American Indians—we touched on the boarding schools created in locations throughout the United States to "civilize" Indians. The intent was assimilation. At these boarding schools, managed and regulated by either the federal government or various religious organizations, young American Indians were exposed to white culture and expected to return home taking these new skills with them. The legacy of these "places" is generally characterized as negative and stories of loneliness, fear, or disease can be found at each.

Yet in spite of these conditions and various hardships, American Indian people survived. They formed lifelong friendships (and intertribal marriages);

they retained their cultural identity and preserved their languages. The places, which were established to create assimilated Indians, found resiliency; Indian children may have had their hair cut and their clothes changed to uniforms, but the place that white people created for them did not change them. Instead, they changed the place. This country's whole history of boarding schools is mirrored in Haskell's history. In spite of concentrated efforts and various prison-like techniques, boarding schools did not erase the identity of Indian children. Recognizing this resiliency, the coalition began an initial convening in late October 2008 at Haskell Indian Nations University in Lawrence, Kansas, to begin the process of formal acknowledgement of recovery. The objectives of the convention were:

1. To identify key contemporary issues (education, sovereignty, cultural assimilation) in American Indian/Alaska Native, Native Hawaiian, and First Nations communities, as well as the larger community, that can be found in the history of the boarding and residential school era that current school sites can address in potential educational programs.
2. To identify possible program strategies of how the boarding and residential schools sites will address their contemporary legacies.
3. To better understand the challenges and identify the needs of boarding and residential school sites to help support the development of programs that confront the schools' contemporary legacies.
4. To identify next steps or special projects for an American Indian Sites of Conscience project (Warner and Sevcenko, 2008).

Haskell was established in 1884 as the United States Indian Industrial Training School, an educational program that focused on agricultural education in grades one through five. Today, Haskell is the site of a tribal university, offering a college curriculum that integrates American Indian/Alaska Native (AI/AN) culture into all of its curricula; it is a national center for Indian education, research, and cultural preservation. Haskell is the only government boarding school that has evolved into a four-year university. The college's alumni can be found in virtually every area of national leadership in Indian affairs in the United States, including the U.S. Congress, state legislatures, the National Indian Education Association, the National Congress of American Indians, as well as various advocacy groups, such as National Indian Gaming Association, the Native American Rights Fund, and the National Council of American Indian Education. Initially established as a vehicle to remove tribal knowledge and culture from students' lives, now Haskell's current leadership works to create an environment where past achievements, particularly in leadership development, can be replicated. The work that the International Coalition of Sites of Conscience has begun can be expanded by further exploration of the link between place, identity, and leadership.

American Indian philosophy, tradition, and culture link individuals across cultures at times. This is particularly true in those places where varied cultures met and interacted. Haskell Indian Nations University is such a place. It is not located on any one traditional tribe's land but is set in what is now eastern Kansas at a physical site that would have been visited and crossed by many tribes. Haskell is home of the longest continuously operated federal commitment to Indian education in the United States. Haskell is regularly host to over 130 tribes, who send their young people for postsecondary education in partial fulfillment of treaty obligations.

Past and present tribal chairs, tribal council members, business and political leaders, military leaders, and business leaders attended Haskell in this storied history. In 1992, as part of the quincentennial year's commemoration of the arrival Columbus. a group of alumni, staff, and students worked to dedicate a medicine wheel on the campus that was created by a local Potawatomi artist and now serves as a gathering place for many contemporary ceremonies. Using stone from the original campus buildings, the mowed design provides a place for quiet reflection. Not all tribes use a medicine wheel, and the recent addition of this artwork to Haskell's campus has begun to claim a part of the history through links to contemporary events. The intertribal nature of such artwork is again an artifact of mixing tribal cultures in one place. In the 125 years of its existence, we ask the question, when did Haskell become a place where the synergy of many peoples made it sacred? The place did not require the addition of the medicine wheel[15] to link it to the lives of children for well over a hundred years. Traditional people tell us that it became sacred the day our children gathered there for the first time. As Coffey (2008) describes the responsibility of tribal leaders to understand the consequences of place to leadership, he notes "Our ancestors cannot speak; our children cannot speak for themselves." His message is directly targeting Native leaders throughout the country; it is important that we continue to honor the traditions of our ancestors. Many tribes believe that leadership is linked to seven generations in the future, reflecting on seven generations in the past. It is this link that provides the robustness of tribal decision making on issues of place and identity, particularly as those decisions relate to cultural survival.

The exploration of Haskell as a site of conscience among emerging Native leaders may create dialogues that will inform our discussion of the sacred and place as we seek to further refine the link to the leadership. Retrospectives from alumni and a serious review of the historic artifacts throughout 2009 added to that discussion and provided awareness for Indian and non-Indians on the impact of place, specifically the boarding school in fostering cross-cultural identities for over a century.

Contemporary dialogues about *place* and *spirituality* are connected to larger and more complex dialogues from mainstream researchers. This is a dialogue that tribal leaders have always had; essentially it is a dialogue about how this place will sustain us. Tribal leaders have advocated for the care of Mother Earth and especially to maintain this spiritual connection to their peoples. Recent attention to phenomena such as global warming and climate change has moved their concerns to mainstream advocacy. For tribal leaders, it is a dialogue about balance and again fuses tribal leadership to the land they use or their situated place.

Tribal lands are rich in mineral resources; two-thirds of the uranium ore, one-fourth of the readily accessible low sulfur coal, and one-fifth of the oil and natural gas that the United States possesses is located within the boundaries of American Indian reservations (Pickering, 2005). This does not include those resources owned by tribal members privately and not considered reservation or communal land. Many reservations encompass hundreds of thousands of acres of valuable natural resources. For example, in the 1980s the Crow tribe had approximately $27 billion in coal; roughly $3 million per tribal member (Anderson, 2004). Economic wealth tied to the land and the management of its resources is the source of concern to traditional tribal leaders.

Tribal efforts to reclaim lands have evolved from the 1960s activism, which resisted efforts to force environmentalism into a narrow distributive paradigm of environmental racism and sought to focus on the ability of tribes to exercise their unique sovereignty (Kanner, Casey, and Ristroph, 2003). Tribal leadership now contends with environmental laws that accord the tribes with different degrees of power and wide latitude for confusion. These general assertions are relative to tribally owned land and are separate from land tenure issues and individual property rights related to the land and natural resources (see www.indianlandtenure.org).

LEADERSHIP AND SACRED PLACE

As we reviewed the literature on Indigenous place within the context of the sacred, the concept *sacred place* and *home* merged. The question became: Where is this place that imbues a leader with the strength to lead, or how do leaders acknowledge a place as sacred? Kenney (2012) writes, "A sense of place brings coherence to suggests an aesthetic engagement with the land—an intimate spiritual commitment to relationships with all living things. . . . To maintain this sense of coherence, we can accept the earth as our first embodied concept of leadership" (p. 3).

So another question to be asked is: How do leaders identify located space that is tribally specific; or do they? Connecting Indigenous leadership to place allows us to explore the collective memory of the place within a tribal nation. Key constituencies, who wish to investigate their own tribal identities and how leadership can be linked to place, can pose the following questions for the knowledge bearers of the tribe:

1. Can you identify a place associated with the nation's history and define how it is currently linked to a tribal identity?
2. What stories are linked to this place by tribal leaders? How are these stories relevant to current tribal decision making?
3. What difference would it make (does it make) to have a dialogue at this place?
4. How do you think remembering the history of this place shapes the future of the nation?
5. What perspectives do tribal members have of this place? What would people feel or learn by being in this place?

Linking the research and practice of leadership to connectedness and place allows for dialogues that have practical implications for better understanding historical context and tribal leadership. American Indian scholars propose a curricular integration focusing on research within an Indigenous framework or Native ways of knowing. Recent efforts to reclaim and assert the holistic nature of tribal research has produced a growing, but narrow, body of work by Native scholars who advocate not only the relevance of Indigenous perspectives but who actively research the complexity of American Indian identity, leadership, and place. American Indian culture, traditions, languages and practices have survived an unusual number of oppressive federal policies and yet, despite being treated as misplaced objects, mascots, and stereotypes, American Indian scholars work to create a counternarrative research that can bridge the gaps among the reality of place, the identity of the sacred, and the practice of leadership.[16]

NOTES

1. These periods of history and consequences have been well documented in the literature and from a variety of paradigms and perspectives.

2. Hämäläinen (2008) provides extensive evidence based on his examination of the archives of Austin and Spanish officials during that historical era in the 1800s. See Hämäläinen's chapter notes referencing the numerous historical documents that were examined for the purposes of his book (pp. 409, 426–29).

3. Jefferson advocated for coercion and establishing federal policies for removing Indigenous peoples from their lands. Sources are the Library of Congress's documents and research literature describing Jefferson's actions and documents evidencing his impetus for the Indian Removal Act, which was signed by Andrew Jackson, www.loc.gov/rr/program/bib/ourdocs/Indian.html. See Mark Hirsch's (Summer 2009) paper, Thomas Jefferson, founding father of Indian removal. Retrieved on December 18, 2012, from http://westgatehouse.com/art263.html.

4. See more at http://gulaghistory.org/nps/onlineexhibit/museum/beyond.php.

5. See more at www.sitesofconscience.org/ and www.wmd.org/resources/whats -being-done/memory-projects/interview-liz-sevcenko-director-secretariat -international#sthash.JJgShktI.dpuf.

6. This act, PL 95–341 (42 USC 1996), states the policy of the United States is to protect and preserve American Indians' inherent rights of freedom to believe, express, and exercise the traditional religions of the American Indian, Eskimo, Aleut, and Native Hawaiians. These rights include, but are not limited to, access to sites, use and possession of sacred objects, and the freedom to worship through ceremony and traditional rites. The act was amended in 1994. See more at www .gpo.gov/fdsys/pkg/USCODE-1994-title42/pdf/USCODE-1994-title42-chap20A -subchapI-sec1996.pdf.

7. See more about this legislation including current programming at www.nps .gov/nagpra/MANDATES/INDEX.HTM.

8. Manifest Destiny is widely interpreted as the belief that the United States was destined to expand from the Atlantic seaboard to the Pacific Ocean and used to advocate and justify territorial acquisition.

9. A preliminary injunction serves to preserve the status quo pending a final determination of the case on the merits. *MacArthur v. San Juan County*, 497 F.3d 1057, 1006 (10th Cir., 2007).

10. See more at H.R. 1308—103rd Congress: Religious Freedom Restoration Act of 1993, in www.GovTrack.us.Access and www.govtrack.us/congress/bills/103/hr 1308. Additional information about similar legislation is provided at www.gov track.us/congress/bills/browse?congress=103#similar_to=H.R.1308%2F103. These include: S. 1021 (103rd): Native American Free Exercise of Religion Act of 1993, sponsor: Sen. Daniel Inouye (D-HI, 1963–2012), introduced: May 25, 1993, re- ferred to committee: May 25, 1993. H.R. 4155 (103rd): American Indian Religious Freedom Act Amendments of 1994, sponsor: Rep. William Richardson (D-NM3, 1983–1997), introduced: March 24, 1994, referred to committee: March 24, 1994. H.R. 4230 (103rd): American Indian Religious Freedom Act Amendments of 1994, sponsor: Rep. William Richardson (D-NM3, 1983–1997), introduced: April 14, 1994, signed by the president: October 6, 1994.

11. MOWA is a geographical identity for this band of Choctaw people living on their lands situated across Mobile (MO) and Washington (WA) Counties in Mount Vernon, Alabama. Read more about the MOWA band of Choctaw Indians at www.mowa-choctaw.com/index.html.

12. See more about the Choctaw Nation of Oklahoma at www.choctawnation .com/.

13. Lezotte's effective schools model correlates are strong instructional leader- ship, a clear and focused mission, a climate of high expectations for success, a safe and orderly environment, frequent monitoring of student progress, opportunity to learn/student time on task, and positive home-school relations. Through its school improvement initiatives, the Bureau of Indian Education's Effective Schools

Team expanded the effective schools model to include three additional correlates including cultural relevance, a challenging curriculum and appropriate instruction, and shared governance and participatory management. To implement the bureau's model, National Indian School Board Association developed a culturally relevant curricula—Creating Sacred Places for Children—and conducted research in the fifteen schools using this curriculum in grades three through five from 2001 to 2003. Findings showed significant gains in reading as compared to students in other Bureau of Indian Education schools. Retrieved December 2, 2011, from jan .ucc.nau.edu/~jar/AIE/IETplaces.htm.

14. The International Coalition of Historic Site Museums of Conscience is a global network of historic museums on four continents committed to "presenting and interpreting a wide variety of historic issues, events and people . . . hold[ing] in common the belief that it is the obligation of historic sites to assist the public in drawing connections between the history of our site and its contemporary implications" (Sevcenko, 2004). Museums are linked through a website of conscience, staff exchange programs, Coalition conferences, capacity building, and dialogues for democracy. See more at www.sitesofconscience.org/ and www.wmd.org /resources/whats-being-done/memory-projects/interview-liz-sevcenko-director -secretariat-international#sthash.JJgShktI.dpuf.

15. The epistemology of the Medicine Wheel teachings, which is embedded in the harmonious relationships of all living things, can be achieved by humans when they create and sustain a balance among their mental, physical, spiritual, and emotional aspects of their lives.

16. This chapter is an expansion of a paper presented at the 7th International Conference on Studying Leadership, The locales of leadership: Foregrounding context, December 8–9, 2008, at the University of Auckland, Auckland, New Zealand.

REFERENCES

American Indian Religious Freedom Act, P.L. 95-341, 42 U.S.C.A. 1996.

Anderson, O. (1981). Charting new directions. In S. Verble (Ed.), *Words of today's American Indian women: Ohoyo Makachi*. Washington, DC: U.S. Department of Education.

Anderson, T. (2004).The wealth of Indian nations. *Hoover Digest*, no. 3. Retrieved February 20, 2015, from www.hoover.org/research/wealth-indian-nations-0.

Bull, A. A. (2008, November 17). Personal email and interview.

Cherrington, M. (2007, Summer). The language of success. *Cultural Survival Quarterly*, 31(2), 30–35.

Coffey, W. (2008, October 5). Personal communication.

Colchester, M. (2004). Conservation policy and Indigenous peoples. *Cultural Survival Quarterly*, 28(1), 17–22.

Comanche Nation v. United States of America, No. CIV-08-849-D 38 (Oklahoma).

Deloria, V., Jr., and Wildcat, D. (2001). *Power and place: Indian education in America*. Golden, Colorado: Fulcrum Publishing.

Friends Committee on National Legislation (2005). *Religious freedom for Native Americans*. Washington, DC: Author.

Geertz, W. A. (1990). Hopi hermeneutics: Ritual person among the Hopi Indians of Arizona. In Hans G. Kippenberg, Wme B. Kuiper, and Andy F. Sanders (Eds.), *Concept of person in religion and thought* (pp. 309–35). Berlin: Mouton de Gruyer.

Glowacka, M. D. (1998). Commentary ritual knowledge in Hopi tradition. *American Indian Quarterly*, 22(3), 387–92.

Griffin-Pierce, T. (1992). *Earth is my mother, sky is my father: Space, time, and astronomy in Navajo sandpainting*. Albuquerque: University of New Mexico Press.

Hämäläinen, P. (2008). *The Comanche empire*. New Haven, CT: Yale University Press.

Indian Land Tenure. www.indianlandtenure.org/.

H.R. 1308—103rd Congress: Religious Freedom Restoration Act of 1993. (1993). In www.GovTrack.us. Retrieved January 22, 2014, from www.govtrack.us /congress/bills/103/hr1308.

Kanner, A., Casey, R., and Ristroph, B. (2003). New opportunities for Native American tribes to pursue environmental and natural resource claims. *Duke Environmental Law and Policy Forum*, 14, 155–83.

Kenny, C., and Ngaroimata Fraser, T. (2012). *Living Indigenous leadership: Native narratives on building strong communities*. Vancouver: University of British Columbia Press.

Kill the Indian and save the man: Captain Richard H. Pratt on the education of Native Americans (1892). Retrieved on December 28, 2008, from http:// historymatters.gmu.edu/d/4929/.

Locke, J. (1960). *Two treatises of government*. Cambridge: Cambridge University Press.

Lyng v. Northwest Indian Cemetery Protective Association, 485 U.S. 439 (1988).

McGregor, D. P. (2007). *Na Kuaʻāina: Living Hawaiian Culture*. Hawaiʻi: University of Hawaiʻi Press.

Native American Graves Protection and Repatriation Act (NAGPRA) (1996). Pub.L. 101–601, 104 Stat. 3048, National Historic Preservation Act of 1966 (NHPA). 16 U.S.C. § 470 et seq. Retrieved January 15, 2014, from www.law .cornell.edu/usc-cgi/get_external.cgi?type=pubL&target=101-601

Pickering, K. (2005). Culture and reservation economics. In Thomas Bilosi (Ed.), *A companion to the anthropology of American Indians*. Hoboken, NJ: Wiley-Blackwell Publishing.

Religious Freedom Restoration Act of 1993 (RFRA), 42 U.S.C. § 2000bb *et seq*.

Reyhner, J. (2006). Creating sacred places for children. *Indian education today*, *1*(6), 19–20. Retrieved December 2, 2011, from http://jan.ucc.nau.edu/~jar /AIE/IETplaces.htm.

Schonchin, J. (2008, October). *The Comanche Nation News* (Lawton, OK), *7*(10), 1–3.

Sevcenko, L. (2004). *The power of place*. Minneapolis: New Tactics.

S.J. Res. (1977). 102—95th Congress: Joint resolution on American Indians religious freedom. Retrieved January 24, 2014, from www.govtrack.us/congress /bills/95/sjres102.

Snyder, G. (1999). *At home on the earth. Becoming Native to our place: A multicultural anthology*. Berkeley: University of California Press.

Terrell, J. U., and Terrell, D. (1974). *Indian women of the Western morning: Their life in early America*. New York: Dial Press.

Turner, J. W. (1997). Continuity and constraint: Reconstructing the concept of tradition from a Pacific perspective. *Contemporary Pacific, 9*(2), 345.

U.S. Department of Interior (1979, August). President's report to Congress on American Indian religious freedom, pursuant to the AIRFA, P.L. 95-341.

Warner, L. S., and Sevcenko, L. (2008). Indian boarding school sites of conscience: American Indian/First Nations sites of conscience project. Unpublished paper. October 31–November 2, 2008, Lawrence, KS.

Whiteman, H. V. (1978). Native American studies, the university, and the Indian student. In Thomas Thompson (Ed.), *The schooling of Native America*. Washington, DC: American Association of Colleges for Teacher Education.

Wilson, M. D. (2008). *Writing home: Indigenous narratives of resistance*. East Lansing: Michigan State University Press.

2

Wōksaṗe

The Identity of Tribal Colleges and Universities

CHERYL CRAZY BULL

Wōksaṗe is the Lakota value of wisdom. It is the sharing of the knowledge of the people, especially of elders, so that others may learn and have good health and happiness. In this sharing it is hoped that good advice is offered so that others will benefit. It is in the spirit of wōksaṗe that this chapter is offered.

Tribal colleges and universities (TCUs) are described in many ways: unique, culturally rich, culturally relevant, reservation based, even as underfunded miracles. They are the best-kept secret in higher education. This chapter focuses on the many aspects of TCUs that inform their identity as tribal institutions. These are the qualities that make them distinctive institutions—distinctive and different from other higher education institutions that educate and serve Indigenous peoples in the United States. I will use the term "tribal colleges," as the encompassing term for tribally chartered institutions of higher education located on Indian reservations. I also use the terms, "Native," "tribe," "Indigenous" and "American Indian" interchangeably. As well, I mean to include Alaska Natives in these terms.

The history of higher education among American Indians traces its roots back to the early days of the colonization of the Americas. This history will not be explored here except to call attention to the fact that many of the early higher education institutions included a mission to serve American Indians. As public education grew in the United States simultaneous with the termination and relocation periods in Native historical experience, the intention of assimilation of Native peoples became more entrenched in educational practice. American Indian history was minimally addressed, if at all, in curriculum and teaching, and no Native culture or language was addressed in any institution of higher education throughout the country.[1] Over time, especially after military service in World War II and the Korean War, Native people became increasingly exposed to American society. This, along with the impact of relocation and termination and the rise of the civil and Native rights movement, caused many Native leaders on reservations to examine how their tribal communities had been impacted by the assimilation experience, what the status of development and management of tribal resources and programs was, and whether there was any positive value in sending young people off to college. College entrance rates were dismal and successful attainment of degrees practically nonexistent.

In preparing this chapter, I considered the identifiers of tribal colleges to be those that are obvious—mission, location, student demographics, tribal charter—and those that are contextual and therefore more subtle as definers of a separate and distinct identity—such as the vision of the founders of the tribal college movement, the character and nature of our students and the experiences that they bring into our settings, and the ways that the spiritual life of the people is integrated into the daily life of tribal colleges.

"Tribally controlled colleges" and "tribally chartered colleges" are terms often used to describe the institutions discussed here. The foundational characteristic of these institutions is that they are established by a tribal government through a charter using the governance authority of the respective tribe. I do not include institutions whose charters or incorporation exist under other authorities, such as a corporate or federal charter, or which are operated by the federal government. The establishment of a tribally chartered institution is inherently a distinct experience because it establishes the tribes as governments in charge of their own higher education experiences. TCUs are the result of tribal sovereignty.

The first tribal college emerged on the Navajo Reservation in 1968 with the establishment of Navajo Community College, now Diné College. Quickly following were several institutions in the northern Plains including Sinte Gleska University, Oglala Lakota College, Turtle Mountain Community College, Standing Rock Community College (now Sitting Bull College), and D-Q (Deganawidah-Queztalcoatl) University in northern California. In 1973, the first six TCUs formed the American Indian Higher Education Consortium (AIHEC), a membership association supporting advocacy and shared development among the colleges. There are currently thirty-seven members of AIHEC, including one Canadian institution and thirty-one tribally chartered institutions. Five nontribally chartered higher education institutions were "grandfathered" into the original membership rolls of AIHEC—two Bureau of Indian Education colleges (Haskell Indian Nations University and Southwest Indian Polytechnic Institute), one federally chartered college (Institute of American Indian Arts), and two career and technical colleges (Navajo Technical University and United Tribes Technical College).

TCU leadership identified our collective voice as one of our unique characteristics. Through the solid leadership of the founders and current members of AIHEC, the TCUs have been able to maintain a cohesive voice for the preservation of the tribal college identity and the tribal college movement. The voice of the TCUs calls attention to the unique government-to-government relationship of tribal governments with the federal government and reinforces the establishment of the tribal colleges as an act of tribal self-governance. AIHEC has evolved from a consortium with a focus on legislative funding to an organization with a broad policy and educational agenda that has significant national influence in higher education. New TCUs continuously emerge across Indian country. Tribal colleges have also played an important role in the international Indigenous education community, particularly with the establishment of the World Indigenous Nations Higher Education Consortium (WINHEC), an organization that promotes collaboration among Indigenous higher education programs and institutions.

This chapter focuses on TCU identity, but there are many related areas of discussion in which the identity and role of the TCUs is a significant factor, including accreditation, academic assessment and institutional effectiveness, Native language restoration, land acquisition and development, and protection of inherent and acquired rights. All of these issues and many others—such as our land-grant status—must relate to the identity of the TCUs to be relevant.

VISION AND PURPOSES

Tribal colleges have an identity that is distinct from other higher education institutions and from other Native-serving institutions. Although the mission statements of the tribal colleges describe the cultural, social, and economic roles of the institutions, they only touch upon the true intention of tribal colleges, which is the preservation of our identities as tribal people for all of eternity. Not only do TCUs maintain existing cultural practice and traditions, in many instances, they are places for restoration of hidden or lost knowledge. As Native people our knowledge not only is what we learn and discover but also is what we acquire through spiritual engagement and practice. In LaFrance and Nichols's *Indigenous Evaluation Framework: Telling Our Story in Our Place and Time* (2008), the authors provide a theoretical description of what the founders of TCUs knew—that a tribal college education would be a source of both learned and acquired knowledge. The TCU founders defined their vision as the preservation of the traditional practices, belief systems, languages, and values of Indigenous people. They saw the importance of this in the development of leaders of tribal nations who would be called upon to negotiate challenging environments, heavily influenced by Western knowledge and experiences. They wanted TCUs to ensure that those qualities that make each tribal people unique are valued and promoted in the educational and community life of the institution. No other educational institution, regardless of its public or private mission, has this vision of tribal survival as its deepest and most heartfelt intention. This values-based mission is also well grounded in the understanding that spiritual life is embedded in the everyday life of American Indian people and thus cannot be "taught" as a separate educational function.

It is well documented that the early founders of the TCUs looked at the whole picture of higher education for Native people and found it sorely lacking in both quality and quantity. There is some evidence that discussions of establishing junior colleges or higher education programs on reservations were first held in the 1950s, probably as a result of the returning war veterans who sought more opportunities for themselves and their people and the recognition that termination was encroaching dramatically on Native rights and identity. With the advent of antipoverty programs and the civil rights movement came increased access across the country to higher education through community college systems and workforce training programs. This, combined with the rise of the American Indian Movement and renewed federal and tribal commitment to tribal self-governance, resulted in the establishment of the first tribally controlled education institutions, including Diné College (formerly Navajo Community College) as the first tribal college. Diné College was quickly followed by the Lakota Higher Education Center (Oglala Lakota College) and the Rosebud College Center (Sinte Gleska University) in 1969 and the early 1970s.

The founders of the TCUs described their vision in their founding documents as well as various speeches and writings—both published and unpublished. Many of the stories of the establishment of the tribal colleges are housed in the archives of AIHEC and at the various institutions themselves. It is important to note that the strong and dynamic oral history of the tribal colleges is another of the distinctive characteristics of the TCUs. The use of oral history, especially through storytelling, is a valued and accepted means of remembering both TCU identity and the vision of historic and contemporary founders of tribal colleges. Among the written accounts about the founding of the TCUs are statements contained in the book *Tribally Controlled Colleges: Making Good Medicine* (1992) by Dr. Wayne Stein, former president of Sitting Bull College and professor emeritus at Montana State University. Examples of founders' statements from Navajo Community College, Oglala Sioux Community College, and Rosebud Tribal College illustrate the early definition of the distinct tribal college mission. For example, among the founding principles of Navajo Community College (Roessel and Board of Regents, 1968–69) are the following:

1. For any community or society to grow and prosper, it must have its own means for educating its citizens. And it is essential that these educational systems be directed and controlled by the society it is intended to serve.
2. If a community or society is to continue to grow and prosper, each member of that society must be provided with an opportunity to acquire a positive self-image and a clear sense of identity. This can be achieved only when each individual's capacities are developed and

used to the fullest possible extent. It is absolutely necessary for every individual to respect and understand his culture and his heritage; and he must have faith in the future of his society.

3. Members of different cultures must develop their abilities to operate effectively, not only in their own immediate societies, but also in the complexities of varied cultures that make up the larger society of man.

The early mission statement of Oglala Sioux Community College (1971) (as cited in Stein, 1992) includes these categories:

Tribe: to provide the Oglala Sioux as a sovereign people with trained human resources and personnel (and) to assist people with being active, productive members of their communities and the Oglala Sioux Tribe.

Cultural: to present the Lakota view in teaching within the professional, occupational and community programs (and) to develop the Lakota culture as an area of study in itself (and) to research, study and disseminate the Lakota language, culture and philosophy.

Academic: high academic standards, open enrollment, access, basic skills and human values, work with other institutions and agencies.

Community: assist with determination of development needs of the reservation districts and communities in furthering their goals (and) to provide sound, basic education or GED. (pp. 50–51)

In keeping with the intention of the founders for their tribal college to be truly tribally controlled through Native leadership, the late Jerry Mohatt, a non-Indian and founding president of Sinte Gleska College, spoke to the importance of his stepping aside in favor of an American Indian president, Lionel Bordeaux, in order "to be true to the mission and goals of serving the Rosebud People: providing quality higher education, always listening to the grassroots people of the communities, being locally and Indian controlled, and preserving and promoting the Lakota language and culture" (as cited in Stein, 1992, p. 66).[2]

Many similar statements and related stories exist for all of the tribal colleges, regardless of whether they were established in the early years of the movement or more recently, as evidenced by the founding mission of a newer tribal college member of AIHEC (College of Muscogee Nation Self-study, 2014):[3]

The College of the Muscogee Nation is the institution of higher education for the Muscogee Creek Nation emphasizing native culture, values, language and self-determination. The College will provide a positive learning environment for tribal and non-tribal students as citizens of a tribal and global society, supported by teaching excellence, and will offer exemplary academic programs that meet student, tribal, and societal needs. Through instructional quality and visionary leadership, the College of the Muscogee Nation will encourage lifelong learners, for personal growth, professional development, and intellectual advancement. (p. 40)

The vision of the founders included preserving the cultural vitality of tribal people—as evidenced by strong tribal identity, social and economic prosperity, and maintaining the integrity of knowledge and practice. Tribal colleges are the only higher education institutions established with this vision.

DEFINING THE PLACE-BASED IDENTITY OF THE TCUS

TCUs are reservation-based institutions whose identity is irrevocably linked to the nature of the reservation experience. Whether established as institutions on reservations that are the traditional homelands of Native people or on other lands whose existence is a function of being dispossessed from their original homelands, the joys and sorrows of the lives of Native people permeate the lands and the resources on which TCUs thrive. Until the establishment of tribal colleges in Oklahoma, tribal colleges arose primarily in the historic homelands of Native people. This historical and contemporary experience includes the knowledge of how the people originated, how the land and resources came to be, and how the other nations joined humans in the time of creation. Each tribe is unique in its understanding of creation and possesses all the knowledge of its identity in the language, experiences, and history associated with the place of their origin. TCUs established in places where their people have been located as the result of forced removal have the challenge of reaching back to the lands of their people's birth for their understanding of their world.

Also important in the description of the TCUs is the commitment to both the sense of being a nation of tribal people and the sense of community and kinship that are inherent in tribal life. Tribal colleges fill the need of Native people to "be at home" and to go college with each other. TCUs reach out to the people of tribal communities, who, despite a rich and abundant tribal culture, are often left behind in the allocation of resources and services. The grassroots people of the reservations often are those people with the richest cultural lifestyles and those who have been disenfranchised from services, including employment, health, and education. Sometimes those two sets of characteristics are held by the same group of people. Regardless of the situation, TCUs reach out into tribal communities in ways that other institutions cannot, both because of their location and because of the nature of their educational services. As TCUs have matured, they now experience multigenerational educational communities where the children and grandchildren of early tribal college programs now are current students. This multigenerational experience tied to the place-based TCUs is not easily replicated in other educational environments: it is most unique to TCUs.

Stein (2008) also references the many challenging experiences that the early tribal college founders had as they promoted their institutions throughout higher education. In the contexts of those experiences lie important descriptors of what the TCUs are. For example, when asked at a news conference in Washington in 1974, "Why a tribal college? What makes a tribal college different?" Dr. Ned Hatathli of Navajo Community College answered after some thought by replying, "For one thing, we don't teach that Columbus discovered America" (as cited by Stein, 1992, p.15). This statement is indicative of an understanding that what TCUs teach is the history and knowledge of the world from tribal perspectives.

Over the years, the experience of education at TCUs has evolved as Native scholars emerge more fully in the world of academia, bringing research and curricular skills and improved teaching skills. However, the evolving philosophy of education at TCUs remains solidly rooted in tribal knowledge and scholarship—as defined by tribal ways of thinking and of knowing the world.

Native studies thrives in the TCUs in ways that are unknown in other settings. These studies are place based and deeply interwoven with the spiritual life of the people. Native students at TCUs and the Native scholars and teachers who work with them have constructed an understanding of Native knowledge that interprets traditional knowledge and life for the contemporary settings that tribal people live in today.

In America today, most public education is solidly grounded in the development of productive citizenship, which generally means the development of individuals who are economically prepared to contribute to mainstream society. Although there is debate over the role of the university and public higher education, it is difficult to challenge the perception of education as an economic tool when examining the allocation of resources and the priorities associated with innovation, technology, business, and other economic engines. Certainly, institutions with religious missions generally promote religious values and may or may not be in the practice of the promotion of a specific religion. They will often have core academic programs that are mission based from a religious perspective, but they will still focus considerable resources on economic outcomes. During the time of the Indian Nations at Risk Task Force Final Report (Department of Education, 1991), which included the task force's commissioned papers, the U.S. educational and political agenda titled Goals 2000 (H.R. 1804, 1994) aspired to achieve a competitive edge for America by strengthening economic drivers such as education in math, science, and technology. TCUs, as part of the overall tribally controlled education movement, rejected that notion. The task force report began to clearly define what had long been known in our tribal communities: that our goal is to develop human beings as tribes describe humanness. Tribal citizens recognized that economic contributions are but one aspect of wholeness as human beings.

Another way in which the TCUs are particularly unique is that the early founders established their institutions out of a genuine understanding of and experience with Native spirituality. The founders called upon their spiritual practices for guidance and to assure success. This intentional spiritual focus does not exist in public education today. Faith-based institutions may have similar foundational qualities with missions that are focused on spiritual and religious ways of living, but, in general, they do not exist to preserve the identity and life ways of particular racial groups (in this case, Indigenous people). This is not to imply that spirituality does not exist for people involved in public higher education; rather it recognizes that spirituality is generally viewed as an external or at best peripheral endeavor for higher education.

Integrated in the spiritual practices inherent at TCUs is the necessary role of natural and customary law in the fulfillment of social relationships and in the governance of the institutions. Most institutions practice a form of shared governance that empowers Native leadership and offers a consultative model of decision making. Family, extended family, and tribally defined relationships such as society and clan relationships are inherent parts of the tribal college experience, given the cultural life and place-based location of the colleges.

SOCIAL, POLITICAL, AND ECONOMIC IMPACT

Also critical to understanding the identity of TCUs is knowledge of how they impact the social, economic, and political climates of the reservations in ways that off- reservation and mainstream institutions cannot. Due both to their missions and their locations, TCUs are naturally influential in community life. One aspect of the university in Western society as a place of study and critical thought has translated itself well into the expression of activism at the TCUs. Students learn how their tribal history and identity is not only critical to their tribe's survival but also is interwoven with the lives of other tribal nations and in the more global experience of human beings. TCUs help students, staff, and community members find their voice as Natives and as part of creation.

TCUs are catalysts for community transformation, fostering economic growth and the development of the knowledge bases of the tribes. TCUs model economic prosperity, often thriving in economic situations where the standard of living is significantly below the poverty level. They can provide a steady source of tribal employment, and they pour millions of dollars into local economies through financial aid, payrolls, and direct services such as construction projects. TCUs are often a primary driver of business development through incubation projects and technical assistance services.

In many instances, TCUs are places where students learn about their family history and develop a strong sense of kinship. They may learn for the first time about the history of tribes in the United States, about Indian education, or about how to conduct themselves in tribal settings. Poverty, disenfranchisement, and oppression, along with mainstream media and transitory populations, have severely hampered the ability of families to pass along tribal knowledge and skills. TCUs are a source for recapturing this knowledge. They also afford students access to different opportunities to practice traditional ways.

Political activism is another key characteristic of tribal colleges. Ranging from advocacy for wellness and healthy living to educational reform to the reform of tribal government, TCU students and staff are fully engaged tribal citizens when addressing the myriad of needs and issues in their tribal communities. Lionel Bordeaux, president of Sinte Gleska University and the longest serving tribal college president, is a clear voice articulating the intention of the founders of the TCU movement in its effort to bring governmental reform to tribal nations through a return to more traditional practices and values within the governance and social systems of the reservations.

In Paul Higbee's (2014) *South Dakota Magazine* article, "A Lion on Campus," Bordeaux is quoted as saying, "Original mandates included redesigning schooling so . . . we have true ownership of education, unlike traditional 'Indian education' that took away our identities and values. . . . The system of government imposed on reservations divided us. . . . And every election there is more division. . . . We have traditionally been a people of consensus" (p. 54). The TCUs not only provide higher education access to tribal communities but also "promote education that would increase local economic development and productivity, and become a platform for eventually redesigning tribal government" (p. 54).

Participating in mainstream educational institutions in the United States is a political act for Indigenous people and especially for Native students; there they are taught a curriculum that promotes American/Western culture, capitalism, and individualism. They are taught with methodologies that do not honor their ways of knowing and that are not effective for their learning. Most Native studies classes at nontribal college institutions are designed to be taught to non-Native students. Native studies at TCUs is for Native students and is a collective experience with Indigenous ways of knowing at the core of its design. The experience of education at TCUs evolves out of the best practices of teaching and learning with Native students.

TCUs also offer critical community outreach and education services to tribal communities. Often they are the only source of adult education including providing GED services to individuals for whom a high school diploma was an elusive goal. Financial literacy, health and wellness programs, arts education, entrepreneurial training, family engagement activities, and similar programs are provided by TCUs at nearly twice the rate of their academic programs. The reach of the TCUs into communities is deep and broad. No other higher education institutions provide such comprehensive support to tribal families. Often TCUs are a bridge to higher education for younger students who participate with camps, weekend and summer programs, and enrollment in college classes while still in high school.

Fifteen of the current TCUs offer bachelor's degrees. All of the TCUs create transition experiences for their students so their pursuit of advanced education—either within their own institution or with transfer institutions—is successful. The personnel of TCUs are experts at preparing students for college courses and for transfer through first-year and first-generation student programs, developmental education, capstone and transfer courses.

RESEARCH AND SCHOLARSHIP

In 1994, when TCUs were given land-grant status by Congress, they became part of a specific family of higher education institutions—those institutions recognized by Congress as providing the education, research, and extension services necessary to a healthy society and productive use of land. Even in this family of institutions, TCUs stand out—they are the only institutions on tribal homelands and the only institutions that did not receive land as part of their designation. All other state land-grant institutions, including the historically black colleges and universities land-grant colleges, received land on which to conduct research and deliver academic programs. In lieu of land, TCUs receive interest from an endowment.

Significant to the land-grant designation, and with increased investment in behavioral and science-based programming, has been the emerging contribution of TCUs to the body of research and scholarship surrounding tribal people and their resources. TCUs are frontrunners in the use of community-based research practices that focus on identifying the research needs of tribal people, conducting research with the input and involvement of tribal people and having tribal people evaluate the results themselves, specifically for the purpose of identifying and creating interventions and programs that address community needs. TCUs conduct important research about plants and animals, about the land, water, and air, and about how to maintain and strengthen sustainability and food sovereignty. TCUs bring the knowledge and experiences of tribal elders and cultural informants to this research. Often elders and cultural informants are right there in the classroom as teachers, students, and resource people.

CONSTITUENCIES AND LEADERSHIP

TCUs serve an exceptional student population. TCU students are reservation based, usually with limited or no access to higher education, and often with limited or no access to many other resources such as government services, housing, health care, and business services. They are almost always rural and have little family history of higher education. Their historical experiences with education are likely to be filled with trauma. Their successful experiences at the tribal college foster a strong sense of accomplishment and a feeling of ownership of both their educational experience and of the TCU. The deepest cultural knowledge of their tribes is usually held by them or someone in their family, and they are eager to take advantage of the education offered by TCUs because it resonates with their cultural and familial experiences. The people served by TCUs are not only students, they are also the teachers and scholars of their tribal nations.

Students at TCUs share that they are a sanctuary, a safe place, often a place where a student feels that his or her life is being saved and transformed. Students share that they have more opportunities to participate in the college experience at TCUs because they are not just a number there—they are among relatives, both literally and figuratively.

Similar to our student population are the characteristics of the faculty and staff at TCUs. Because TCUs are reservation-based institutions, our total Native employee population is high while the percentage of faculty who are not Native is significant. This is primarily due to the limited number of available trained Native individuals for faculty positions, and the challenges associated with offering competitive opportunities for Native educators. Underrecognized across the academy is that at the TCUs are some of the most knowledgeable Native faculty and scholars in the country. The faculty and staff of the TCUs are experts at the education of American Indian adults and often possess the greatest amount of knowledge about how to provide a seamless education experience in tribal communities.

Because of the community-based nature of TCUs, the academic and community programs are accountable to the community's elders and leaders. This accountability goes beyond the expectations of any external evaluator, including accreditation agencies. Accountability often is rigorous and challenging because the expectations and hopes of the tribal elders and leaders for the future of their children rest with the opportunities and resources of the TCU. Whether or not they are members of the community or tribe, faculty and staff are responsible for a very close-up form of accountability. At any moment, a student's auntie might come to visit the campus or a young mother may bring her children to class. This is almost unheard of in other educational settings.

A case study of Cankdeska Cikana Community College (CCCC) on the Spirit Lake Reservation in North Dakota (Longie and Rousey, 2001) demonstrates the crucial role of the place-based tribal college in support of Native student success. Their study discusses the ways CCCC supports students in a manner quite distinct from nontribal institutions. This includes the fact that central to the college's place-based role is expression of cultural and family support through the college's mission and programs, the social services support provided by the college to its students, and the ability of the college to be responsive to the students' familial and social obligations. Longie and Rousey examine the impact of this central characteristic of family and social support on the higher student retention and successful graduation of at-risk students at TCUs. It reinforces that the reservation or place-based focus is critical to student identity and achievement.

The governing boards of TCUs also are reflective of this community experience. Regardless of whether elected or appointed, board members have governance roles at TCUs because of political, social, cultural, and familial relationships. Many board members are graduates of TCUs (as are an increasing number of TCU presidents), but they may also have more experience with a traditional upbringing or local knowledge-based education. Often they have deep ties to the grassroots members of tribal communities, to the cultural and spiritual leadership, and to the extended families who comprise most of our tribes. They also live in the communities served by the colleges.

Finally, presidents of TCUs also bring critical leadership and knowledge to the identity of the colleges. As Janine Pease identified in her 1994 study of TCU leaders, the (Plains Indian) warrior traditions of spiritual strength and courageous dedication are notable characteristics of the TCU president. Her description of the leadership prior to 1994 applies still today: "They were raised up in the tribal community with the values of family sharing, generosity, warrior commitment and spiritual dedication" (p. 224). Rarely does the opportunity exist in mainstream colleges for a college president to significantly influence the future of a cohesive and defined group of people in the way that a TCU president can impact the people served by his or her institution, where the presidency is very personal.

HONORING THE TCU IDENTITY

Native people are becoming increasing multitribal or multiracial, and the majority now live in urban areas. Few opportunities for employment exist on many reservations, so economic hardship has caused more Natives to move to cities for jobs. Tribes also have multigenerational residency in population centers where their relatives were sent during relocation. Because of access to media through television and the Internet, Native young people increasingly are becoming global citizens. Tribal nations are at a critical period with regard to protecting their national identity as tribal people. It is important that all Native people and their allies recommit to the preservation and restoration of tribal languages and cultural knowledge and practices. Tribal citizens should do everything possible to preserve tribal homelands and to teach children and their families about their inherent rights and about the protections and rights afforded to us by treaties. Tribal citizens must honor and practice traditional and customary laws, Indigenous ways of governing, and spiritual teachings. Without these qualities, Indigenous peoples do not exist as a people and as Nations, at least not in a way that tribal ancestors would recognize.

Other institutions educate American Indian/Alaska Native (AI/AN) and other Indigenous students. They provide opportunities for research and scholarship and build lasting and productive relationships with tribal communities. They employ some of the most talented and well-educated Native people in the country in their various colleges and programs. As tribal colleges and universities, we honor and respect the work of Native faculty and staff at those institutions. We support our Native students who attend those institutions and defend their right to a high quality education at whatever place they choose. However, no matter how many Native students attend them, no matter how well intentioned, and no matter how long their relationships with surrounding tribes, these institutions are not tribally controlled colleges.

TCUs are distinct because they are institutions of a specific place. Tribal knowledge is gathered and taught from the context of the tribe's place—with all the teachings that go with that. Traditional knowledge is taught in a contemporary setting, just as the founders intended. TCUs are places where scholars and teachers have found strategies for preservation and restoration of knowledge in a place that might be a called a "living laboratory." They are places where Native students go to school with each other and learn and work toward living a life of balance—one that honors identity while developing skills and abilities needed to lead our tribes, manage our resources, and take care of our families.

NOTES

1. Except, of course, in anthropology and linguistics classes that studied Native peoples and their languages as artifacts.

2. Original source document is Mohatt, G. (1978). Sinte Gleska College: Issues and dilemmas in the development of an alternative setting in a Native American college. University Microfilms International. Ann Arbor, Michigan.

3. See more information about the College of Muscogee Nation at www.mvsktc .org/mission.html.

REFERENCES

Department of Education. (1991, October). Indian nations at risk task force. Washington, DC. Retrieved February 16, 2015, from U.S. Department of Education, http://eric.ed.gov/?id=ED339587.

Higbee, P. (2014, March/April). A lion on campus. *South Dakota Magazine, 29*(6), 51–56.

H.R. 1804. (1994). Goals 2000: Educate America Act. Washington, DC: U.S. Department of Education. Retrieved February 15, 2015, from www2.ed.gov/legislation/GOALS2000/TheAct/index.html.

LaFrance, J., and Nichols, R. (2008). *Indigenous evaluation framework: Telling our story in our place and time.* Washington, DC: American Indian Higher Education Consortium (AIHEC).

Longie, E., and Rousey, A. (2001, May) The tribal college as family support system. *American Behavioral Scientist, 44*(9), 1492–1504.

Pease, J. (1994). The tribally controlled community colleges act of 1978: An expansion of Indian trust responsibility (Doctoral dissertation). Montana State University–Bozeman.

Preserving the vision of our ancestors: An educational legacy self-study of the College of the Muscogee Nation, March 2014.

Roessel and Board of Regents. (1968–69). Internal document. Navajo Community College, Tsaile, AZ.

Stein, Wayne J. (1992). *Tribally controlled colleges: Making good medicine.* Peter Lang Publishing. New York, NY.

ADDITIONAL RESOURCES

American Indian Higher Education Consortium (www.aihec.org).

American Indian College Fund (www.collegefund.org).

Carnegie Foundation for the Advancement of Teaching. (1989). *Tribal colleges: Shaping the future of Native America.* Princeton, NJ.: Ivy Lane.

Carnegie Foundation for the Advancement of Teaching. (1997). *Native American colleges: Progress and prospects.* Princeton, NJ.: Ivy Lane.

Tribal College Journal of American Indian Higher Education (www.tribalcollege journal.org).

Warner, L., and Gipp, G. (Eds.). (2009). *Tradition and culture in the millennium: Tribal colleges and universities.* Charlotte, NC: Information Age Publishing.

3
Guiding Principles of Indigenous Leadership from a Hawaiian Perspective

ALOHALANI HOUSMAN

In order to clearly define what leadership is from a Hawaiian perspective, it is necessary to look at our Native language. In Hawaiian, the word for leadership, *alaka'i,* is actually derived from two smaller words, *ala* and *ka'i.* "Ala" is a path, road, or trail, and "ka'i" means to lead, direct, lift up, and carry (Pukui and Elbert, 1986). So from the Hawaiian worldview, a leader leads, directs, lifts up, and carries the people around him on a journey down a pathway, which leads to a common goal.

This chapter will look at three legendary journeys of the Hawaiian people that illuminate the essence of what it means to be a leader in the Hawaiian mindset. The journeys include the analyses of long-distant voyaging canoes, Kamehameha's prowess as premier chief, and the emergence of the Hawaiian language revitalization movement.

Academic research on the specific topic of Hawaiian Indigenous leadership has been virtually nonexistent until recently and is being built upon the work of Hawaiian academic scholars. Their contributions in Hawaiian ways of knowing, cultural identity, and strengths-based research are laying the grounds to begin defining the attributes of Hawaiian leadership today. Meyer (1997) is well known for her research in the area of Hawaiian epistemology. She identified six philosophic structures in her dissertation: (a) spirituality and knowing, (b) culturally defined senses, (c) relationships and knowledge, (d) utility and knowledge, (e) words and knowledge, (f) the na'au or, in other words, the seat of both thinking and feeling for Hawaiians. Kamana'opono Crabbe (2003) developed the Hawaiian Ethnic Identity (HEI) scale as a means for assessing acculturation and identity in people of Hawaiian ancestry. Kana'iaupuni (2004) admonishes educators to adopt a Hawaiian research methodology built on the strengths of the culture not its deficiencies. Kana'iaupuni also suggests that the pursuit of science needs to be completed using a Hawaiian worldview and in a manner that strengthens scientific knowledge through a cultural diversity and Hawaiian epistemological lens.

Kaulukukui and Nāhoʻopiʻi (2008) developed an Inventory of Exemplary Hawaiian Leadership Behaviors based on the prior research of Meyers (1997), Crabbe (2003), Kanaʻiaupuni (2004), Smith (1999), and Kouzes and Posner (1987). The inventory included ninety-five items of various leadership behaviors, which were rated using a five-point Likert scale. Two hundred seventy-six surveys were included in the analysis. Following is a summary of their findings:

> The items showed that the exemplary Hawaiian leader acknowledges the Hawaiian culture as the source of leadership. Additionally, the exemplary Hawaiian leader must be able to apply cultural values in leadership activities and understand the balance of relationships that support a thriving community for future generations. These exemplary Hawaiians also are leaders who are guided by a higher power. Finally, exemplary Hawaiian leaders must exhibit a personal strength and aptitude for leadership. (Kaulukukui and Nāhoʻopiʻi, 2008, p. 130)

The Hawaiian leadership behaviors identified by Kaulukukui and Nāhoʻopiʻi (2008) support the principles that emerged from the analysis of the three journeys included in this chapter. The first step of the strengths-based approach taken to identify the guiding principles was to decide which influential leaders in the history of the Hawaiʻi have been able to unite people together to fulfill a particular vision that embraces the values and practices of its Indigenous people. Three examples came to mind quickly: canoe voyaging, Kamehameha the Great, and the Hawaiian language revitalization movement. Once these were identified, the next step was to analyze the reasons why each one of these groups was able to surmount obstacles to rise to positions of influence to fulfill their goals. The process for identifying guiding principles of leadership included the gathering of information from books, journals, and research and then looking at commonalities between the three movements.

THREE JOURNEYS

In analyzing the lessons learned from traditional transoceanic voyaging canoes, the achievements of Kamehameha the Great, and, more recently, the Hawaiian language revitalization movement, several important components of leadership have emerged from the experiences of these three distinct facets of the Hawaiian people. Based on the three historic journeys, successful Indigenous leaders exhibit eight leadership principles. Principles are:

- clear vision
- strong cultural identity

- ability to unite others in a common purpose
- ability to overcome hardships and challenges
- commitment to the whole journey
- sensitivity to spirituality
- respect for mentors
- legacy to pass on

In a later section in this chapter these eight guiding principles of leadership are examined and described within the Hawaiian worldview termed the *Kumu Honua Mauli Ola* Philosophy.

VOYAGING CANOES

A stellar example of such a journey-based definition of leadership from the history of our Hawaiian ancestors is found in the collective wisdom and experience of the navigators of the voyaging canoes that crossed thousands of miles of ocean to settle new lands throughout the vast Pacific region. The navigator plays a very important role on the canoe and must have a clear vision of the target in mind. He/she needs to be knowledgeable, skilled, prepared, resourceful, inspiring, caring, and a respected leader. A good understanding of the elements and the environment surrounding the canoe is imperative. Observation skills must be keen. Elements such as the stars, the clouds, the sky, the currents, and the birds are there to guide and must be respected. These signs given from the environment must be heeded with reverence if the journey is to be made safely. The navigator inspires the entire crew to work together in common purpose to fulfill the mission of the voyage. The needs of the entire group on the canoe must supersede the wants and desires of individuals. Otherwise the canoe could possibly wander aimlessly in the deep ocean instead of moving in a well thought out plan of action. The canoe, as the vessel transporting groups from one place to another, needs to be culturally viable, relevant, and of value to those on the canoe. If not, the group members will become disillusioned and feel hopeless. As a result, catastrophic consequences could occur and result in the loss of life along the way. The children aboard the educational canoe are our legacy. They are our hope and our future. Life, language, and culture will fail to continue without them. Therefore, contemporary leaders, like traditional ocean navigators, must do all that is within their power to make the journey the epitome of success. The well-being of our ancestors in the past, along with continued flourishing of the people of this generation and future generations, depends on visionary leaders who can take us on arduous journeys to new lands of promise, where our people can grow and prosper in an environment that values and nurtures the Native worldview.

KAMEHAMEHA THE GREAT (1736–1819)

Another decisive journey in the history of the Hawaiian people is the unification of the Hawaiian Islands under the rule of one chief. Kamehameha the Great was the paramount leader to accomplish such a task. According to the writings of Kamakau (1992) and ʻĪʻī (1993), Kamehameha I was prepared from the time he was born to become a strong and great leader. He was skilled in many different aspects: religious rites, athletics, games, warfare, family matters, government, and politics. It is because of the qualities that he possessed that he became the most famous and honored Hawaiian chief of all time. Throughout his life, he showed respect to the gods, leaders, teachers, community, and family. He had very strong beliefs in the spiritual realm and therefore adhered to prophecies, omens, and signs in order to bring good to the land and avoid bad fortune. He listened intently to teachings from leaders and followed instructions precisely as commanded to him. He was fearless in battle and is considered to be one of the greatest warriors of his time. His many battles settled power and land rights. Poepoe (1906) informs us that Kamehameha united all of the Hawaiian Islands in 1810, after which he served the people of the kingdom for the remainder of his life. He is well-known for the establishment of the *Māmalahoa Kānāwai* (Law of the Splintered Paddle); which protected the weak, especially the old, the women, and children. Kamehameha had good relationships with foreigners and demonstrated a curiosity to new ideas and concepts, but his beliefs, values, and foundations in his cultural identity are what guided him throughout his long and prosperous life.

THE HAWAIIAN LANGUAGE
REVITALIZATION MOVEMENT

In the past thirty years, another significant journey has taken place in Hawaiʻi. That journey of leadership is the Hawaiian language revitalization movement. The primary goal of the movement is to speak the Hawaiian language fluently in our families, in schools, and in the community. Many leaders in this language revitalization movement find a philosophical underpinning for their efforts in the Kumu Honua Mauli Ola (Foundations of Cultural Identity), a Native philosophy built upon ancient wisdoms and understandings useful in a contemporary setting (Ka Haka ʻUla o Keʻelikōlani a me ka ʻAha Pūnana Leo, 2009). The Kumu Honua Mauli Ola serves as a conceptual framework to guide Hawaiian revitalization efforts and is an articulated vision of what education at all levels should seek to accomplish (Silva, Alencastre, Kawaiʻaeʻa, and Housman, 2008). The philosophical template provides direction for Hawaiian-medium education and contains universal elements that might be useful in other cultural contexts. The philosophy provides the lens through which leaders can focus their efforts to provide culturally healthy and responsive learning experiences for all (Kawaiʻaeʻa 2006).

The Kumu Honua Mauli Ola helps to identify and preserve the essence of who we are as Native Hawaiians. The philosophy is comprised of three major aspects—the *mauli*, the *piko*, and the *honua*. Each of these features will be described in detail in this section.

"Mauli" is an old word that can be defined as the life, heart, spirit, or seat of life (Pukui and Elbert, 1986). It can be compared to a fire that burns deep within the soul. Just as a fire can be extinguished, if we neglect our mauli, our life force can also diminish greatly and we can become lost as a Native people. On the other hand, if nourished and cultivated properly, the mauli, like a well-tended fire, can burn brilliantly (Silva et al., 2008). As we stand strong in our cultural identity as individuals and as an entire Native group, the fire becomes even more illuminated, and well-being follows thereafter.

According to the Kumu Honua Mauli Ola, there are four major elements of an individual's life-giving mauli: spirituality, language, traditional knowledge, and behavior. As each one of these components is nourished and developed, the fire burns brighter and pride in oneself and in one's culture flourishes. Following is a short summary of each individual element and its relationship to different parts of the body where they are tended. After each synopsis is an explanation of how that particular element can be applied in today's world:

> *Ka ʻAoʻao Pili ʻUhane*—**the spiritual element**, that is, the spirit with which we are all born, which is seated in the head, the most sacred part of the body, recognizes right from wrong, good from bad, and creates a relationship with everything in the universe, both seen and unseen. (Silva et al., 2008, p. 30)

Spirituality has always been an important aspect of the Hawaiian culture. Dreams, visions, omens, signs, a feeling in the gut, or hair-raising sensations of the skin can warn of imminent danger, bring serenity to a troubled mind, or answer a perplexing question. From ancient days, prayers, religious rules, and rituals have been an important part of everyday living. Even today, showing respect for a higher being and all creation in the heavens and on the earth is believed by many contemporary Hawaiians to be essential for ultimate success. For example, before going into the rain forest to gather foliage to make a lei, one should ask permission through an *oli* or prayer. When gathering ferns, leaves, and flowers, collecting should be done with the utmost care so that native ecosystems are not disrupted. One should never be wasteful and take more than is needed to accomplish the task. After the lei adornment is used, the garland is returned back to the earth and not carelessly disposed of in a rubbish can.

The second essential element of the mauli (life force) is language. There is a Hawaiian wise saying, *"I ka 'ōlelo nō ke ola, i ka 'ōlelo nō ka make"* (Pukui, 1983). It means that there is life in speech and there is death in speech. Therefore, it is very important to choose words wisely, since language has the power to heal and the power to destroy.

> *Ka 'Ao'ao 'Ōlelo*—the language element, found in the ears, the mouth, and the tongue. Language can be used in many different ways and may be soft, rough, gentle, harsh, forthright, or secretive, but perhaps its greatest strength lies in its ability to transmit mauli to future generations. (Silva et al., 2008, p. 30)

Language is the fiber that binds us to our cultural identity. It provides an important worldview in terms of understanding culture, traditional ways of thinking, and values. Language is the mode for communicating everyday ideas and thoughts along with revealing information from the past such as the meaning of place names, wise sayings, riddles, songs, folklore, and other literary forms. Without language, the comprehension of these beautiful art forms of culture would eventually cease to exist. Evidence over generations and across diverse cultural settings has demonstrated that when a native tongue is a vibrant living language, the people of that nation are also strong. However, when foreign languages are imposed on native inhabitants, a decline in the fortitude of that people follows. Therefore, for the resiliency of the population it is critical that the native tongue return to a position of high status as a fluent, dynamic, and viable language spoken on a daily basis between several generations. Language can be destroyed in one generation, but it takes at least three generations for it to become well established again. Revitalization is not an easy task but is possible with great effort and commitment on the part of dedicated people.

The third essential element of the mauli (life force) is traditional knowledge, which is knowledge that has been passed down from ancestors over many generations of time and is still being utilized today. Following is the description for this element:

> *Ka 'Ao'ao 'Ike Ku'una*—the traditional knowledge element is seated in the intestines, where knowledge and emotions lie. It is expressed in traditional values and practices like the hula, poetry, and prayer. Such practices have creative aspects and, like language, can reflect misrepresentations. Thus, the true power of traditional knowledge lies in authentic practices carried out by mature people who recognize their cultural responsibility to others who share their mauli. (Silva et al., 2008, p. 30)

Traditional knowledge holds essential keys that are critical to understanding the Native worldview. Cultural practices in the area of genealogy, history, religion, traditional stories, farming, fishing, canoe making, navigation, sports, martial arts, hula, lei-making, food preparation, and medicine are still vital parts of modern-day living. An example of using traditional knowledge in the realm of fishing and farming is following the different phases of the moon to determine the optimal time to plant certain vegetation or catch certain fish to bring a high yield of subsistence. The keen observation skills of early ancestors were critical in providing the necessities of life to relatives and to the community. Fortunately, traditional knowledge and wisdom gained from years of experience in the past can still greatly benefit families in present-day situations.

The fourth essential element of the mauli is physical behavior. Each ethnic group has its own particular way of behaving. For instance, when first meeting a Hawaiian person, a warm hug and kiss of aloha would graciously welcome a person, whereas the bowing of the head would be the behavior demonstrated by a traditional Japanese person and a handshake would be an appropriate greeting by Americans. These particular behaviors are what identify us with a particular group of people.

> *Ka 'Ao'ao Lawena*—the physical behavior element is found in the limbs of the body, in gestures, in the way one stands or moves the feet while walking, in a facial expression, in a smile. This element of one's mauli usually is learned at a young age through unconscious imitation and is easily recognized and appreciated by those who share the same mauli. (Silva et al., 2008, p. 31)

Behaviors vary from culture to culture. What is appropriate in one culture may not be appropriate in another. There is a code of conduct in each ethnic group that includes certain behaviors that are acceptable and not acceptable. For example, hospitality has always been an important part of the Hawaiian culture. Many traditional stories are based on this customary practice. Inviting travelers into one's home, providing food, water, and shelter for sleeping represented hospitality among Hawaiian people. In legends, when hosts were gracious and welcoming, gods rewarded them with something such as new fresh springs of drinking water. However, when the opposite occurred, stingy residents were punished by the gods with the stripping of precious natural resources or the destruction of possessions by devastating natural disasters. Therefore, even today, it is very natural for Native Hawaiians to be very hospitable. Other examples of appropriate behavior include listening and observing, being respectful to people and nature, giving up a seat to sit on the floor so someone older can sit down, keeping things clean and tidy, greeting someone while passing, not arguing at dinner time, taking food to someone's house when invited for dinner, not interrupting someone else's conversation, and taking off shoes before entering a home. These are just a few examples of proper behavior from a Hawaiian perspective.

Another important aspect of the Kumu Honua Mauli Ola is the piko. The piko are connecting centers of the mauli (Ka Haka 'Ula o Ke'elikōlani a me ka 'Aha Pūnana Leo, 2009). Although each person has a mauli or life force that can grow strong or dim based on his or her cultural identity, the piko are physical centers on the body that connect the mauli to the divine, to preceding generations, and generations to come. This idea demonstrates the extension of relationships that go beyond the here and now. Following are the three centers of the body:

Piko 'Ī—the fontanel or soft spot at the top of our heads when we are babies and through which we become physically connected to the spiritual beliefs of our people.

Piko 'Ō—the navel, attached to the umbilical cord and placenta, which connects us to our ancestors, and is closest to the na'au or gut, the seat of our knowledge and emotions.

Piko 'Ā—the reproductive organs, which create future generations and, by extension, all that we create and establish. (Silva et al., 2008, p. 31)

These piko centers connect us to the past, the present, and the future and by extension, to time, space, people, and place. Maintaining our connections enables us to understand the knowledge of the past as a foundation for the present to continue our legacy and further develop it for future generations (Kawai'ae'a, 2006).

The last important aspect of the Kumu Honua Mauli Ola is the honua, places where our mauli is nurtured and developed. They are the environments that foster our connections to the people and places that solidify our cultural identity. Life can be seen as having three basic honua as follows:

Honua 'Iewe—the highly protected placenta in the mother's womb representing the close ties of family and kinship that are the foundation of one's mauli.

Honua Kīpuka—a kīpuka is a clear place or oasis where a lava flow has left an area of uncovered forest, thus representing the ties of community, an extended protected environment in which one develops the mauli of the family.

Honua Ao Holo'oko'a—the world at large, where an adult who has been raised with a strong cultural identity expresses and shares the distinctiveness of that mauli with others from diverse backgrounds. (Silva et al., 2008, p. 31)

It is important to note that as a child grows and develops learning takes place first in the family and works outwardly from the home to the community and to the broader world. There is a wise saying, "*'O ke kahua ma mua, ma hope ke kūkulu*" (Pukui, 1983, p. 268) that means "The foundation is first, then the building." Far too often, well-intentioned educators introduce foreign ideas and concepts, before acknowledging the foundations of a child's own culture. The result can be disastrous when Native knowledge and experience are not taken into consideration before developing new constructs of knowledge. Therefore, the base must be well established in order for the structure to be assembled properly and advantageously. The Native worldview is the foundation through which the Native child should see the world and discover new ideas. It is the place where the mauli is nurtured and confidence is developed, so that, as a child matures, he or she will have the ability to not only respect and share the Native perspective but also to respect and learn from other cultures of the world.

GUIDING PRINCIPLES OF INDIGENOUS LEADERSHIP

The guiding principles of Indigenous leaders listed earlier in this chapter will be examined in this section through the lens of the Kumu Honua Mauli Ola philosophy (see table 3.1). If Indigenous leadership models are to be developed for Native people, the worldview of that people must first be understood. It is critical to the survival of Indigenous ways of thinking, knowing, and behaving. Examples from the three historical journeys will be used to expand on each of these qualities in greater detail.

CLEAR VISION

The leader must possess a mental image of the target in mind in order to accomplish the vision. For navigators of canoe voyaging, the target is an island destination that lays thousands of miles away in the vast Pacific Ocean. For Kamehameha, the vision was the uniting of all the Hawaiian Islands under one rule. For leaders of the Hawaiian language revitalization movement, the vision, "*E Ola Ka 'Ōlelo Hawai'i*," which means "the Hawaiian language shall live," is the driving force. The vision is what drives the leaders to accomplish the goal, especially in times of difficulty and hardship. To lose track of the vision would be a great compromise and significant adverse consequences would surely follow.

The vision must be clearly defined and visible in the mind, heart, and soul as illustrated in the following excerpt taken from the writings of Nainoa Thompson, navigator of the double-hulled canoe called *Hōkūle'a*.

Mau said, "Can you see the island?" You know, Tahiti is smaller than Maui. You cannot see Tahiti from Hawai'i. But his question was not asking about what your eyes see, as I understood it. He said, "Can you see the island?" And I didn't know the answer, so I had to wait. Finally

Table 3.1 The Guiding Principles of Indigenous Leadership through the Lens of the Kumu Honua Mauli Ola Philosophy

Guiding Principle	Kumu Honua Mauli Ola	Voyaging	Kamehameha the Great	Hawaiian Language Revitalization Movement
Clear Vision	The leader has a clear vision that promotes the mauli (life force) of the Indigenous group.	The transporting of individuals with precision between small islands that lay thousands of miles away in the grand Pacific Ocean without the use of modern day instruments and by relying solely on traditional voyaging practices.	The unification of the Hawaiian islands into one rule so that interisland warfare would end and the people would prosper in a united, harmonious kingdom.	"E Ola Ka ʻŌlelo Hawaiʻi" (The Hawaiian Language Shall Live). The native Hawaiian language is returned to its status of being the everyday language of its people and therefore found in every context of life.
Strong Cultural Identity	The cultural identity of the leader strongly correlates with the mauli of the Indigenous people that he/she represents.	Leaders of voyaging canoes today remain true to the traditional navigational beliefs and practices of early Hawaiian ancestors.	Literature written by Hawaiians and westerners regarding Kamehameha confirms that he remained steadfast in his traditional Hawaiian beliefs and practices until the day he died.	The Kumu Honua Mauli Ola philosophical statement was written by leaders of the language revitalization movement based on practices and beliefs of early Hawaiian ancestors.
Ability to Unite Others in a Common Purpose	The leader is able to clearly articulate the vision, which is built upon the mauli, to others and unite them to fulfill the vision.	In the 1970s, the dream of Hōkūleʻa started with a handful of people. Over the past thirty-two years, the Hōkūleʻa has sailed over 125,000 miles. Now there are seventeen or eighteen deep-sea voyaging canoes. Before Hōkūleʻa there were none.	Kamehameha united the high chiefs and warriors from Kona to fight against rivals of other districts and islands in the Hawaiian chain. After thirty-five years, the islands were united under one rule.	The Pūnana Leo Preschools have grown from one school in 1984 to eleven schools today. The Hawaiian language immersion schools have grown from two K–1 classes in 1987 to twenty-one schools today with over two thousand students statewide.

Ability to Overcome Hardships and Challenges	The leader does not let hardships and challenges become obstacles in achieving the vision but rather uses them as a means to strengthen the mauli.	"Fear has become my best friend. It's not about being fearless, it's about not being afraid of fear. It helps me get ready. It helps me train." This statement by Nainoa Thompson is a classic example of how to use a challenge to achieve positive outcomes.	*ʻImua e nā pōkiʻi a inu i ka wai ʻawaʻawa* (Forward my younger brothers until you drink the bitter water). A statement made by Kamehameha before winning the battle on the island of Maui. It is still used today as an encouragement when facing difficult challenges.	Laws that banned the use of Hawaiian in schools were changed, hours of service to prepare materials were rendered, the lack of money and resources were overcome through the cooperation of the ʻAha Pūnana Leo, teachers, parents, children, and community.
Commitment to the Whole Journey	The leader has an unwavering resolve to fulfill the vision, even in the face of adversity, and therefore demonstrates a lifelong commitment to building up the mauli of the people.	At least 95 percent of the voyage is before you leave. It is in the training, preparation, competence, unity, and strength. The journey begins with the commitment to the vision. The voyage is just a piece of that.	Kamehameha trained diligently to become the strongest warrior and remained steadfast in protecting his people during his entire life.	Graduating classes over a ten-year span have proven that students who began their education in the Hawaiian language immersion movement as small children have become extremely fluent in two or more languages. They also have higher test scores, graduation rates, and college attendance rates when compared to Hawaiian students in regular public schools.
Sensitivity to Spirituality	The leader recognizes that he/she is part of a greater force in the world. Through honoring and respecting that greater force, the mauli is cultivated and the vision is fulfilled.	Observance of star constellations, ocean rhythms, wind patterns, cloud formations, and flight patterns of seabirds all play an important part of traditional navigational practices.	Kamehameha adhered to signs, omens, promptings, and prophesies from his spiritual counselors. He also performed regular rituals to honor his gods.	Listening to the internal compass provides the direction in which to make good choices in moving the program forward successfully and to bring about harmony among stakeholders.

Table 3.1 continued

Guiding Principle	Kumu Honua Mauli Ola	Voyaging	Kamehameha the Great	Hawaiian Language Revitalization Movement
Respect for Mentors	The leader recognizes and honors mentors who emulate the mauli passed down from ancestors and who play an instrumental role in achieving the vision.	Master navigators are shown respect and are valued for their wisdom, knowledge, strength, and expertise. They play an important role in the teaching and nurturing process, especially when difficulties arise. Nainoa pays tribute to Mau Piailug, Herb Kane, Eddie Akau, and his father, Myron Thompson.	Kamehameha showed respect to his mentors by listening, following their instructions, and defending them with his life. Keaweheulu, Keʻeaumoku, Kamanawa, Kameʻeiamoku, and Kekūhaupiʻo, who were his greatest teachers and supporters, became the premier regents under Kamehameha's rule.	Native speakers of the grandparent generation are highly respected for their expertise in the language, cultural practices, music, and storytelling. Members of the ʻAha Pūnana Leo Board are master teachers who are also highly respected for the contributions that they have made to ensure the continuation of the Hawaiian language.
Legacy to Pass on	The mauli of the leader lives on in others as the vision is realized and perpetuated through generations.	Voyaging meetings and conferences are held on a regular basis to prepare the upcoming generation to become the next navigators and leaders. Hundreds of participants are enthusiastically involved with learning traditional practices with a dream to sail around the entire world in the near future.	Kamehameha was the ultimate Hawaiian leader of all time in the history of Hawaiʻi. He was highly respected in his day by Natives and foreigners alike, and his life is still honored and his memory lives on in the hearts of the Hawaiian people today.	A survey conducted in 1983 estimated that only 1,500 people could speak Hawaiian, most of them elderly. However, today there are between six thousand to eight thousand Hawaiian language speakers throughout the state, most of them under thirty.

I said, "You know, Mau, I can see the image of the island in my mind." And he said, "Okay, good." . . . We sailed down to Tahiti, we sailed back, we were successful. And when I look back at that defining moment, Mau knew that the journey needed to be mine. That day at Lānaʻi Lookout, Mau said to me, "Nainoa, you keep that image in your mind because if you forget what it looks like, you'll be lost." And I always remember that second comment because he knew I was going to be tested more than I had ever been in my life. He knew that the ocean would be unforgiving, and he knew it was going to be harder than anything I ever did. The only way I would find Tahiti was if I believed in it enough, if I cared about it enough. That it was more than my sense of inabilities, it was beyond my weaknesses, that it would draw on my sense of purpose, all the things that are meaningful. Mau knew, "Keep the image of the island in your mind because that's what you care about, that's what is meaningful to you." That was an extraordinarily powerful learning experience for me. (Thompson, 2007, p. 32)

STRONG CULTURAL IDENTITY

The vision is the dream that carries one to loftier ideals and places, where a strong cultural identity is the anchor that grounds a leader. Both are equally important and necessary to be successful. Cultural identity was not in question when the first canoes landed in Hawaiʻi, nor was it an issue during the time of Kamehameha. Hawaiians naturally exhibited spirituality, language, traditional knowledge, culturally authentic behavior, binding relationships, and value of place through a Hawaiian perspective. Hawaiians were the majority and so the Hawaiian worldview permeated all aspects of life.

When Captain Cook arrived, there were approximately eight hundred thousand Native Hawaiians. Westerners brought diseases, which decimated the Hawaiian population until only about twenty-four thousand Hawaiians remained. Only about one in thirty-four people survived (Thompson, 2007). American businessmen forced their belief systems on the people; these beliefs required the overthrow of the Hawaiian monarchy and banning of the Hawaiian language. A quick downward decline in the quality of life of the Native population followed shortly thereafter. Hawaiians have never fully recovered and still feel disadvantaged today as a minority group in their own homeland. Society at large teaches native people that they must push their cultural identity aside in order to be successful. Yet, examples throughout history have shown that loss of cultural identity is detrimental to one's well-being and even one's existence. This is evident in the high statistics for health problems, alcoholism, prison rates, and welfare enrollment among Hawaiians today, as well as the lowest statistics for educational attainment (Kanaʻiaupuni, Malone, and Ishibashi, 2005).

In the area of physical well-being, a study conducted by the Kamehameha Policy Analysis and Systems Evaluation (PASE) team found that almost three-quarters of Native Hawaiian adults (71.8 percent) are overweight or obese, compared with 51.8 percent of the total adult population. Native Hawaiian mortality rates for cancer, diabetes, and heart disease are the highest among the major ethnic groups in the state. In 2001, 25.2 percent of Native Hawaiian high school students had smoked cigarettes during the previous month, compared with 17.1 percent of non-Hawaiian students. Current smokers account for 31.1 percent of Native Hawaiian adults versus 20.4 percent of the state's total adult population (Kana'iaupuni et al., 2005).

Compared with other families in the state, according to the PASE team (Kana'iaupuni et al., 2005), in the area of social and cultural well-being Native Hawaiian households have the highest incidence of single-parent families with minor children (15.8 percent versus 8.1 percent). Such families more often struggle with financial insecurity and family tensions. The research team also found that Native Hawaiians on the whole have disproportionately high rates of substance abuse, arrest, and incarceration; these are areas that might benefit from engaging the support of *kūpuna* (elders) and the cohesive aspects of Hawaiian cultural practices and active community involvement.

In the area of material and economic well-being the PASE team found that Native Hawaiian families with children have the lowest mean income ($55,865 versus the statewide average of $66,413) and the highest poverty rates (18.3 percent versus 11.3 percent statewide) among the major ethnic groups in the state of Hawai'i. Poverty among Native Hawaiians is highest in rural areas such as Moloka'i and the eastern side of Hawai'i island, where the concentration of native Hawaiians is high. In the Leeward district on O'ahu, almost one-third (32.4 percent) of school-age native Hawaiian children live in poverty (Kana'iaupuni et al., 2005).

Even though statistics for Native Hawaiians have been dismal in the past, new research gives hope for change in a positive direction in the future. Recent statistics from the PASE team have found evidence that students who attend Hawaiian language immersion and culture-based charter schools are outperforming Hawaiian students in mainstream education. Native Hawaiians in charter schools score higher in math and reading tests compared with their counterparts in mainstream public schools. For example, from 2001 to 2003, Native Hawaiian tenth graders in charter schools scored one and a half times higher than Native Hawaiians in mainstream public schools on the state standardized test in reading. In addition, just 4.1 percent of Native Hawaiians in language and cultural-based charter schools are excessively absent from school, compared with 17.3 percent of Native Hawaiians in mainstream public schools (Kana'iaupuni et al., 2005).

Research shows that having a strong cultural identity has a positive impact on achievement and well-being. It is the foundation upon which everything else should be built. When the foundation is strong, one is confident and is able to contribute to the society. Nainoa's father sums it up in his advice to his son:

> My father said, "Carry your culture on your canoe." He said, "Your people need it. They're going to need that sense of your direction and your commitment to your heritage and your ancestors. They're going to need to know that it counts and it's important." My father said, "Make sure when you carry that identity and dignity of who you were and who you're going to become, make sure you do it in a way that doesn't compromise anyone of a different culture." He said, "We need everyone." (Thompson, 2007, p. 23)

UNITING OTHERS IN A COMMON PURPOSE

Every successful journey begins with a dream, a vision that unites others in a common purpose (Thompson, 2007). Therefore, the Indigenous leaders must have the ability to inspire others to work together harmoniously to achieve goals. In more recent days, another kind of uniting of minds and hearts in a common purpose has taken place. The dream of sailing to Tahiti began with just a few but eventually increased in numbers. Nainoa Thompson was inspired by the words of his father: "Give them your vision. Articulate your values. Let them come. Never allow your community to be defined and split off by geography or by race. Hold them together by common vision and shared values. They will come. Define them as a people who want to give back. Go build your community" (Thompson, 2007, p. 22).

In 1976, the *Hōkūleʻa* accomplished a miraculous feat. It was the first time that a double-hulled canoe sailed from Hawaiʻi to Tahiti in the modern day using traditional navigation practices from many centuries earlier. Since then, voyaging leaders have not only united the Hawaiian people in many subsequent trips but have inspired other Polynesian and Indigenous groups to return to traditional voyaging practices. Over the past thirty-two years, the *Hōkūleʻa* has sailed over 125,000 miles (Thompson, 2007). Now there are seventeen or eighteen modern deep-sea voyaging canoes where previously there were none. Knowledge and pride has been restored to Native people throughout the Pacific and beyond.

It was prophesied at Kamehameha's birth and also at other times during his life that he would become a great leader and that he would triumph over the other island chiefs. Although the prophecy was significant, it was Kamehameha's character and inspirational qualities that influenced the chiefs and the warriors from his homeland on the Hawaiʻi island to unite together. Kamehameha I had great respect for Hawaiian tradition. This asset guided him throughout his life and served him well as he developed into a strong, fearless, unwavering leader. He carried out his duties with obedience, dedication, steadfastness, and honor. He demonstrated dedication to his gods, to his chiefs, and to his people. His attributes and determination set him apart from others and helped him rise as a favorite amongst the regents. Keaweaheulu, Keʻeaumoku, Kamanawa, Kameʻeiamoku, and Kekūhaupiʻo—high chiefs from Kona—were instrumental in placing Kamehameha in power (Kamakau and ʻAhahui ʻŌlelo Hawaiʻi, 1996). They united their warriors to do something that had never before been accomplished: the unification of the individual islands under a single rule, thus installing Kamehameha as the first king of Hawaiʻi.

The third example of uniting in a common purpose took place in 1983. The ʻAha Pūnana Leo was established when a small group of friends who are Hawaiian-speaking educators met on Kauaʻi to discuss the dismal state of the Hawaiian language, then near the brink of extinction (ʻAha Pūnana Leo, 2014). Following the model established by the Māori people in New Zealand, the group decided to open a preschool where children would be educated through the medium of Hawaiian. The school was named the Pūnana Leo, which means the "nest of voices." From one small preschool, the program has now grown to include eleven Pūnana Leo sites on five of the major islands with a current enrollment of 226 children (ʻAha Pūnana Leo, 2009). Stemming from the successes of the Hawaiian language nests, in 1987, the first Hawaiian language immersion programs opened up in the public school system. Two combination classes of kindergarten and first-grade students opened their doors with a total enrollment of thirty-four students the first year. Today there are over two thousand students in twenty Hawaiian language immersion schools with over four hundred graduates in the past fifteen years (Hale Kuamoʻo, 2014). One of the strengths of the program, as identified by outside contracted evaluators, is the involvement of parents in the education of their children (Slaughter, 1988). This is a significant finding, since prior to the establishment of Hawaiian language immersion program, widespread Hawaiian family participation in the education system was basically nonexistent. The evidence of the success of this program echo the words of wisdom that were uttered by Nainoa's father, "Give them your vision, articulate your values. . . . They will come, define them as a people who want to give back, go build your community."

ABILITY TO OVERCOME HARDSHIPS AND CHALLENGES

Hardships and challenges make people strong and help them to grow. "When you are under the most strain, a time when you experience the strongest crisis, it's the time when you need leadership. That's when leadership needs to stand up—when it's hard, not when it's easy" (Thompson, 2007, p. 25). Voyaging has made enormous strides in the past thirty-two years, due to leaders who are able to stand up and face obstacles. Thompson acknowledges that challenges can come from many sources, but perhaps the greatest challenge is facing fears that come from within: "It is true that every voyage has its share of hardships. Sometimes the challenges come from outside the community, and other times they come from within. Most often, they come from inside ourselves, stemming from feelings of fear and inadequacy" (Thompson, 2007, p. 9). Fear can conquer people, or people can conquer fear. A good leader is able to face fear head-on and use it to an advantage. Thompson has said, "Fear has become my best friend. It's not about being fearless, it's about not being afraid of fear. It helps me get ready. It helps me train" (Thompson, 2007, p. 32).

One of Kamehameha's famous sayings to his warriors as they went to battle against the formidable forces of Maui was, "*I mua e nā pōkiʻi a inu i ka wai ʻawaʻawa*": "Forward, my younger brothers, until you drink the bitter water" (Pukui, 1983, p. 135). Kamehameha knew that the battle would be difficult and there would be loss of life, but there was no turning back. He and his warriors united and faced their challenge with strength and tenacity. This simple phrase demonstrated the commitment Kamehameha's forces had to the mission. Kamehameha's warriors won the battle and his opponents fled (Kamakau and ʻAhahui ʻŌlelo Hawaiʻi, 1996). This was a decisive battle in moving the armies of Kamehameha forward in accomplishing their goal.

In the Hawaiian language revitalization movement, challenges, and obstacles presented themselves from the very beginning. For one, the state's laws had to be changed. The ban on the Hawaiian language that was instituted in 1896 had to be lifted in order for the Native language to become a medium of instruction in the public school system once more. Teachers were few and resources were limited. Many hours of service on the part of the ʻAha Pūnana Leo volunteers, university professors, immersion teachers, and Hawaiian families to produce books and curriculum were dedicated to the fulfillment of the shared vision. The odds were stacked against the success of the program, but challenges made all parties involved strong and resilient in the face of adversity. Year after year, evaluators hired by the Hawaiʻi Department of Education to assess the progress of the students found the pilot program to be a huge success story for the Hawaiian community (Slaughter, 1988). Leaders had the ability to endure and overcome challenges and so the pilot program became a permanent program in 1989 (Office of Instructional Services, General Education Branch, 1994).

COMMITMENT TO THE WHOLE JOURNEY

Commitment needs to be a conscious decision at the very beginning of the journey, that way when difficult times arise, leaders will be able to hold steadfast and not be easily swayed to abandon the mission. To be committed, one needs to plan meticulously, prepare diligently, and remain firm even when difficulties arise. Nainoa Thompson clearly describes the importance of training and preparing for a voyage as advised by his father, who said,

> 95% of your voyage is before you leave. It's in the training, it's in the preparation. That's where you guarantee success. Give me your plan for success. Give me every single step. That's where I will hold you to your steps. Do not talk to me about departure. Talk to me about getting ready. Talk to me about competence. Talk to me about unity. Talk to me about strength. Do the whole journey. The journey begins with the commitment to the vision. The voyage is just a piece of that. (Thompson, 2007, p. 22)

Some people are enticed by the romantic thought of sailing in the deep blue sea, and many think that you can just go aboard without training properly for the voyage. However, the double-hulled canoe is a small floating community on the ocean in which everyone has a responsibility to work together harmoniously in order to preserve the safety of all members and to arrive at the predetermined destination.

Kamehameha demonstrated a commitment to the whole journey by training diligently. He became one of the strongest warriors of Kalaniʻōpuʻu, the high chief of the Hawaiʻi island.[1] When Kalaniʻōpuʻu died, his son Kīwalaʻō ascended as the high chief in 1782. Keōuakūahuʻula, the brother of Kīwalaʻō, was dissatisfied with how the land was divided among the chiefs by their uncle Keaweaheulu, a Hilo chief, who reserved the largest portions for himself. Keōuakūahuʻula went to Keʻei, a land under the rule of the Kona chiefs, and he cut down coconut trees, which was an outright sign of war. Kamakau (1992) describes this historical event: "When the party reached Keʻei, some of the chiefs and others were out surfing, and a quarrel arose in which Keōua's party killed some of the men belonging to Kamehameha's party. Their bodies were taken to Kīwalaʻō to offer up at the heiau, and Kīwalaʻō offered up these war victims of Keōuakūahuʻula" (p. 120).

It can be assumed that Keōuakūahuʻula was trying to stir up a war between Kīwalaʻō and Kamehameha, so that he could strategically acquire more land and more power if one of them were to be killed. Several skirmishes took place for four days. During that time, several of the chiefs of Kamehameha's party deserted him for Kīwalaʻō. The outcome of the battle must have looked bleak for Kamehameha's side since Kīwalaʻō and Keōuakūahuʻula joined their forces together. Kamehameha and his warriors stayed committed to protecting their people and protecting their land even though the odds were against them. On the fifth day, the battle continued into the afternoon. Keōua had canoes ready in the event that Kamehameha should win. Kīwalaʻō was killed in that battle and Keōua fled when he heard the news of his brother's defeat (Kamakau and 'Ahahui 'Ōlelo Hawai'i, 1996).[2] The lesson that can be learned from this historical event is to stay committed even when the going gets tough. Some of the chiefs that deserted Kamehameha were favorites of the chief, but they chose to follow the side that seemed to have the greatest power at that moment in time. To their dismay, in the end, Kamehameha was victorious and eventually became the high chief of the island and king of the entire island chain.

Unwavering commitment needs to be present in any kind of program, if it is to be successful. The evaluation report for the first year of the Hawaiian language immersion program in 1988 stated that the program was successful in providing a total Hawaiian language immersion experience to participating students, and by the end of the year all students had attained a functional to proficient degree of fluency in the Hawaiian language (Slaughter, 1988). It was also noted in the evaluation report that parental involvement was exemplary in the program and was one factor to its success. Parent participation in the program was due partly to the innovative and unique features of the program and partly due to the 'ohana (family) spirit of the immersion classrooms and the Hawaiian language movement as a whole (Slaughter, 1988). The Hawaiian language immersion program was well on its journey. Students were speaking Hawaiian; pride in one's culture and in oneself was being restored; Hawaiian families were involved in the education of their children; and yet, some of the biggest challenges of the program came from critics, both Hawaiian and non-Hawaiian. They confidently (but incorrectly) predicted a dismal future for the children in the program, assumed that they would be illiterate in the English language and would not be able to go to college, all contrary to solid research in other places that indicates otherwise. Some teachers and families gave in to the pressures of critics and left the program to follow easier and longer established educational choices. Fortunately, many more stayed. They are to be applauded for working tirelessly to save the Native tongue and preserve the Hawaiian way of knowing and living. Commitment and hard work in the program has paid off. Graduating classes over a fifteen-year time span have now proven for Hawaiians what researchers for other language groups have shown. Students have graduated from high school proficient in both Hawaiian and English. Nāwahīokalani'ōpu'u Hawaiian Medium School on the Big Island has the prestigious status of a 100 percent graduation rate and 80 percent college attendance since its first class graduated in 1999. This is an incredible statistic when compared to the state averages of a 69 percent graduation rate for students of Native Hawaiian ancestry (Hawaii State Department of Education, 2008). At the tertiary level, Nāwahī graduates attend local institutions of higher education, as well as prominent out-of-state universities such as Stanford and Loyola Marymount. One former student earned an M.A. and a Ph.D. at Oxford. In 2003, Nāwahī students made up less than 2 percent of the Hilo High School senior class but accounted for 16 percent of its summa cum laude graduates (Wilson and Kamanā, 2006). This confirms that if one stays committed to the entire journey, extraordinary things can be achieved.

SENSITIVITY TO SPIRITUALITY

Sensitivity to things of a spiritual nature can be likened to an internal compass that provides guidance and direction. Observation of star constellations, ocean rhythms, wind patterns, cloud formations, and flight patterns of seabirds aided in the successful navigational practices of the early Polynesians. Failure to be observant led to life and death situations with tragic results. Ancestral stories and anthropological artifacts prove that voyaging occurred on a large scale between the Polynesian islands. The navigational skills of the Polynesian people far surpassed the skills of Westerners at the same period in history. Early European explorers had difficulty in finding the large American continents, whereas the Polynesian people could find small islands scattered throughout the Pacific with precision. The difference is that Westerners depended on scientific instruments made by men, whereas the Polynesians depended on their spiritual sense and keen observation skills to guide them on their voyages.

Kamehameha consistently adhered to signs, omens, promptings, and prophesies from his spiritual counselors. This strong attention to spirituality is one of the things that separated him from his rival Kīwalaʻō. A clear example of this is notable in the battle in which Kīwalaʻō was slain.

> At about nine in the morning of the fifth day the decisive battle was fought, Kamahemaha's side was defeated, some of his men were killed, their bodies taken before Kīwalaʻō, and offered as a sacrifice by him and his kāhuna. At the close of the offering a kahuna named Kālaikuʻiʻaha said to the chief, "The flood tide is yours in the morning, but it will ebb in the afternoon. Postpone the fighting until tomorrow." Kīwalaʻō would not listen to this advice, believing that Kamehameha's side would be defeated. (Kamakau, 1992, p. 121)

All the chiefs went to battle except Kamehameha. He was detained at Kealakekua by Holoʻae and the prophetess Pine to perform the ceremony of divination with sacred calabashes. Holoʻae said to Kamehameha: "It is a day of misfortune, with defeat for both sides. One chief in your party will be killed, but when the god turns the defeat to that side, then the ruling chief will be killed. But the tide is still rising; when the sun begins to decline the other side will meet defeat" (Kamakau, 1992, p. 121). The revelation was fulfilled as it was prophesied. Kīwalaʻō was killed and the warriors of Kamehameha were victorious. If Kīwalaʻō had listened to his spiritual advisor, perhaps the outcome would have been different. During the time of Kamehameha, respect for spirituality was a matter of life or death, so strict adherence was vital.

In other circumstances, such as the language revitalization movement, adhering to spirituality is not physically life threatening. However, an understanding that the movement is in the hands of a force greater than the participants themselves and that individuals are merely instruments in accomplishing the dream has been substantial. Listening to that internal compass is important, for it provides the direction to make good choices in moving the program forward successfully. It assists in knowing when it is the best time to approach a person or organization for help and support. It is a common thread with the power to bring harmony of thought among stakeholders.

RESPECT FOR MENTORS

In the voyaging community, respect is shown to master navigators. Mentors are valued for their wisdom, knowledge, strength, and expertise. They play an important role in the teaching and nurturing process, especially when difficulties arise. Thompson says, "We rely on our teachers and leaders to guide us through times of crisis, to inspire hope, and to point us toward new horizons" (Thompson, 2007, p. 9). For the voyaging crew, Mau Piailug was that teacher and mentor.

> Our leadership talked to Mau, [asking him to help us find Tahiti]. and Mau said yes. I always wondered what drove him to make that kind of decision, that kind of commitment. In some ways, Mau is a fierce man because, as the navigator, you must be. He's a strong man, and he certainly had the knowledge, but I think that Mau, in his genius beyond all his capabilities, knew that when he was asked the question, "Will you help us find Tahiti?" it wasn't just about getting Hōkūleʻa there, it was about helping save the Hawaiian people by bringing back our traditions, our heritage, and our culture. I think Mau knew he had to be there. . . . Mau was what everybody believed in and followed. He was the strength, he was everything. (Thompson, 2007, p. 15)

Good leaders realize that they don't have all of the answers and are humble enough to go to mentors for advice and help. In doing so, one shows respect and demonstrates that one is teachable.

Kamehameha not only showed respect for his mentors by listening and following their instructions, but he also demonstrated his devotion to them to the point of placing his own life in danger to protect them. Kekūhaupiʻo, who was Kamehameha's instructor in the matters of warfare, also became his close companion. They fought side by side in battles and the two of them became famous warriors under the high chief Kalaniʻōpuʻu. On one occasion,

Kalaniʻōpuʻu's forces went to battle the chiefs of Maui, Oʻahu, and Kauaʻi. Kalaniʻōpuʻu was losing, so he and his warriors retreated to their canoes. Kekūhaupiʻo was the only one still fighting on shore. When Kamehameha heard that his mentor was in danger of being killed, he ran ashore to help Kekūhaupiʻo escape death. Kalaniʻōpuʻu was amazed by Kamehameha's act of bravery and commanded all of his warriors to return to shore. The fighting continued until it was dark and the battle ended. Kekūhaupiʻo survived because of the respect and devotion that Kamehameha had for him (ʻĪʻī, 1993).

Mentors of the Hawaiian language revitalization movement are highly respected Native speakers, particularly the *kūpuna* of the grandparent generation. The value of the elders' expertise was recognized early on, and laws were changed so that they could be hired to teach in classroom settings. In addition to supporting language goals of immersion education, kūpuna have also enriched the classroom experience by sharing a wealth of knowledge in music, cultural practices and traditional storytelling. They not only play a crucial role by providing excellent models of language for children in the Pūnana Leo Preschools and Hawaiian language immersion schools, they are also the mentors of teachers who are primarily second language learners. Leaders look to these experts for suggestions and approval. Other mentors include master teachers, such as those on the ʻAha Pūnana Leo Board, who have made monumental contributions to the movement. They have worked diligently over the last twenty-five years to insure that the Hawaiian language will continue to grow on all levels from infancy through the doctorate degree and beyond.

LEGACY TO PASS ON

The legacy of long-distance voyaging has continued. The ancestors of the Hawaiian people first came to Hawaiʻi around two thousand years ago. They are clearly the greatest explorers of their time. As noted by Herb Kāne:

> The Pacific Ocean is the largest single feature we have on the planet. The Polynesian Triangle is the region anchored by Hawaiʻi in the north, Aotearoa [New Zealand] in the southwest, and Rapa Nui [Easter Island] in the east. It is 10 million square miles, bigger than Russia, and three times the size of the continental United States. If you do not include the landmass of Aotearoa, all the other islands in Polynesian have a land area equal to one third the state of New York. There is 600 times more water than there is land. (Thompson, 2007, p. 15)

Amazingly, Polynesian explorers were able to build deep-sea voyaging canoes from limited resources on small islands and were able to sail them in open-ocean passages of 2,500 miles with accuracy without the use of modern day instruments. Who would not find pride in such a heritage?

The revival of voyaging and the use of traditional navigational practices is a gift that was bestowed upon Nainoa Thompson from Mau Piailug, a man considered to be one of the six great master navigators, from Satawal, Micronesia. Although Nainoa was the initial recipient of this gift, the beneficiaries of this knowledge are far-reaching in Hawai'i and beyond. Nainoa's father expressed the importance of leaving a legacy:

> This voyage is not about you. It's about children not born. It's about the voyage helping to change the way we look at ourselves and look at the world. Your ultimate role as voyagers will be to become teachers. If it only stays with you, you have done nothing over time. Make sure you keep in mind, along the path of the vision, that you see children all the way. (Thompson, 2007, p. 23)

In order for the legacy to continue, the knowledge must be passed on from one generation to another. That goal is being accomplished through voyaging meetings and conferences. Hundreds of participants are enthusiastically involved with learning traditional practices with a dream to sail around the entire world in a double-hulled canoe in the near future.

Kamehameha was the ultimate Hawaiian leader of all time. He left his legacy to benefit future generations. He was not only highly respected in his day by Hawaiians and foreigners alike, but his life is still honored and his memory lives on in the hearts of the people of Hawai'i today. "He was a father to the orphan, a savior to the old and weak, a helper to the destitute, a farmer, a fisherman, and cloth maker for the needy" (Kamakau, 1992, p. 210). The historian Ralph Kuykendall said this about Kamehameha

> He was a man of powerful physique, agile, supple, fearless and of sound mind . . . well filled with the accumulated learning of his race and capable of thinking clearly and effectively. He was an excellent judge of men and had . . . the faculty of inspiring loyalty in his followers. Ruthless in war, he was kind and forgiving when the need for fighting was past. He had foreigners in his service, . . . but they were always his servants, never his masters; his was the better mind and the stronger will. (Williams, 1996, p. 111)

According to Kamakau (1992, p. 210) Kamehameha lived to be eighty-three years old, and "when he died his body was still strong, his eyes were not dimmed, his head unbowed, nor did he lean upon a cane; it was only by his gray hair that one could tell his age." During his life he saw the rise and fall of high chiefs. He fought fourteen years to unite the islands, and he ruled for twenty-three years afterward. He went on to serve the people and to build up the kingdom of Hawai'i. Before he passed on, he uttered the words, "*E na'i wale nō ʻoukou i kuʻu pono ʻaʻole pau*" (Williams, 1996, p. 109) It means, "End-less is the good that I have given you to enjoy." Even today, many Hawaiians are inspired by his words, his deeds, his accomplishments, and the legacy that he has left for future generations. In 1969, bronze statues of two great persons in the history of Hawaiʻi were placed in the National Statuary Hall in Wash-ington, DC: Kamehameha and Father Damien.[3] They were selected to repre-sent Hawaiʻi among the greatest heroes of the United States (Williams, 1996).

The leaders of the Hawaiian language revitalization movement also are cre-ating a legacy. It was illegal for Hawaiian to be used in Hawaiian schools from 1896 to 1986. The result was the decline of the Hawaiian language in all facets of life. According to Dr. Kalena Silva (*Honolulu Star Bulletin*, March 14, 2005), a 1983 survey estimated that only 1,500 people could speak Hawaiian, most of them elderly. Today, there are approximately 6,000 to 8,000 Hawaiian lan-guage speakers throughout the state, most of them under 30. Twenty-five or so years ago, when the Hawaiian language immersion program began, young parents hoped that their children would embrace the vision of the language movement when they themselves became adults. That dream is being ful-filled as a second generation of children is being raised in Hawaiian-speaking homes and attending immersion schools throughout the state. It has become more common to see three generations of speakers in the family setting and in the community. The legacy of language lives on—of critical importance, because without language, the culture will eventually cease to exist, and the Native people known as Hawaiians will be no more.

CONCLUSION

Three journeys, represented by transoceanic voyaging canoes, Kamehameha the Great, and the contemporary Hawaiian language revitalization movement, provide concrete and practical examples of leadership based on traditional practices that are embedded in the Hawaiian culture. Based on research, these journeys have been highly successful and have positively impacted the re-cipients of these movements. Each one personifies the meaning of leadership from a Hawaiian perspective; to lead, direct, lift up, and carry others on a journey down a pathway, which leads to a common goal.

These examples demonstrate how the philosophy of the Indigenous group must be the cultural lens in which to view leadership. Native people can move forward by recognizing the attributes of Native heroes and role models. Soci-ety is inundated with commercial books, tapes, CDs, and programs to develop leadership skills. Even though some information may be well intentioned, most of these products represent Western thinking and may not be culturally appropriate for Indigenous people. Where Indigenous leadership models have not been well established as in the case of Native Hawaiians, it is important to look at highly respected leaders who have effected change for the betterment of their people. Analyzing the principles that guide such leaders gives insights on developing Indigenous models that can be utilized in contemporary times.

Indigenous educational leaders today have the notable responsibility of developing effective leadership skills in the next generation. There are various opportunities in which to teach, learn, and practice the qualities of leadership. One such experience could include the interaction with mentors. Mentors have a wealth of knowledge and expertise in which they can share. Another avenue could include providing service to the community. Skills can be developed from practical experience with family, school, and community interactions.

Indigenous leadership models must promote the cultural identity of the Indigenous group. If this is not an outcome of the model, than the model needs to be reexamined. Well-being on all levels: social and cultural, material and economic, physical, emotional, and cognitive can only be achieved by nourishing the mauli (life force). It is through the strengthening of the mauli that pride is restored and potential as leaders is realized.

NOTES

1. Learn more about the history at www.hawaiianencyclopedia.com/part-1 -complete-timeline-of-ha.asp.

2. Find this book at the World Catalog website: http://www.worldcat.org/title /kumu-aupuni-ka-moolelo-hawaii-no-kamehameha-ka-nai-aupuni-a-me-kana -aupuni-i-hookumu-ai/oclc/39283370.

3. Read more about the honoring and lives of these two men at http://content .lib.umt.edu/cdm/ref/collection/mansfieldspeeches/id/992.

REFERENCES

'Aha Pūnana Leo, Inc. (2009). Nā kula pūnana leo 2008–2009. Statistics for the Pūnana Leo preschools. Unpublished raw data.

'Aha Pūnana Leo, Inc. (2014). *A timeline of Hawaiian language revitalization.* Retrieved from www.ahapunanaleo.org/en/index.php?/about/a_timeline_of _revitalization/

Crabbe, K. (2003). Initial psychometric validation of He Ana Mana'o o Nā Mo'omeheu Hawai'i: A Hawaiian ethnocultural inventory of cultural practices (Doctoral dissertation). University of Hawai'i.

Hale Kuamo'o, University of Hawai'i at Hilo (2014). Nā kula kaiapuni Hawai'i 2013–2014. Statistics for Hawaiian language immersion schools. Unpublished raw data.

Hawaii State Department of Education. No Child Left Behind state report. School Year 2007–2008. Retrieved June 2009, arch.k12.hi.us/school/nclb/targets .html#.

'Ī'ī, J. P. (1993). *Fragments of Hawaiian history*. 2nd rev. ed. Honolulu: Bishop Museum Press.

Ka Haka 'Ula o Ke'elikōlani a me ka 'Aha Pūnana Leo. (2009). *Kumu honua mauli ola: He kālaimana'o ho'ona'auao 'ōiwi Hawai'i*. Hilo, Hawai'i: 'Aha Pūnana Leo and Ka Haka 'Ula o Ke'elikōlani.

Kamakau, S. M. (1992). *Ruling chiefs of Hawai'i* (Moolelo o Kamehameha I.). Rev ed. Honolulu: Kamehameha Schools Press.

Kamakau, S. M., and 'Ahahui 'Ōlelo Hawai'i. (1996). *Ke kumu aupuni: Ka mo'olelo Hawai'i no Kamehameha ka na'i aupuni a me kāna aupuni i ho'okumu ai*. Honolulu: 'Ahahui Olelo Hawai'i.

Kana'iaupuni, S. (2004). Ka'akālai Kū Kanaka: A call for strength-bases approaches from a Native Hawaiian perspective. *Educational Researcher, 33*(9), 26–32.

Kana'iaupuni, S. M., Malone, N., and Ishibashi, K. (2005). *Ka huaka'i: 2005 Native Hawaiian educational assessment*. Honolulu: Policy Analysis and System Evaluation (PASE), Kamehameha Schools, Pauahi Publications.

Kaulukukui, G., and Nāho'opi'i, D. (2008). The development of an inventory of exemplary Hawaiian leadership behaviors. *Hūlili: Multidisciplinary Research on Hawaiian Well-being, 5*, 95–151.

Kawai'ae'a, K. (2006). Ke kumu honua mauli ola: Foundations of cultural identity. Power Point presentation at He 'Ōlelo Ola Conference. Hilo, Hawai'i.

Kawai'ae'a, K., Housman, A., and Alencastre, M. (2007). Pū'ā i ka 'ōlelo, ola ka 'ohana: Three generations of Hawaiian language revitalization. *Hūlili: Multidisciplinary Research on Hawaiian Well-being, 5*, 183.

Kouzes. J., and Posner, B. (1987). *The leadership challenge*. San Francisco: Jossey-Bass.

Meyer, M. (1997). Native Hawaiian epistemology: Sites of empowerment and resistance. *Equity and Excellence in Education, 31*(1), 22–28.

Office of Instructional Services, General Education Branch. (1994). *Long-range plan for the Hawaiian language immersion program: Papahana kaiapuni Hawai'i*. Hawai'i State Department of Education, RS 94–5555.

Poepoe, J. (27 Nowemapa 1905–16 Nowemapa 1906). "Ka Mo'olelo o Kamehameha I, Ka Na-i Aupuni o Hawaii, Ka Liona o ka Pakipika." *Ka Na'i Aupuni*.

Pukui, M. K. (1983). *'Ōlelo no'eau: Hawaiian proverbs and poetical sayings*. Bernice P. Bishop Museum special publication; no. 71. Honolulu: Bishop Museum Press.

Pukui, M. K., and Elbert, S. H. (1986). *Hawaiian dictionary: Hawaiian-English, English-Hawaiian*. Honolulu: University of Hawaii Press.

Silva, K., Alencastre, M., Kawai'ae'a, K., and Housman, A. (2008). Generating a sustainable legacy: Teaching founded upon the kumu honua mauli ola. In M. A. Nee-Benham (Ed.) *Indigenous educational models for contemporary practice: In our mother's voice* (2:29). Mahwah, NJ: L. Erlbaum.

Slaughter, H. (1988). *Evaluation study of the . . . year of the Hawaiian language immersion program: A report to the Hawaiian language immersion program, state of Hawaiʻi, department of education.* Honolulu: University of Hawaiʻi, Mānoa.

Smith, L. T. (1999). *Decolonizing methodologies: Research and Indigenous people.* Dunedin, New Zealand: University of Otago Press.

Staton, R. (2005). Language revival: Hawaiian rates as the nation's only growing Indigenous tongue. *Honolulu Star Bulletin,* March 14, 2005. Retrieved October 2009 from http://starbulletin.com/2005/03/14/news/story7.html.

Thompson, N. (2007). E hoʻi mau: Honoring the past, caring for the present. *Hūlili: Multidisciplinary Research on Hawaiian Well-being, 6,* 9.

Williams, J. S. (1996). *Kamehameha the great.* Honolulu: Kamehameha Publishing.

Wilson, W., and Kamanā. K. (2006). For the interest of the Hawaiians themselves: Reclaiming the benefits of Hawaiian-medium education. *Hūlili: Multidisciplinary Research on Hawaiian Well-being, 3,* 153.

4

A Raven's Story

Leadership Teachings for an Indigenous Teacher Education Program

JO-ANN ARCHIBALD

I live on the west coast of British Columbia, Canada, where the Pacific Ocean greets the traditional and unceded land of the Indigenous peoples every day. Ravens and Eagles watch over this land. I write from the perspective of a Sto:lo[1] woman scholar who has worked at the University of British Columbia (UBC) for three decades. As I write my reflections about Indigenous[2] leadership and Indigenous teacher education, many memories come to my mind and to my heart. These memories are about those who created solid educational pathways in a mainstream university such as UBC. They include the Indigenous Raven; Indigenous community-based educator and elder, the late hereditary chief Joan Ryan; Dr. Verna Kirkness, the first Indigenous director of the first Indigenous program established at UBC, the Native Indian Teacher Education Program (NITEP); and DeDe DeRose, a NITEP alum.

This chapter presents the story of lived experience in the NITEP[3] at the Faculty of Education, University of British Columbia. This story focuses on ways that Indigenous educational leadership has created and sustains a teacher education program that is relevant to Indigenous communities. It is a story that is based primarily on my experiences and reflections. I am a member of the Sto:lo First Nation and have worked with NITEP for seventeen years as an instructor, course developer, coordinator of a NITEP field center, and director of the program. In 2006–2007, NITEP students, faculty/coordinators, and I, as the director of NITEP, participated in the development of a self-study document in which each group discussed the ways that NITEP addressed Indigenous knowledge in addition to the challenges and successes in this regard. This information and various NITEP historical documents provide additional information for this chapter. The first part presents the historical story of creating NITEP; then it describes how NITEP addresses indigeneity and Indigenous communities. The second part highlights some leadership stories and my own reflections about those who have ensured that a university teacher education program is relevant to Indigenous communities.

NITEP'S CREATION STORY

NITEP was established in 1974 as a Bachelor of Education degree program at the University of British Columbia's Faculty of Education, following pressure by Indigenous activists for improvements to Canadian educational systems. During the 1960s, Indian people in Canada began exercising stronger political agency in reaction to the significant failure of schools to provide an adequate education for their children and the federal government's attempt to extinguish Indigenous rights (Royal Commission on Aboriginal Peoples, 1996). The failure rate of the public educational system in the late 1960s was evidenced by the fact that 96 percent of Indian students failed to complete high school (Hawthorn, 1967). Indian people felt that "enough was enough." A national political movement to address the crisis in Indian education resulted in the development of the 1972 Indian Control of Indian Education Policy (ICIE) by the National Indian Brotherhood (now Assembly of First Nations). The Canadian federal government accepted the ICIE in principle.

This policy was based upon the two fundamental principles of local control of education and parental engagement. The ICIE policy also emphasized the importance of building upon Indian students' cultures and values and stressed the need to have more Indian teachers and to increase the cultural sensitivity of non-Indian teachers. The development of Indian teacher education programs across Canada was one of the first outcomes of the ICIE (Royal Commission on Aboriginal Teachers, 1996). The founding NITEP group, called the British Columbia Native Indian Teachers' Association, argued that an Indian teacher education program was needed in order to increase the numbers of Indian teachers and that such a program needed to be delivered in or near Indian communities. One member of the founding group, the late Robert Sterling, was a highly respected educational leader, who in 1983 attributed NITEP's success to Indigenous peoples' leadership. Sterling stressed: "Programs in which Native people have been actively involved in the planning and throughout the developmental phases have shown the greatest success. Among these, our Native Indian Teacher Education Program, NITEP stands at the forefront of our successes. The program is an Indian idea, is Indian-controlled and its philosophy is Indian, although the program falls under the jurisdiction of the University of British Columbia" (cited in Archibald, 1986, p. 33). It took five years to get both federal and provincial government funding and university support before NITEP became a university degree program (Joan Ryan, cited in B.C. College of Teachers, 2004, p. 7). Today, this B.Ed. degree is of a concurrent nature, requiring students to take arts and sciences courses along with education courses throughout their program.

When NITEP began, there were approximately twenty-six Indigenous teachers in the province of British Columbia out of a total population of twenty-three thousand teachers (0.11 percent) (Native Indian Teacher Education Program, 1974). Four decades later, 372 Indigenous people have graduated from NITEP with B.Ed. degrees. Today, the actual numbers of Indigenous teachers in British Columbia are still not known, which is a continuing problem. There is no requirement for any educational professional association or teacher accreditation body to keep annual records about Indigenous teachers. Yet Aboriginal children in the British Columbian public school system comprise just over 11 percent of the kindergarten through grade twelve student population.[4] Increasing the numbers of Aboriginal teachers in British Columbia and across Canada has become a priority for many Aboriginal educational organizations, professional educational associations such as the Association of Canadian Deans of Education, and provincial and federal governments.[5]

The founding group left NITEP with a visible and meaningful legacy when it chose the program logo of Raven holding the sun in its beak, superimposed over a circle that symbolizes the hole in the sky. This logo was designed by Opie Oppenheim of the Nlaka'pamux First Nations of the interior region of British Columbia. A traditional Indigenous story forms the basis of the logo, and most importantly this story told in the oral tradition provides guidance and vision to the work of NITEP (see figure 4.1).

> Raven is an Indigenous trickster character that often gets into trouble because it does not follow good cultural teachings, but sometimes Raven does good things to help others. In the NITEP story, Raven pitied the people who were living in darkness and decided that he would find the sun for them so that they would have a better life. Raven went on a journey and after lots of effort and trickery, he found a hole in the sky, and captured the sun. He brought it back to the people of the earth.[6] (Archibald, 1986)

NITEP is like the sun in Raven's beak that brings light to improve education, especially Indigenous education. The *light* is an Indigenous teacher education program based on Indigenous knowledges that prepares Indigenous people to be effective educators. This important story reminds the faculty, students, and community members associated with NITEP to find ways to ensure that its teacher education program meets the learning needs of all learners in the K–12 schools and in other educational contexts, but especially, the learning needs of Indigenous learners. The NITEP story also challenges its graduates to use their "Indigenous heart and mind" to transform Indigenous education. Close to one's heart is the well-being of family and community.

Figure 4.1. The NITEP logo, *The Raven and the Sun*, by Opie Oppenheim of the Nlaka'pamux First Nations of British Columbia. Courtesy of the Native Indian Teacher Education Program (NITEP), Faculty of Education, University of British Columbia, Vancouver.

NITEP: ADDRESSING INDIGENEITY AND INDIGENOUS COMMUNITIES

Besides NITEP's logo and story, the holistic learning model informing NITEP is another Indigenous framework that has been used to guide the overall programmatic nature of NITEP, particularly its Indigenous courses and mentoring of its teacher candidates (see figure 4.2). Holistic learning involves developing the spiritual, emotional, physical, and intellectual aspects of human growth. Because Indigenous knowledge is often relational and interdependent, the aforementioned four realms are acknowledged as distinct entities, but the interrelationships among these realms are what creates a holistic approach (Archibald, 2008a; Armstrong, 2000; Brown, 2006; Cajete, 2000; Castellano, 2000; Little Bear, 2000). The principle of interrelatedness extends to one's self, one's family, one's community/environment, and the wider world.

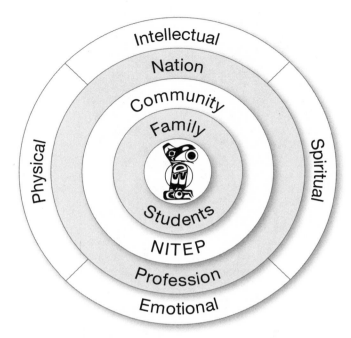

Figure 4.2. The NITEP Holistic Model. Courtesy of the Native Indian Teacher Education Program (NITEP), Faculty of Education, University of British Columbia, Vancouver.

Jeannette Armstrong, an Okanagan scholar, describes her understanding of holistic relationships using the physical realm and its relationship to self, family, community, and land as follows:

> the physical self—the "me" underneath my skin. The first concentric circle, "self," says that I must do everything I have to do to keep my physical health. I need to exercise and get the best nutrition to be well. In terms of education, if I am well I have the best chance of being accomplished at anything. Wellness impacts my learning. . . . Physical self also means the physical health of my family members. This is the second circle of family. We are referring to how we are physically connected to our family in terms of what we do together, so that we are all contributing members of the family. . . . We learn relational skills from our experiences with our family. . . . How to contribute physically to one's family is an important lesson that must be learned in order to be able to contribute to community—our third circle. We are talking about participating physically in ceremony, the work of the community, and in the growth and caretakership of the community. It also means the

protection of the land on which our community is based. All of this is built on a strong foundation of physical self and family. It is at the community level that we interface with the land. (2000, pp. 37–38)

Specific examples of how NITEP uses the holistic model, particularly its relationships with Indigenous communities will be discussed in the next section.

COMMUNITY-BASED RELATIONSHIPS

NITEP establishes and maintains community-based relationships through its two- and three-year regional field centers, located in various areas of British Columbia (B.C.). Students begin their teacher education program close to their home or in a location that has strong Indigenous community support and relationships. After these initial years, the students move to the main university campus located in Vancouver, B.C., to complete the remainder of their B.Ed. degree. Over its forty years of operation, NITEP has had seventeen[7] field centers located in both rural and urban areas. In 2014–15, NITEP ran four regional field centers. A field center can be established if an Indigenous community requests one, but there must be a minimum of twelve students, sufficient funding, a college or university nearby that will offer the arts and sciences course requirements, and a variety of sites for the educational placement experiences. If these conditions are satisfied, a partnership between NITEP and an Indigenous community organization then is formed. The local college or university often enters into this partnership. The community partner assists with recruitment, helps to provide physical classroom and office space, gives program advice, and participates in the program's governance council.

Each field center works with local Indigenous community groups and engages community resource people such as elders to mentor the NITEP students. At the field centers, the NITEP students complete educational placements that are often sponsored by various community groups such as Indigenous early childhood education centers, First Nations–run schools, adult education programs, and cultural centers. The local public school districts also offer educational placements.

The governance of NITEP includes significant community-based representation. A First Nations Education Council (FNEC) guides NITEP's program and curriculum policy and other pertinent program matters. Community representatives from the regional sites, an elder, alumni, and professional educational associations comprise the FNEC, along with student representatives from the field center and on campus groups and the associate deans for Teacher Education and Indigenous Education from the UBC Faculty of Education. The FNEC and the NITEP faculty have major the responsibility of ensuring that Indigenous-oriented courses and community-oriented learning experiences comprise a core part of the teacher education program.

ADDRESSING INDIGENEITY   \

NITEP addresses indigeneity through its holistic programmatic structure, academic courses, Indigenous values, extended family/cohort approaches, and community relationships, which will be exemplified in this section. Indigenous courses, seminars, and educational experiences are required in each year of the current four-year degree program. NITEP has authority over the course development, delivery, and selection of Indigenous faculty to teach its courses.[8] These courses include:

EDUC 140, Introduction to Indigenous Studies
EDUC 141, Cultural Studies
EDUC 143, Seminar and Educational Experiences
EDUC 240, Issues in Indigenous Education
EDUC 244, Seminar and Educational Experiences
EDUC 344, Seminar
EDUC 345, Indigenous Curriculum Field Experience
EDCP 396, Curriculum Development and Evaluation: Indigenous Focus
EDUC 440, Aboriginal Education in Canada
EDUC 442, Critical Issues in Indigenous Education

Students are given opportunities to complete a total of six weeks of educational placements in Indigenous educational contexts that are organized and supervised by NITEP coordinators during the first three years of the program.

The above-noted required courses build upon a foundation of Indigenous knowledge that students bring with them into the program. They also learn more about Indigenous knowledge from each other and from community-based cultural knowledge holders, and they are introduced to the work of Indigenous scholars. Through these courses, they also begin to understand the intergenerational impact of colonization. As well, students often engage in further development of their Aboriginal identity during these courses. Some have not had the opportunity to learn much about their Aboriginal culture because their parents went to residential schools where Aboriginal culture- and language-suppression policies were enacted or where they were separated from their families and communities through foster care or adoption. By completing all the aforementioned courses, NITEP students develop a teaching specialization in Indigenous education.

The NITEP holistic model discussed earlier also is an important part of the students' course learning. They learn to understand the dimensions of the model and they are challenged to apply it to their everyday living and to use it for their learning and teaching. To demonstrate this point, the Urban NITEP field center student group wrote this response in answer to the question, "What does the term 'transformative Aboriginal educators' mean?"

Realizing that being a part of NITEP truly means we will make a difference in the educational realm, but we are striving to take that a step higher. How will we evoke the most "change" in elementary and in secondary school students?—this is our mission. Identity is crucial. We understand that as Aboriginal people we are able to connect with Aboriginal students on levels that surpass both empathy and sympathy. We identify with these Aboriginal students, in a holistic mode, in every aspect of the students' being: spiritually, physically, intellectually and emotionally. (NITEP, 2007, p. 9)

Indigenous people typically teach the Indigenous education courses, which is another fundamental principle of NITEP. It is a crucial aspect of professional modeling and mentoring for NITEP students to learn from Indigenous educators who have completed their B.Ed. degrees and more, and most importantly, to learn from faculty members who have a critical consciousness about the impact of colonization and who understand the need to embrace transformative educational philosophies and practices. During their courses in Indigenous culture, NITEP students, as a caring cohort, have opportunities to explore and develop their cultural identities through cultural research and experiential projects. They can learn about and heal from the intergenerational trauma caused by the impact of residential schooling and assimilationist approaches of the public education system. As well, they can develop relevant educational understandings, competencies, and concrete educational resources that are based in Indigenous knowledges.

In the first three years the students develop an interactive learning community where they learn from each other, pose probing questions of each other, and work both individually and cooperatively on learning projects, which often have a holistic framework. For example, one NITEP group organized a potlatch for their kindergarten to grade twelve school and community to recognize the anniversary and positive impact of the First Nations' school. They publicly acknowledged the support that families, teachers, and community leaders gave to the school students so that their school could develop into a welcoming and caring learning environment. During the potlatch they provided food (physical), organized speeches, songs, and dances (spiritual and emotional), and created student learning units about the Indigenous knowledge associated with a potlatch[9] (intellectual).

During NITEP courses and student events at both field centers and UBC's main campus, Indigenous cultural practices such as prayer, talking circles, feasts, ceremony, land-based/environmental experiences, traditional arts, and storytelling are integral to students' learning activities. Elders and cultural resource speakers often give talks and tell stories to share their knowledge with the students. The students take field trips to the local Indigenous community gatherings. The NITEP cohort becomes an extended family, which is formed at the regional field center and expanded when students move to the main university campus and merge with other NITEP cohorts (Archibald, 2008b, pp. 91–92).

NITEP graduates also speak at the NITEP courses and annual student gatherings, thereby continuing the extended family and intergenerational learning process. The students note that they have a safe and comfortable learning environment in which they do not have to defend Indigenous culture to others. They can talk about the importance of such matters as Indigenous spirituality and learn more about it without fear of ridicule or skepticism from non-Aboriginal students. They can also talk about their concerns regarding community leadership and schooling in their community, which they would not disclose in a mixed Indigenous and non-Indigenous group. NITEP graduates are loyal to this program because for many it helps them to recognize their internal gifts and to develop a sustained network of educator-friends to draw upon once they are out in the field. For some it is a life-altering experience, as described by a graduate of the program: "[Before UBC] I was curled up, not feeling too good about who I was. . . . Also I didn't quite feel I knew who I was, . . . and after attending NITEP . . . and working, it was like the rose has bloomed. . . . That's what it was like for me" (Archibald, Selkirk Bowman, Pepper, et al., 1995, p. 160).

In the last ten plus years the topic of decolonization in education has become more prominent in the scholarly literature (Battiste, 2000; Smith, 1999). In NITEP, decolonization starts by raising questions about power relations between the school and Indigenous parents and Indigenous communities; raising questions about the suitability of educational policies, curriculum choices, and pedagogies used in the school systems; and challenging the teacher candidates to develop a critical community-oriented consciousness. These crucial discussions take place in the NITEP courses and NITEP educational seminars. Those who develop this type of consciousness take on roles as change agents in various educational contexts once they are working in the educational field.

Since 2006, the NITEP coordinators have agreed upon various themes that are used as a common program thread and addressed in the NITEP education seminars, the annual NITEP newsletter, and the annual NITEP student gathering. For example, one theme about transformation included the following iterations: "Transformative Aboriginal Educators," "Transforming Aboriginal Education," and "Transformative Action: Holistic Teaching and Learning." Such themes challenge students to question the existing educational systems for relevance to Indigenous education and to develop ideas, perspectives, and concrete plans to improve Indigenous education. We also recognize that engaging in transformative education is an ongoing process, which is implied in the themes that covered a three-year period. The NITEP Raven reminds us about the Indigenous teachings and values that are the foundation of our teacher education program: respect, caring, extended family, community orientation, and relationships. The Raven can also represent NITEP leaders who have brought light and strength to this program through their Indigenous philosophies, tenacity, commitment, resilience, and bold actions. The next section highlights the Indigenous foundations of NITEP leadership.

RAVEN'S LEADERS:
COMMUNITY-BASED LEADERSHIP

NITEP was fortunate to have long-term community-based leadership from educators such as the late Joan Ryan, a hereditary clan chief of the Gitxsan First Nation of northern British Columbia. Elder Ryan was one of the original founders of NITEP. She served for many years as the cochair of the First Nations Education Council with another noted educational leader, the late Bert McKay of the Nisga'a First Nation. Both McKay and Ryan were respected leaders and elders of their Indigenous nations. Both gave endless hours of volunteer leadership to ensure that NITEP met the educational needs of Indigenous communities as identified by those communities. Joan Ryan's persistence and impact was recounted by De De DeRose, a NITEP graduate and current cochair of the FNEC:

> Joan has been committed to NITEP since it was a vision. For many years, at least four times a year, she travelled by bus to Vancouver to attend our advisory meetings. She did this through rain, snow, sleet, while the fish were running and when the berries were ready. The bus ride alone takes 17 hours in good weather. All items on the agenda, under her leadership, were thoroughly discussed and debated. Joan especially enjoyed hearing from NITEP student representatives about how things were going, their areas of concern and their recommendations for improving the program. (DeRose, 2005, p. 13)

Elder Ryan demonstrated humility, often not wanting to be acknowledged for her leadership role:

> Joan was asked for permission to acknowledge her exceptional contributions to NITEP. She replied that she was uncomfortable about being singled out and recognized, because she did not do the work alone and she did not do it for recognition. She did it because it was important. She was acknowledged at NITEP's 30th Anniversary Celebration, surrounded by NITEP graduates who are products of her vision, dedication, and commitment. It is to Joan that so many of us owe our careers and, more importantly, it is because of her work that so many Aboriginal

children and all children have positive learning experiences. (DeRose, 2006, p. 8)

My relationship with Joan Ryan took on a new dimension when I became the head of NITEP in 1985, which was my first major leadership position. Leading a fairly large province-wide Indigenous teacher education program of approximately 120 students, with four regional field centers and a large on-campus contingent seemed a daunting task for me at that time. NITEP was changing from a four-year to a five-year program, which created much anxiety for the coordinators and students because they were concerned about the impact of additional finances for students, the additional year that students would be away from their home community, and uncertainty about what would be lost with the new programmatic changes. The NITEP group did not have any decision-making power about the increased program length and additional arts and sciences courses that were required for teacher certification. In addition, I had ongoing concerns about funding for the program because the Faculty of Education was experiencing major funding cuts in the mid-to late 1980s. Joan's steadfast leadership as cochair of the FNEC gave me comfort, knowing that I could phone her to ask for policy and programmatic advice. She had a calm, thoughtful, and thorough way of thinking through matters. Over the years, she rarely missed a council meeting. She always attended the student graduation ceremonies and felt great pride to see the growing numbers of NITEP graduates. She posed challenging questions that made those of us who worked with the program strive to ensure that we addressed Indigenous knowledge and culture and community access at the same time that we ensured that NITEP students learned knowledge and skills to enable them to be effective teachers. She would ask if NITEP was delivering a top quality academic and cultural program. She would ask the Faculty of Education leadership what their commitment was to NITEP and how they would ensure its adequate funding or how they would address some of the systemic barriers related to admissions that students experienced.

In 2006, I attended Elder Joan Ryan's memorial in her home community. She was acknowledged by many for her community-based and province-wide leadership in areas such as Indigenous language, health and healing, land claims, justice, and education. Her leadership impact and commitment to NITEP was acknowledged not only by me but more importantly by the many Gitxsan teachers whom she had mentored over the years. She truly lived her Gitxsan teachings and passed these on to others, thereby demonstrating the power of intergenerational learning and teaching. In her words: "We are given *aatxyasxw* by the Creator which are tools for our earthly journey. These are intuition, inner knowing and visions. Gitxsan Elders took on the task of preparing for the future through their visions and prayers. . . . The Gitxsan are expected to leave earth in a better state than when they first arrived for their physical journey" (cited by Smith, 2007, p. 11).

Leaving a place or a program in a better state than when we first encountered it is a foundational teaching that can result in transformative changes to improve Indigenous education in significant ways. Elder Joan Ryan exemplified this teaching in her community-based leadership with NITEP. The next NITEP leader also left this program in much better shape than when she first was introduced to it.

PROGRAMMATIC LEADERSHIP

Verna J. Kirkness, of Cree ancestry from Fisher River, Manitoba, became the first Indigenous director of NITEP in 1981. In the early years of the program, non-Indigenous UBC faculty members led the program. They were committed to the program's philosophy and ensured that the program addressed the overall teacher education requirements so that NITEP became the first degree program at UBC specifically for Indigenous people.

I remember that in 1979–80, regional Indian education conferences were held throughout British Columbia. This was an exciting time. Those of us who were educators teaching in schools had the opportunity to talk with each other, to give workshops about our programs and our curricula, and to hear inspiring speakers such as Verna J. Kirkness, who was known nationally for her work on developing the Indian Control of Indian Education Policy. She was a keynote speaker at these regional conferences, which is where I first met Verna.

Verna began to make some major policy and programmatic changes shortly after she was appointed to the NITEP director position. The Indigenous education courses under NITEP's auspices were revised, Indigenous educators were hired to teach these courses, and more regional field centers were established in both rural and urban areas. Verna became well-known for her ability to raise substantial program development funds, for writing articles about the importance of Indigenous teachers, and for finding ways to address the teacher educational needs of Indigenous communities. She always found a way for the university leadership to say "yes" to her requests. One important example was hiring Indigenous educators who did not have Ph.D.s to teach the NITEP courses. In the 1980s, there were a few Indigenous teachers with bachelor's degrees and substantial years of teaching experience; even fewer had master's degrees and those with doctorates were very hard to find. Verna challenged the university to acknowledge the Indigenous knowledge expertise of these Indigenous educators and she succeeded. The NITEP leadership was given the authority to appoint the instructors that were most appropriate and most qualified, using Indigenous criteria, such as Indigenous knowledge expertise, community leadership, and educational work experience.

As the following two quotations document, Verna's scholarship often challenged educators to question the status quo, to have vision, and to keep community needs and Indigenous culture at the forefront of their consciousness. She asserted:

> Most Indian teachers . . . realize the challenge that confronts them. Their challenge is to be role models for their students, "change agents" in Indian education and culture-brokers in society. They are the key to progress. (1999, p. 62)

> Although the education of our people has not been entirely one of gloom and doom, at least over the last 25 years, we are still faced with the monumental challenge of creating a meaningful education that will not only give hope, but a promise of a better life for our future generations. I believe that this means that we must cut the shackles, cut the crap, and cut the mustard." (1998, p. 10)

Cutting the shackles means disengaging from colonial educational approaches and defining education on our terms. Cutting the crap challenges us to move from rhetoric to practice regarding Indigenous culture and language: practice that is meaningful and sustainable. Cutting the mustard encourages community members and other educational stakeholders to work together in truly strategic ways. Verna emphasized the importance of personal and community agency:

> Our independence education will be based on the marriage of the past and the present. It will honour our cultures, which include our values, our languages, and our peoples' contributions to the development and progress of this vast country. Most importantly, [if you follow these principles] you will have found in your quest for a meaningful education for your school or community that the answers you have been seeking can be found within yourselves, within your own communities. (Kirkness, 1998, p. 15)

After leaving the NITEP leadership position, Verna moved on to make other substantial institutional changes at the University of British Columbia. Most notably, she founded an Indigenous graduate studies program called Ts"kel, a university-wide academic and student service unit called the First Nations House of Learning, and an academic, cultural, and social facility known as the First Nations Longhouse.[10] Verna's NITEP leadership created a pivotal moment in the program, turning its original Indigenous philosophy and community orientation into strong systemic hiring policies and teaching practices that continue to this day. In addition, Indigenous educators became much more involved in the daily teaching and leadership of the program. Numerous NITEP graduates have taught and worked for NITEP, many of whom were mentored by Verna during her NITEP leadership tenure. Now, it is their turn to mentor and lead.

NITEP ALUMNI LEADERSHIP

NITEP graduates often take on leadership roles as teachers, school principals, school district principals, government educational directors, community education coordinators, and curriculum developers. Approximately, thirty-two (9 percent) have been public school principals, First Nation school principals, or public Aboriginal school district principals. Many work to make institutional changes to public schools, First Nations schools, and at governmental levels. Approximately forty-seven (13 percent) have worked at Indigenous and public colleges and universities in teaching, program coordination, student service, or management positions. Many have gone on to complete master's degrees and a few are now enrolled in doctoral degree programs (see table 4.1).[11]

NITEP graduates often are change agents. For example, they started an Aboriginal educational specialist group within the provincial teachers' union and have tried to implement employment equity mechanisms despite the tight control that teacher unions often have through their collective agreements regarding these matters. NITEP graduates have worked as NITEP field center coordinators and faculty teachers. NITEP graduates also helped to develop some courses for a master's program (UBC's Ts"kel graduate studies) in the 1980s that first focused on educational leadership. Often NITEP alumni speak of the importance of the program for facilitating their access to higher education, for helping them strengthen their indigeneity, and for facilitating their careers in education. They willingly volunteer their time and expertise to NITEP. A key role for some has included being on the FNEC. One of the NITEP alumni, DeDe DeRose will be highlighted in this section to exemplify the important leadership contributions that Indigenous educators with a university education can make in improving Indigenous education.

DeDe DeRose graduated from NITEP in 1981. Since graduation she has worked in the educational field as a classroom teacher, a school principal, and with the provincial Ministry of Education. She was the first Aboriginal principal in the public school district where she has worked for many years. DeDe

Table 4.1 NITEP Graduates' Levels of Education

B.Ed. degrees	Master's degrees	Doctoral degrees	Doctoral degrees in progress
371	79 (21%)	3 (0.8%)	7 (2%)

served on NITEP's FNEC first as a regional community representative, then as cochair with Joan Ryan, and then, after Joan's passing, as chair until 2009. At that time Victor Jim, a member of the first NITEP graduating class became cochair with DeDe. The cochair structure maintains the NITEP philosophy of shared leadership for the FNEC.

In addition to work on this council, DeDe has served on province-wide committees that addressed teachers' professional certification, curriculum, policy, and research. In 2006, the Association of British Columbia Deans of Education recognized her leadership impact by selecting her as the first recipient of their annual Teacher Education Award (NITEP, 2006, p. 18). In 2012, DeDe was seconded from her principalship to become the first superintendent of Aboriginal Achievement for the B.C. Ministry of Education, the first position of its kind in Canada. In this new role, she reviews the public school districts' progress or lack of it for increasing Aboriginal student success. She continues to advance the need to prepare and hire Indigenous teachers.

Since 2008, I have returned to the NITEP director position for various periods and have continued to work closely with DeDe. She brings an important sense of school reality and school-community relationship to my thinking, along with an emphasis on the importance of developing and maintaining professional teaching standards that our program must continually achieve. Students have more appreciation and respect/regard for the advice and challenge of someone "who has been there." For DeDe, graduating from NITEP, earning a master's degree, teaching in various schools, and holding school leadership positions all contributed to her practitioner knowledge, an impact that is important to our program. DeDe also works with teaching associations on systemic changes to accreditation policy so that all teachers become better informed about Indigenous education and better prepared to teach Indigenous learners. An important outcome of her work with these associations is that in 2012 the B.C. provincial certification unit announced that a three-credit course or equivalent on Aboriginal education had to be completed in order to receive a professional teacher certificate. The Faculties of Education in British Columbia now must offer mandatory Aboriginal education courses or equivalent learning for all their teacher candidates. DeDe's leadership demonstrates commitment, tenacity, professionalism, and critical engagement in order to make a difference.

Now we turn to the future Indigenous educational leaders. Each year, various students take on leadership roles in their NITEP cohorts by representing their group on the First Nations Education Council, organizing special events such as a workshop or conference, leading Indigenous student associations, and educating non-Indigenous students and faculty about Indigenous education. Another indication of potential leadership comes from their thoughts about topics such as transforming Indigenous education through their roles as future teachers. These are noted below.

PREPARING RAVEN'S FUTURE LEADERS

There are many milestones of success for NITEP students, beginning with admission into the program followed by attending courses, successfully completing the courses and the educational placements/practica, from moving from the field center to the Vancouver campus, and then to graduating. However, each transition phase often presents financial, personal, and systemic difficulties to students because of their demographic characteristics: for the majority of the NITEP students, they are among the first in their families to attend a university; there are more women than men; and they are older than the typical students enrolled in teacher education programs. In 2014–15, the majority (89 percent) of the NITEP students were female and 11 percent were male; one-third (33 percent) were under twenty-five years of age, while two-thirds (67 percent) were over twenty-five; and the average age of the students was thirty-one. In addition to these characteristics, the majority of the NITEP students have children and important responsibilities to family and community, and, as the first generation to attend a university, students are usually unfamiliar with higher education institutions. Because of these reasons, NITEP students, with the assistance of the field center coordinator cultivate an ethos of extended family among their peers and help support one another—practices that contribute to student retention. For example, I have witnessed students holding a fund-raising luncheon or contributing food baskets to those who have unexpected financial difficulties. Many deaths occur in the NITEP students' families and communities during their program, which means that they must return home for the cultural ceremonies. The NITEP coordinators and fellow students provide emotional and academic support in these difficult times. Often, non-Indigenous university instructors do not understand these cultural and community responsibilities, so our program staff members spend much time educating them and mediating course and program completion.

A crucial benchmark of success is not only academic achievement but maintaining and developing an Indigenous "heart and mind" in which the teacher candidates build upon their Indigenous knowledges and maintain pride in their indigeneity. Students live such Indigenous values as caring, sharing, and helping one another as members of an extended family/cohort. NITEP teacher candidates and graduates often speak about their goals of maintaining and strengthening their indigeneity while completing their bachelor of education degree, despite encounters with racism, institutional disinterest, and marginalization from non-Indigenous teacher candidates and some instructors.

Personal growth is another important benchmark of student success. Through the NITEP courses and program activities, many students develop perseverance, self-confidence, leadership, and agency. This personal growth is also connected to their professional growth as teachers. The NITEP teacher

candidates often talk about their desire to make a positive impact on their future students' lives, as is exemplified in this student quote. Rupert Richardson
was a third-year NITEP student, when he wrote:

> Transformation can have many different meanings when it comes to
> education. There are the questions of what is being transformed, who is
> being transformed and who is doing the transforming. . . . In my future
> job as a transformative teacher; I must consider three important ideas
> regarding transformative teaching. First, education is constantly chang-
> ing. My mother's education is different from my own and in turn will be
> different from my future children's. In order to give the best educational
> experience, I must constantly be transforming with the times. Second,
> with the changing curriculum there has to be a middle ground regard-
> ing Aboriginal curriculum and the mainstream educational curricu-
> lum, with the same importance being given to each set of educational
> values. This will help Aboriginal students to realize that their ways of
> learning and teaching are just as important as the dominant educational
> system's values. I feel this will help to instill a sense of pride within the
> Aboriginal students. Thirdly, education must be taught in a way that is
> relevant to Aboriginal students. . . . I can't wait to become a transformer!
> (NITEP, 2009, p. 24)

Rupert graduated from NITEP, then completed an educational master's degree, and has begun his teaching career.

Through their membership on the FNEC, students gain leadership experience, they meet experienced NITEP educators, they gain an understanding
of how policy and program matters are determined, reviewed, and revised,
and they get to know other NITEP student leaders. The student representatives participate in NITEP decision making through their involvement at
FNEC meetings. Many of the NITEP graduates become educational leaders
in their communities, schools, professional associations, and in other careers
they may undertake. I often travel around British Columbia and, when I stop
at any urban or rural community, it does not take long before I find a NITEP
graduate. I think that Raven has a very large extended family that has been
given good teachings. These teachings serve family members well because the
challenges that confront Indigenous education are daunting and require both
individual and collective transformative efforts.

RAVEN'S CHALLENGES

For forty years, those who govern, work for, and study within NITEP have continued to examine its purpose, structure, courses, and policies in order to ensure
that it remains relevant and beneficial to its Indigenous learners, Indigenous

communities, and education in general. In order to ensure that NITEP is still responsive to Indigenous communities and to receive community-oriented feedback on how the program could be improved, regional Indigenous community consultations were held in 2006–2007 and in 2010. Invitations were sent to those who worked in education or who had decision-making positions at the reserve level, in urban and rural settings, in schools, at local colleges and universities, and with provincial professional associations. These sessions were held because the student enrollment had declined substantially at the field centers, thereby affecting the program's overall enrollment.

We asked participants in these consultations if NITEP was still needed in these regions. We asked about issues and questions they had regarding NITEP. We wondered how we could work cooperatively to increase student enrollment and how we could ensure that we were meeting their teacher education needs. Participants responded that NITEP was needed and that they wanted to help with recruitment by encouraging their community members to apply to NITEP and to complete the program. However, they identified two problems that resulted in two major programmatic changes.

First, we were asked to develop a part-time program option for those who were employed as teaching assistants so that they could keep their jobs while working on their degree program. This part-time program option was put into place the following year and has given a few more people an opportunity to take NITEP.

Second, the participants in the consultation wondered what NITEP could do to offer more of the program locally so that their community members did not have to relocate, and why NITEP could not work cooperatively with local universities that offered teacher education. In response, we found a way to offer one more year at the regional centers. However, we could not offer the entire bachelor of education degree because the last year of NITEP focuses on numerous pedagogical courses and senior education courses, which would be too expensive to offer at each regional center. Instead, we developed agreements with two other universities located on or near the field center sites to have NITEP students transfer into their teacher education programs after they completed their field center courses. These universities offer the additional courses and students are thus able to complete their degree requirements closer to home.

Some of the concerns of the Indigenous communities have yet to be resolved, however. Over the years, Indigenous communities have asked the NITEP leadership to address Indigenous language instruction and curriculum development. One part-time field center was established for a few years and it focused on Indigenous language preparation. However, this important area still needs to be addressed in a sustainable and relevant manner. Another issue relates to teacher education accessibility where Indigenous people cannot relocate to a regional center or to the Vancouver campus because of financial, work, family, and community concerns. We will soon implement flexible learning approaches that combine online and face-to-face options.

There have been many ongoing challenges that confront NITEP leaders and students alike. Substantial examples include limited programmatic and student funding, racism experienced by students, criticism that NITEP is not as good as the mainstream teacher education programs, and the intergenerational impact of colonization through education and social services. Dealing with these challenges is a daily and ongoing struggle. Sometimes when these issues become too stressful or too overwhelming, it feels like living in a world of darkness. But, we know that Raven is still flying overhead watching over us and the land.

RAVEN NEVER STOPS

NITEP as noted above began as an "Indian idea" although it found some support through non-Indigenous faculty allies and deans. NITEP will continue to face programmatic challenges that come from students' personal, family and community circumstances stained by a colonial legacy that for decades excluded Indigenous culture and language from formal education. Systemic challenges still confront NITEP students and those who run the program, including nonsupport or fear of including Indigenous knowledge in courses and criticism that NITEP is not a credible teacher education program, implying that its graduates are not qualified to teach in public schools. But those who have graduated from NITEP show that they have the resilience, determination, and ability to move beyond these challenges, complete a high-quality education degree program, and then take on leadership roles in various education contexts, often addressing Indigenous education in some way.

The Indigenous course component, the use of field centers, the cohort/extended family structure, Indigenous programmatic leadership, and an Indigenous community orientation help fulfill the "Indian idea"—the original NITEP vision. Indigenous leadership values and teachings such as caring, respect, extended family, community orientation, tenacity, and critical engagement are embedded in the program's Indigenous courses, cohort experiences, community interactions, and its governance structure. These leadership teachings have been experienced by students, individually and holistically. They are given many opportunities to understand the spiritual, emotional, physical, and intellectual dimensions of Indigenous knowledges and of education in general. NITEP students are challenged to think deeply about the effective learning relationships they will create with their future students, the students' families, and the larger professional education community of which they will be a part. They often approach this challenge with a mixture of enthusiasm and anxiety; however, they usually do not waiver in their conviction that they can make an educational difference.

Over a forty-year history, NITEP has created a new legacy for Indigenous teacher education in British Columbia, Canada. It is a legacy that values Indigenous knowledge, that is committed to providing Indigenous communities with access to teacher education, and that promotes Indigenous educational leadership. Many of the NITEP graduates are working to improve Indigenous education at all levels, creating a vibrant provincial network of NITEP alumni.

The Raven and the Sun story is as important today as it was when the program first started. The reflective stories of NITEP leadership that I have shared in this chapter are only a small sample of what can be told about how university education can address the needs of Indigenous communities. I know that the Raven never stops in the quest for making the world a better place. I know that many more Indigenous educational leadership stories will be lived and shared in the days to come.

NOTES

1. The Sto:lo people live along the Fraser River and its tributaries in southwestern British Columbia from Langley to Yale. "Sto:lo" means river.

2. The terms, Native, Indigenous, Aboriginal, and Indian will be used interchangeably in this chapter. When referring to names of programs and scholarly literature, the term used for these purposes will also be used in the textual discussion. The author's preference is to use Indigenous in order to show the common local and global matters that link Indigenous peoples around the world.

3. NITEP is a five-year Bachelor of Education degree program that prepares Indigenous people to teach at the kindergarten to grade twelve levels. The program may also be completed in just over four years. The Indigenous portion of the program will be discussed in this chapter.

4. See Ministry of Education, www.bced.gov.bc.ca/abed/perf2008.pdf for Aboriginal student data. Accessed April 12, 2014.

5. See the following web sites: First Nations Education Steering Committee (www.fnesc.ca), First Nations Leadership Council (www.fns.bc.ca), B.C. Deans of Education (www.educ.sfu.ca/abcde), and B.C. Teachers' Federation (www.bctf .ca). The Canadian Association of Deans of Education (ACDE), www.csse.ca /CADE/home.htm, has developed a national accord on Indigenous education that can be used for improving Indigenous education in Faculties of Education across the country. Sites accessed January 25, 2010.

6. This story or a version of it has been told by many different people associated with NITEP. It is italicized to indicate its orality. One version is offered by Archibald (1986).

7. The field centers have been or are located at Terrace, Hazelton, Prince George, Williams Lake, Penticton, Kamloops, Merritt, Sardis, Chilliwack, East Vancouver, North Vancouver, UBC Vancouver campus, Victoria, Duncan, Campbell River, Waglisla (Bella Bella), and Bella Coola.

8. For the purposes of this chapter, the NITEP concentration of its bachelor of education degree program is discussed. Students must complete many arts and sciences courses, as well as professional education courses and practica to receive a B.Ed. degree, which are not under the purview of NITEP. For more detail about the B.Ed. degree requirements see http://nitep.educ.ubc.ca (accessed April 12, 2014).

9. The purpose, protocols, and practices associated with Indigenous potlatches in British Columbia vary. Potlatches are an example of a holistic approach where oral history is practiced, cultural knowledges, values, and teachings are shared, extended families work cooperatively, food and gifts are given to participants, and ceremony is a key part of the activity.

10. See www.longhouse.ubc.ca for information about these programs and initiatives. Accessed April 12, 2014.

11. This data is based on communications from NITEP alumni and knowledge that the author and NITEP coordinators have of many of the graduates. Many, but not all, NITEP alumni often send emails and write articles for the annual NITEP newsletter, indicating their work contexts and graduate education. The actual numbers of NITEP alumni with magistral degrees is probably higher than what is reported in this chapter.

REFERENCES

Archibald, J. (1986). Completing a vision: The Native Indian teacher education program at the University of British Columbia. *Canadian Journal of Native Education, 13*(1), 33–46.

———. (2008a). Indigenous storywork: Educating the heart, mind, body, and spirit. Vancouver: University of British Columbia Press.

———. (2008b). Self-study and report: Aboriginal ways of knowing in teacher education. Native Indian Teacher Education Program (NITEP). In S. Niessen (Ed.), *Aboriginal knowledge exchange project. Self-study compilation and report: Aboriginal ways of knowing in teacher education* (pp. 86–98). Regina: Saskatchewan Instructional Development and Research Unit, Faculty of Education, University of Regina.

Archibald, J., Selkirk Bowman, S., Pepper, F., Urion, C., Mirehouse, G., and Shortt, R. (1995). Honoring what they say: Postsecondary experiences of First Nations graduates. *Canadian Journal of Native Education, 21*(1), 1–248.

Armstrong, J. (2000). A holistic education, teachings from the Dance House: "We Cannot Afford to Lose One Native Child." In M. Nee-Benham and J. Cooper (Eds.), *Indigenous educational models for contemporary practice* (pp. 35–43). Mahwah, NJ: Lawrence Erlbaum Associates.

Battiste, M. (2000). *Reclaiming Indigenous voice and vision.* Vancouver: University of British Columbia Press.

B.C. College of Teachers. (2004). NITEP celebrates 30 years. UBC's teacher education program puts Aboriginal teachers in front of the class. Vancouver: B.C.
College of Teachers.

Brown, L. (2006). The Native raining institute: A place of holistic learning and
health. *Canadian Journal of Native Education, 29*(1), 102–16.

Cajete, G. (2000). Indigenous knowledge: The Pueblo metaphor of Indigenous
education. In M. Battiste (Ed.), *Reclaiming Indigenous voice and vision* (pp.
181–91). Vancouver: University of British Columbia Press.

Castellano, M. B. (2000). Updating Aboriginal traditions of knowledge. In G. Dei,
B. Hall, and D. Rosenberg (Eds.), *Indigenous knowledges in global contexts:
Multiple readings of our world* (pp. 21–36). Toronto: University of Toronto
Press.

DeRose, D. (2005). Tribute to Joan Ryan, Gitksan elder and one of the founders of
NITEP. *NITEP news.* Vancouver: NITEP.

DeRose, D. (2006). Tribute to Joan Ryan, Gitksan elder, and one of the founders
of NITEP. *NITEP news.* Vancouver: NITEP.

Hawthorn, H. (1967). *A survey of the contemporary Indians of Canada: Economic,
political, and educational needs and policies,* vol. 2. Ottawa: Indian Affairs
Branch. Retrieved February 24, 2015, from the Government of Canada website, www.aadnc-aandc.gc.ca/eng/1291832488245/1291832647702

Kirkness, V. J. (1998). Our peoples' education: Cut the shackles; cut the crap; cut
the mustard. *Canadian Journal of Native Education, 22*(1), 10–15.

———. (1999). Native Indian teachers: A key to progress. *Canadian Journal of Native Education, 23*(1), 57–63.

Little Bear, L. (2000). Jagged worldviews collide. In M. Battiste (Ed.), *Reclaiming
Indigenous voice and vision* (pp. 77–85). Vancouver: University of British
Columbia Press.

National Indian Brotherhood. (1972). Indian control of Indian education. Policy
paper presented to the Minister of Indian Affairs and Northern Development. Ottawa: National Indian Brotherhood.

Native Indian Teacher Education Program (NITEP). (1974). *A proposal for a Native Indian teacher education program.* A report of the dean's committee.
Vancouver: Faculty of Education, University of British Columbia.

———. (1975–85). *Annual reports presented to the NITEP Advisory Committee.*
Vancouver: Faculty of Education, University of British Columbia.

———. (2005a). NITEP meeting at Cowichan Campus, Malaspina University
Campus. November 14, Meeting Minutes. Vancouver: NITEP.

———. (2005b). NITEP regional meeting at the Kamloops Chief Louis Center.
December 12, Minutes. Vancouver: NITEP.

———. (2006). *NITEP news.* Vancouver: NITEP.

———. (2007). *NITEP news.* Vancouver: NITEP.

———. (2008). *NITEP news.* Vancouver: NITEP.

————. (2009). *NITEP news*. Vancouver: NITEP.

Royal Commission on Aboriginal Peoples. (1996). Report of the Royal Commission on Aboriginal Peoples. *Gathering Strength*, vol. 4. Ottawa: Supply and Services Canada.

Smith, J. (2007). Tribute to Joan Ryan. *NITEP news*. Vancouver: NITEP.

Smith, L. T. (1999). *Decolonizing methodologies: Research and Indigenous peoples*. London: Zed Books.

PART II
THE WAY FORWARD
Preparing Indigenous Leaders for the Future

Theoretically, Indigenous leadership has guiding principles and practices that are largely informed by Indigenous epistemologies that shape and facilitate culturally responsive education across educational institutions serving Native students (preK–12 schools to higher education). Native communities continue to take positive steps to control education through community-based leadership to reverse the decades of failed federal education policies. Leadership that enacts the processes critical to self-determination in education is directly linked to Native community members engaged in leadership roles in schools and governance of educational systems serving their communities. This is a first step toward achieving educational sovereignty. Researchers have noted that even with an inadequate number of licensed Native school leaders, the impact of an engaged community in school leadership on the academic and social well-being of tribal children and on tribal sovereignty and self-determination efforts is crucial (Figueira and Beaulieu, 2006). The field of education demands literature that informs how to understand processes and structures in educational institutions, how educational leaders serving Indigenous communities support self-determination, and how they practice the principles of culturally based education that emphasizes localized Indigenous knowledge in schools (Demmert and Towner, 2003). Understanding how to respond to the systemic inequities that stymie self-determination in Native communities and how to create the most effective education system beneficial to Native children are necessary components of an essential curriculum in the preparation programs for Indigenous leaders in education;[1] it is imperative to cultural sovereignty and survival as Indigenous peoples to have leaders who know how to build relationships with the community. It takes leaders with team development skills and courage to transform conventional education into culturally responsive learning and teaching environments that support the goals and visions of Indigenous peoples. Developing professional development programs for educators and administrators in schools serving Indigenous students in the foundations (principles and practices) of culturally responsive education also has been essential due to the limited number of Native educators. Historically, mainstream higher education institutions provide teacher preparation programs that are Eurocentric and, even when culturally informed, are rarely culturally relevant to Indigenous children and families, with the exception of the localized culturally relevant teacher education programs at tribal colleges and universities; another exception we would include as Indigenous is the Native Indian Teacher Education Program established at University of British Columbia and described in Archibald's chapter 4. To achieve educational sovereignty involves the preparation of both school leaders and educators from all backgrounds to develop and implement culturally responsive education systems. School leaders also have a responsibility to conduct assessment on teaching and learning resources in their schools and to create and support the professional development plan for teachers so they have the culturally appropriate skills, pedagogy, and curricula to respond to the cultural needs of Indigenous students.

These chapters shed light on preparation programs for Native leaders in shifting what has historically been a deficit model of education toward a culturally responsive model driven by local Indigenous educators. The scholars who have authored these chapters explore Native perspectives about leadership and epistemologies as these relate to educational leadership endeavors and leadership practices relevant to tribal nations' control of education. This in turn requires leadership with the vision for creating culturally responsive education systems that serve Indigenous populations. A number of questions guided the research of these scholars: In what ways do Native educators understand and define leadership practice? How are mainstream educational institutions blending approaches, methodologies, and epistemologies to educate Native leaders? What conceptual frameworks and professional development models are used in preparing educators to serve Indigenous communities? What challenges and tensions exist in the Western worldview institutions that contradict Native leaders' goals for self-determination and educational sovereignty?

NOTE

1. We have written in other volumes about the rights of Native children to their cultures and languages in schools (Aguilera and LeCompte, 2007).

REFERENCES

Aguilera, D. E., and LeCompte, M. D. (2009). Restore my language and treat me justly: Indigenous students' rights to their tribal languages. In J. C. Scott, D. Y. Straker, and L. Katz (Eds.), *Affirming students' right to their own language: Bridging educational policies to language/language arts teaching practices* (pp. 130–72). London: Routledge.

Demmert, W. G., Jr., and Towner, J. C. (2003). A review of the research litera-
    ture on the influences of culturally based education on the academic
    performance of Native American students. Portland, OR: Northwest Re-
    gional Educational Laboratory.
Figueira, A., and Beaulieu, D. (Eds.). (2006). *The power of Native teachers: Lan-
    guage and culture in the classroom*. Center for Indian Education, Arizona
    State University.

5
Theory Z + N

The Role of Alaska Natives
in Administration

RAY BARNHARDT

One year, back in the early 1970s, a new principal/teacher (P/T) assumed his duties in a small Tlingit village on an island in southeast Alaska. He was employed by the State-Operated School System, headquartered in Anchorage, and had taught previously in rural village schools in other areas of the state, though this was the first time he also had principal duties. He was assigned to this particular school because the community had been expressing concern about the lack of cultural sensitivity on the part of previous teachers, and he had shown some interest in the local Native culture in earlier teaching assignments, even though his own cultural roots were still down in the panhandle of Texas.

Cognizant of his superiors' concern that the expectations of these politically aggressive villagers not get out of hand, the new P/T decided to take the initiative and give them what they wanted—a bit of local culture in the school curriculum. The most obvious expression of the local Tlingit culture to an outsider was the presence of totem poles at various locations in the community. What better way to show concern for the local culture than to have the students carve a totem pole as an after-school project; he himself would take responsibility to see that it happened as a sign of official commitment to the community's concerns.

The project did not move along quite as quickly as he had hoped, however, because the purchasing office in Anchorage, through which he had ordered the cedar log that was to be transformed into a totem pole, had difficulty in locating a supplier, and when they did, it took several months to have it shipped from Seattle. It had not occurred to him that local residents might have been able to acquire such a log from nearby forests at little or no expense to the school. Given the late start, and sensing some uncertainty on the part of the community, he decided to move right on in to the carving, so he set aside an area in the back of his classroom, drew a design on the log with a magic marker, and put the students to work with the carving tools.

Each school day for the next six months the P/T and his students put in an hour or so after school chipping away at the log. By late spring they had completed the carving, had colorfully painted the design, and were ready to present the result of their effort to the community. The P/T decided to sponsor an official unveiling and to erect the "totem pole" in front of the school, so he put out notices inviting the villagers to participate in the festive occasion. Finally, people in the community would see that the school did appreciate their culture, and the "totem pole" would be a prominent and permanent symbol of this recognition.

On the appointed day, the P/T assembled all of the students and the other teachers to participate in the ceremony, and they gathered in front of the school and excitedly waited for the villagers to arrive from the community below. An hour or so later, his excitement began to turn to anxiety, as there was still no sign of anyone coming up from the village to attend the ceremony. He was accustomed to community events starting on "Indian time," but this was beginning to try his patience. Finally, he spotted an old man walking by and asked him where everyone was. Why were people not coming up to the school for the unveiling of the "totem pole"? After some hesitation, the man responded, in a slightly admonishing tone, that people were not attending because they were offended by what he had done, and this was their way of showing their displeasure.

After the P/T had regained his composure, the old man proceeded to explain that totem poles were not just carvings that anyone could do at any time for any purpose. They had particular meanings and were designated for very particular occasions. The design was intended to tell a story, incorporating significant mythic and contemporary figures, the selection and sequence of which was determined by the clan affiliation of the sponsor and by the intended purpose of the pole. The presentation of a totem pole was a major event usually involving a ritual exchange between clans and accompanied by a formal potlatch with many reciprocal obligations associated with it. The P/T had violated nearly all of the critical cultural ingredients that go into the transformation of a log into an authentic "totem pole." His effort at cultural sensitivity, rather than appeasing the community, had led to further alienation.

This incident illustrates several problems with the way schools have typically addressed cultural issues in Native American communities. One such problem is viewing Native culture as an artifact—as just another item that can be added to the curriculum as though it were a subject of the past, rather than as a way of life and a way of knowing that exists today and has implications for all subject matter, as well as for when, where, and how subject matter is taught. Another problem illustrated by this story is the tendency of educators to view themselves as the sole proprietors of useful knowledge, not recognizing that theirs is a very specialized and limited way of knowing—so much so that they often overlook the fact that much knowledge is already present in the community that could be effectively built upon to the schools' advantage. These are long-standing problems that have been treated extensively by other authors (Barnhardt, 2002; Barnhardt and Kawagley, 2005, 2004; Kawagley, 2006; Scollon and Scollon, 1981), and need not be further elaborated here. There is a third problem reflected in this story, however, that has not received so much attention, and that is the more pervasive problem of using an administrative framework of Western origin to provide services to a non-Western cultural community. It is to this latter issue that this chapter is addressed.

As Raymond Callahan pointed out long ago in *Education and the Cult of Efficiency* (1962), the administrative framework for American schools has grown out of an industrial model, which typically includes organizational features such as a centralized authority structure, compartmentalization of responsibilities, short-term goal orientation, specialization of skills, standardization of procedures, and an emphasis on efficiency and productivity (No Child Left Behind Act of 2001, Public Law PL 107–110, signed into law by President Bush on January 8, 2002,[1] notwithstanding). These characteristics of administration and organization are somewhat consistent with a society that prides itself in its heterogeneity, mobility, and individualism. However, not all elements of American society have bought into the McDonald's version of the American dream, including many Native American communities.

The Tlingit people on the island in southeast Alaska, for example, have maintained a distinctive lifestyle that is still very much in harmony with the surrounding environment and is based on a strong bond of kinship and sense of mutual obligation, all of which foster a sustained tribal and clan identity, which serves as the primary source of cultural and psychological nurturance and support for its members. All else, including the school, is peripheral to this sense of bonded community. The P/T, however, was an outsider to the tribal community and saw as his primary responsibility allegiance to his employer in Anchorage. He based his actions on the expectations emanating from the detached institutional perspective of the central office. Despite his good intentions to respond to the wishes of the community, he was blinded by his adherence to a monolithic administrative framework that was more likely to reward him for appeasing the restless Natives than for providing a positive educational experience. Instead of recognizing that he was just one more of a long string of well-meaning but culturally deprived educators to pass through the community, he saw the assignment as an opportunity to establish his reputation in the institutional hierarchy as an innovative and responsive educator by demonstrating his commitment to local cultural concerns. His perception of the issue was framed, therefore, by his concern for how his actions might be viewed by his superiors, rather than how he would be viewed by the community. It probably did not even occur to him to check with the villagers before ordering the cedar log through the central office in Anchorage. While his actions may have enhanced his reputation in the eyes of the district administration, he did so at the expense of his credibility in the community.

EMERGENT INSTITUTIONS
FOR NATIVE COMMUNITIES

By the mid-1970s, the Native communities in rural Alaska were no longer willing to serve as proving grounds for aspiring educators. The State-Operated School System was too monolithic, detached, and cumbersome to adequately respond to the disparate educational needs of the various Native groups throughout Alaska, as well as to the needs of the military bases around the state, which also came under its authority. In 1976, largely through the political efforts of Native leaders, the State-Operated System was dissolved, and in its place twenty-one new regional school districts were established in rural Alaska. By placing control of the schools in the hands of regional boards, it was hoped that the educational services would be more responsive to local community concerns.

One of the principal avenues by which this increased responsiveness has been sought has been through an increase in the presence of Native people themselves in the schools, as teacher aides, bilingual instructors, and, to a more limited extent, as certificated teachers and administrators. As these new school districts evolved, with local people getting increasingly involved from the policy-making to the classroom level, the posture of their administration has slowly changed from that of a distant, all-knowing authoritarian regime to a more collaborative, adaptive, and facilitative form of administration. A reflection of this shift is an increased use of local parent committees and policy-advisory boards as well as a greater utilization of local expertise in all facets of the school operations, including the carving of totem poles.

While there still are a few mini-fiefdoms around rural Alaska, most administrators and teachers now recognize that their employer is the community, and their longevity requires a certain degree of sensitivity to community wishes. At the same time, communities are gradually developing a sense of ownership of their schools and are taking an increased interest in what goes on in them.

THEORY Z

This change in the administrative climate in the rural schools of Alaska over the past three decades has run parallel to changes in another sphere of organizational development beyond Alaska—that of national and multinational corporation management. Just as the original administrative structure of the State-Operated School System reflected many of the essential features of the old industrial management model described earlier, the new regional districts

Table 5.1 Contrasting Tendencies of Type A and Type Z Management

Type A	Type Z
Variable reducing	Variable generating
Centralized control	Decentralized control
Formal relationships	Informal relationships
Tight structure	Loose structure
Likeness oriented	Difference oriented
Vertical staff relations	Horizontal staff relations
Information flows out	Information flows in
Managing role	Facilitating role
Explicit rules	Implicit rules
Restrictive communications channels	Open communications channels
Content/product oriented	Process/direction oriented
Converging focus	Diverging focus
Resistant to change	Receptive to change
Static structure and function	Evolving structure and function
Upward responsive	Downward responsive
Impersonal relationships	Personal relationships

adopted administrative practices that were representative of an emerging model of corporate management that began to gain popularity in the 1980s and 1990s, in response to the increasing challenge to American industrial supremacy of companies from Japan, China, India, and other foreign countries.

One of the early proponents of this emerging model of corporate management was William Ouchi, who studied both Japanese and American versions of two contrasting styles of organization and management. He distinguished these as Type A (favored by Americans) and Type Z (favored by the Japanese). Out of his analysis of Type Z organizations, Ouchi identified a set of management practices (table 5.1) that he called a "Theory Z" style of management (Ouchi, 1981).

The most significant distinguishing feature of this style of management is its holistic emphasis on people and the environment in which they work. Employees are treated as integral and central elements in the organization and are given an active role in decision making and self-governance. Employment is viewed as a long-term mutual commitment in which the organization takes responsibility for the social, as well as the economic, well-being of its employees. The theory behind Theory Z is that employees who develop a sense of ownership in and commitment to the organization in which they work will be more dedicated to the goals of the organization and thus will become more productive contributors. To illustrate his point, Ouchi identified Hewlett-Packard, and Procter and Gamble as examples of successful American corporations that use a Theory Z style of management.

Theory Z is not limited in its corporate application to the multinational arena, however. Native regional corporations in Alaska, formed to administer the land and money acquired through the 1971 Alaska Native Claims Settlement Act, have also adopted management principles that reflect aspects of a Theory Z type of philosophy. As corporations with an exclusively Native clientele, they have attempted to employ Native workers, to invest in local enterprises, and to keep their shareholders informed and actively involved in corporate affairs. Their actions have not always been met with enthusiastic acceptance, however, and recurring debates regarding the efficacy of the corporate structure as a vehicle for serving Native interests indicate that a management style that is in the best interest of an organization may not always be in the best interest of its clientele.

In the early years of the Native regional corporations, the boards of directors, and the corporate executives sometimes became so preoccupied with the economic goals of the corporation that they overlooked the larger responsibility of protecting the cultural well-being of their shareholders. For example, in their pursuit of corporate objectives, some of the Native corporations established their main offices in urban centers to be near the financial and commercial markets, but in the process they distanced themselves from their primary constituency—their shareholders. As a result, there has been a backlash against some of the corporation leaders from Native people in the villages, where land and subsistence issues often overshadow concerns over making a profit in the cash economy. From the village shareholder's perspective, the needs of the community are seen as overriding the needs of the corporation, with the corporation expected to be of service to the community, rather than the other way around.

This places the managers of the Native corporations in a fundamentally different role from their counterparts in other corporations because they must deal with multiple constituencies with sometimes competing and conflicting expectations—a role that is not readily accommodated in Theory Z. It has not been enough for Native corporate leaders to attend only to the internal dynamics of employee relations within the corporation. They must also pay careful attention to the external relations with their Native shareholders. And just as Native corporations are seeking to redefine their modus operandi to be more compatible with their cultural constituencies, so too are the regional school districts having to adapt their administrative posture as Native people become more active participants in their operation, particularly as administrators.

THEORY Z + N

In the context of Native controlled institutions serving Native communities, Theory Z requires a Native corollary (which I will refer to as "Theory Z + N"), which takes into account the overriding communal responsibility of such institutions and of those who manage them, particularly if the managers are themselves Native. Theory Z + N takes into account the essential link between the well-being of the institution and the well-being of the community in which it is situated. While it may be possible to establish a management style such that the internal environment of a Native institution is organizationally coherent, operationally efficient, and employee sensitive, all of that will be of no avail if the overall thrust of the institution itself is not perceived by its Native clientele as consistent with the needs it is intended to serve. Such perceptions are created by many subtle features in the way an institution operates, and the way an institution operates is in large part a function of the attitudes and style of its administration.

While administrators, through their own deliberate actions, can influence the way an institution interacts with its clientele, there are many other ways, some obvious and some not so obvious, in which institutions can present unintended structural barriers to the accommodation of Native community concerns and perspectives. Such barriers may exist in any feature of the institution in which there is potential for different cultural beliefs and practices to influence the attitudes and behavior of institutional participants (cf. Barnhardt, 2002; Scollon and Scollon, 1981). This includes implicit behavioral routines, such as the way people are expected to communicate and interact with one another and the way decision making and leadership are exercised. It also includes explicit institutional routines, such as recruitment and selection procedures, the way time and space are structured, and the criteria and techniques used to judge peoples' performances. As can be seen by the experience of the P/T in southeast Alaska, administrative action sometimes speaks louder than the rhetoric that often accompanies it.

It is possible to reduce some of these institutional barriers by training non-Native administrators to recognize how organizational and administrative practices favor some people over others and encourage them to develop practices that take cultural diversity into account (Lindsey, Robins, and Terrell, 2003). Such an approach does not, however, address accompanying inequities in the distribution of power in the institution, nor is it the most effective or efficient means of building cultural sensitivity into institutional practices. Native people, with appropriate training and the opportunity to bring their unique perspective and skills to bear, are generally in a better position to break down institutional barriers to Native participation because they are more likely to have inherent within themselves the necessary cultural predispositions. They must also, however, have the incentive and support to take culturally appropriate initiatives in the restructuring of organizational and administrative practices, or they will simply perpetuate the inequities built into the existing system.

Bringing administrative responsibility for the delivery of services to the level of the Native community is a critical step if those services are to reflect local cultural considerations. In doing so, however, new kinds of demands are placed on the role of the administrator, which require a familiarity with and sensitivity to features of the local cultural system that few people from outside the system are likely to develop. It becomes imperative, therefore, that Native people assume those administrative responsibilities and be given the latitude to introduce their own modus operandi in response to the needs and conditions in the community. Efforts to achieve "cultural fit" may require changes in institutional features ranging from the simple rescheduling of daily activities to a rethinking of the very function of the institution. Persons fully immersed in the cultural community being served are in the best position to recognize and act upon the discrepancies between institutional and cultural practices that interfere with the performance of the institution.

While moving the control of services closer to the community and bringing Native people into decision-making and management roles is a critical and necessary step toward transforming Western bureaucratic institutions, such as schools, corporations, or government agencies, into more culturally sensitive institutions, that step in itself is not sufficient to achieve the equity of services that is needed. In addition to possessing all of the bureaucratic and technical skills necessary to maintain a Western-style institution, the Native administrator must also understand how the institution can be made to fit into the Native world without subverting essential features of that world. When such a transformation of existing institutions is not possible without losing more cultural ground than is gained, the Native administrator must also have the skills to build new kinds of institutions that can respect and be reconciled with the cultural values that are implicit in a Theory Z + N approach to management.

NATIVE PARTICIPATION IN DECISION MAKING

To be truly responsive to Native concerns, an institution must not only reflect an awareness of Native cultural values and practices but it must also convey an attitude of respect for those values and practices. This must be done in such a way that Native people feel a sense of ownership with regard to the institution and see it as incorporating their traditions and perpetuating their interests. So long as the institutional decision-making processes are in the hands of non-Native decision makers (regardless of how well intentioned), Native people will feel shut out as equal participants in those institutions. It is not enough to invite a token Native representative to "bring a Native perspective" to the decision-making arena or to hire a token Native employee to integrate the staff and appease the critics. Nor is it enough to have Native people in professional or supervisory roles using conventional bureaucratic-style criteria to perpetuate Western institutional values. Such gratuitous avenues of participation are too easily subverted by the weight of Western bureaucratic machinery and do little to counteract the cultural distance between Western-style institutions and Native people.

To develop a sense of institutional ownership, Native people must feel they are a part of the action and are a party to decision making from top to bottom, beginning to end. They must be on the delivery end of institutional services, not just on the receiving end. If such a transformation is to take place, institutions must adopt a participatory approach to decision making, whereby everyone that is affected by an institution, whether as producer or consumer of institutional services, has an opportunity to influence the way the institution operates. This requires multiple avenues of access to the decision-making process, so that everyone can contribute in a manner consistent with their relationship to the institution and with their style of participation and decision making. It also involves a horizontal distribution of power, so that all of the decision-making authority is not vested in a top-down hierarchical structure. Participatory decision making is at the heart of any administrative process that seeks to strengthen the degree of control that people have over their lives.

Increased Native participation in institutional decision making can be achieved through a variety of mechanisms. These range from the establishment of affirmative action and career ladder programs that strengthen Native presence in existing institutions, to the creation of new institutions, where Native people sustain their cultural community through their own system of educational and service institutions (e.g., tribal colleges). Other options include contracting with Native organizations to provide services to Native people, establishing Native councils or guardianships to oversee Native interests, employing Native elders to advise in areas of Native cultural and spiritual significance, and creating Native units within existing institutions through which Native people can manage their own affairs. It is through mechanisms such as these and any others that bring Native people into the decision-making arenas that they can begin to wield the power that is needed to shape their own destiny. It is not enough to be the beneficiaries of benevolent institutions. Native people must be full and equal participants in the shaping and operation of those institutions if they are to achieve true self-determination (Barnhardt, 1992).

CULTURAL BUREAUCRATS, ADVOCATES, AND MEDIATORS

Once inside an institution in a professional, supervisory, or decision-making role, Native people often face another set of considerations that extend far beyond those of their non-Native counterpart. Personal aspirations on the part of a Native administrator can be bound to a whole range of cultural expectations and obligations that rarely enter into non-Native considerations. This is in part a function of differences in cultural traditions, but it is also a function of the history of a beneficiary relationship between Native people and the institutions of a dominant society (i.e., the institution is there to provide certain benefits and those who work in the institution are there to administer those benefits for the people). As indicated earlier, Native administrators must not only reconcile themselves to their role within the institution, they are also expected to reconcile the relationship between the institution and its clientele. This may not always be easy because the expectations of a Native community regarding an institution do not always coincide with those of the persons responsible for maintaining the institution. Given such circumstances, the administrator-cum-leader must choose to align either with the community being served or with the institution providing the services or attempt to establish a middle ground as a mediator between the two. Each of these options leads to a different kind of role for the administrator vis-à-vis the community and the institution and, therefore, requires different kinds of skills.

If primary allegiance is granted to the institution, the Native administrator takes on the mantle of a "bureaucrat" and is likely to pursue primarily personal career goals as a matter of survival in the institution with little willingness to challenge any lack of institutional response to the unique concerns of the Native community. Having bought into the bureaucratic system, efforts of such a person in the community are more likely to be directed toward getting the community to understand the needs of the institution than to initiate actions or raise issues that further complicate institutional tasks. The responsibility of the bureaucrat (Native or non-Native) is to maintain the established system as efficiently and effectively as possible by reducing the variables that the system has to deal with to the minimum necessary for survival. It is the rare bureaucrat that willingly introduces new complicating variables to the system. If bureaucratic institutions employ Native personnel with the intent of improving relations with Native communities yet expect them to take on a typical bureaucratic posture, they should not be surprised if the same old issues continue to resurface. While many benefits may be gained from such an arrangement, the greater share of those benefits will go to the individual and the institution rather than to the community. Little is likely to be gained in terms of Native self-determination.

If, on the other hand, a Native person enters a bureaucratic institution as an "advocate" for Native concerns while retaining primary allegiance to the community, a set of skills different from those of the bureaucrat come into play. The concern of the community advocate is to bring community perspectives to the attention of the institution and to mobilize community action to achieve appropriate changes in the system. To achieve community action goals, cultural, political, and legal skills are often more important than administrative or technical bureaucratic skills.

Advocates tend to prefer positions that allow them to keep in close touch with the community (e.g., field offices) so that their institutional ties are often are somewhat tenuous. Faced with a choice between alienation from the community and losing one's job, the advocate is likely to choose the latter option. This can present the institution with a dilemma because, while commitment to institutional goals and procedures is expected, the expertise of the Native community advocate can be vital to effective implementation of those goals and procedures. The root of the dilemma is not, however, in the lack of institutional commitment by the community advocate but rather in the cultural distance between the functioning of the institution and the needs of the community. From the community advocate's point of view, change must occur by bringing institutional practices into closer alignment with the expectations of the community being served rather than the other way around. To the extent that the community advocate adequately represents community perspectives and the institution finds ways to accommodate those perspectives, that institution becomes an instrument of empowerment and service to Native people and thus to all of society.

A third and more difficult posture that a Native person can assume as an administrator in a non-Native–dominated institution is that of "mediator" between the non-Native and Native cultural worlds. While such a posture can lapse into little more than fence straddling, it also has the potential for creative application of the bicultural skills embodied in Native people. To function as mediator, a person must have a firm understanding of the essential qualities that make up the two (or more) worlds represented in the mediating arena. Just as important, however, is an ability to see beyond existing circumstances so as to create new options that reconcile differences in mutually beneficial ways. Bicultural skills must, therefore, be reinforced with institution-building skills as well as with negotiation and persuasion skills. Such a combination of administrator and cultural broker can be a valuable asset to any institution, so long as the institutional power brokers recognize that mediation and accommodation are two-way processes.

To be a successful mediator, a person must be able to establish comembership in both the community and institutional arenas. To be recognized and supported by Native people and to have influence in Native arenas requires the ability to display one's self in ways that are characteristically Native and the ability to articulate issues in terms that make sense to Native people. To have credibility in the bureaucratic institutional arena requires the ability to command authority and display competence in ways that are characteristically non-Native. So, to be an effective mediator as a Native administrator, one has to be able to shift readily back and forth between different authority structures, leadership styles, decision-making processes, communication patterns, and any other cultural variables that enter into the way people get things done. The task of the mediator becomes one of constantly juggling multiple sets of often conflicting expectations and trying to determine where and how to seek changes that will reconcile the differences in a mutually satisfactory manner.

Whether the task is to increase Native participation in decision making, improve communication, or develop culturally appropriate organizational policies, practices, and procedures, there is one set of skills that is paramount above all others and that is a thorough grounding in Native cultural beliefs and practices. Without such grounding, administrators (Native or non-Native) are likely to lack the knowledge and credibility necessary to bridge the gap between existing institutions and Native people, regardless of how well intentioned they might be. Unless they are prepared to add the "N" to Theory Z in their administrative practice, they are likely to experience the same frustration as the P/T in the Tlingit community in southeast Alaska. Priority must be given, therefore, to the preparation of skilled Native administrators who can apply their talents to the development of the kind of culturally sensitive institutional structures and practices that are required if Alaska Natives are to achieve the degree of cultural and institutional independence needed to exercise Native control over Native affairs.

NOTE

1. The No Child Left Behind Act of 2001, Public Law PL 107–110 (NCLB), signed into law by President Bush on January 8, 2002, was a reauthorization of the Elementary and Secondary Education Act (ESEA), the central federal law in pre-collegiate education. The ESEA, first enacted in 1965 and reauthorized in 1994, encompasses Title I, the federal government's flagship aid program for disadvantaged students. Coming at a time of wide public concern about the state of education, the NCLB legislation set in place requirements that reached into virtually every public school in America. It expanded the federal role in education and took particular aim at improving the educational lot of disadvantaged students. At the core of NCLB were a number of measures designed to drive broad gains in student achievement and to hold states and schools more accountable for student progress. They represented significant changes to the education landscape (U.S. Department of Education, 2002). See http://www.edweek.org/ew/issues/no-child-left-behind/.

REFERENCES

Barnhardt, R. (1985). *Maori makes a difference: Human resources for Maori development*. Hamilton, New Zealand: Centre for Maori Studies and Research, University of Waikato.

Barnhardt, R. (1992). Administration across cultures. In V. D'Oyley, A. Blunt and R. Barnhardt (Eds.), *Education and development: Lessons from the third world*. Calgary: Temeron Press.

Barnhardt, R. (2002). Domestication of the ivory tower: Institutional adaptation to cultural distance. *Anthropology and Education Quarterly, 33*(2), 238–49.

Barnhardt, R. (2005). Culture, community and place in Alaska Native education. *Democracy and Education, 16*(2), 44–51.

Barnhardt, R., and Kawagley, A. O. (2004). Culture, chaos and complexity: Catalysts for change in Indigenous education. *Cultural Survival Quarterly*, 27(4): 59-64.

Barnhardt, R., and Kawagley, A. O. (2005). Indigenous knowledge systems and Alaska Native ways of knowing. *Anthropology and Education Quarterly*, 36(1), 8–23.

Callahan, R. E. (1962). *Education and the cult of efficiency*. Chicago: University of Chicago Press.

Kawagley, A. O. (2006). *A Yupiaq worldview: A pathway to ecology and spirit* (2nd ed.). Prospect Heights, IL: Waveland Press.

Lindsey, R. B., Robins, K. N., and Terrell, R. D. (2003).*Cultural proficiency: A manual for school leaders* (2nd ed.). Thousand Oaks, CA: Corwin Press.

Ouchi, W. G. (1981). *Theory Z*. Reading, MA: Addison-Wesley Publishing.

Scollon, R., and Scollon, S. (1981). *Narrative literacy and face in interethnic communication*. Norwood, NJ: Ablex Publishing.

U.S. Department of Education (2002). *No Child Left Behind Act of 2001*. Washington, DC: Author, Office of the Secretary, Office of Public Affairs.

6

Native American Doctoral Students

Establishing Legitimacy in Higher Education

DANA E. CHRISTMAN, DONALD PEPION,
COLLEEN BOWMAN, AND BRIAN DIXON

This chapter reviews the experiences and perceptions of Native American educational leaders as they make their way through educational leadership doctoral programs at large, public research universities. These Native American scholars face enormous challenges as they prepare academically for their roles as advocates for balanced education for Native American students, blending cultural relevance with federal mandates. This case study used open-ended, semi-structured, electronic questionnaires to determine how these Native American cohort students made meaning of their entry and progress through their own doctoral programs. Viewed through an Indigenous lens, this study may help higher education departments shape culturally appropriate doctoral programs in the academy.

In 2004, Native Americans earned 0.07 percent of the entire associate's, bachelor's, and advanced degrees conferred at colleges and universities (National Center of Educational Statistics, 2007). Native American/Alaska Natives from U.S. Indian reservations are only one-half as likely as their white counterparts to persist and attain a postsecondary degree (Pavel, Swisher, and Ward, 1995). Having more Native American leaders serving in Native schools might improve achievement gaps through the affinity these administrators would feel for their communities; it also might produce a more authentic kind of leadership. Also, the existence of Native American leaders serving in their communities may positively affect the overall educational achievement of students by being role models and mentors.

NATIVE LEADERSHIP INFLUENCE ON EDUCATIONAL OUTCOMES

Educational leaders must find answers to the multitude of problems that worsen the dropout rates of Native American students in preK–12 schools and respond directly and culturally to students' difficulties in pursuing post-secondary education. These problems include cultural discontinuity, lack of culturally based education, lack of mentorship and role models, lack of preparedness among education leaders, and a lack of professional development for school administrators. Next, we introduce a series of remedies to which numerous scholars have dedicated decades of research in the name of educational sovereignty and self-determination, especially to improve educational experiences for Native populations.

Culturally Based Education

Worthley (1987) explains that individuals within a culture, such as a Native American culture, develop common learning patterns. Although it is important to state that there is no one specific type of learning pattern among Native tribes (MacIvor, 1999), there is still a teaching and learning relationship between Native American/Alaska Native students and their teachers that must be taken into account (Swisher and Tippeconnic, 1999). Indigenous students learn in their culturally informed ways of knowing and interacting with others (in learning environments) that are characterized by "factors of social/affective emphasis, harmony, holistic perspectives, expressive creativity, and nonverbal communication" (Pewewardy, 2002, p. 22). Thus, teachers and administrators of schools with significant Native American/Alaska Native populations should keep in mind that education must respond to the culture of their students. Other researchers (e.g., McCarty, Lynch, Wallace and Benally, 1991) also report that culture-based education is particularly important for the success of Native American students because of the relative isolation and unique cultural distinctiveness of Native American groups (Demmert, Towner and Yap, 2003). In Native American communities, inclusion is an important part of education, that is, students learn by watching, practicing, and then teaching to others (Tharp, Dalton, and Yamauchi, 1994). Following on this tradition, learning for Native American students would be best accomplished in small groups, rather than in isolation. But instead, today's mainstream schools tend to reward individual responses and competition, rather than cooperative, efforts. Such practices clash with nonconfrontational approaches preferred by Native American students (DuBray, 1993). Culture-based education has been the topic of research among many Indigenous educators and practitioners whose studies show the impact of strong culturally embedded education with Native American/Alaska Native students (Demmert, Towner and Yap, 2003; Aguilera, 2003; Aguilera, Lipka, Demmert, and Tippeconic, 2007).

Mentorship and Role Modeling

Along with culturally based education, continued feedback and support to the students by mentors or role models in the school also has been shown to raise achievement (Weaver, 2000). Further, by establishing tribal members as mentors, they can offer the students ongoing access to role models, hope, vision, and an intergenerational connection to the community (Radda, Iwamoto, and Patrick, 1998). Because of the small numbers of Native Americans who pursue postsecondary education and the decrease in providing opportunities for elders—our culture bearers—to be actively engaged in schools, Native American students often lack access to such role models. Currently, some Native American children in the state where this study takes place likely will go through the entire public school system without ever having had a Native American administrator in charge of their schools or the opportunity to have a tribal member as their teacher. This is unfortunate as Native American/Alaska Native students have unique needs that must be met for them to be successful in schools. The research is clear that Native educators have a positive impact on Native children and their presence is important to student success (Reyhner, 2001; Cleary and Peacock, 1998; Silverman and Demmert, 1986). In the final report on the Indian Nations at Risk Task Force, Charleston (1994) targeted key components for improving Indian education through local control with Native educators and leadership also serving as role models in the public schools, suggesting educational leadership in the context of Native student populations should be oriented in an Indigenous paradigm to support student success (p. 15). In a time when the desire for self-determination among Native American people is high, the lack of appropriate role models for Native American children and teachers is appalling and inexcusable. This gap in mentorship could be offset with educational organizations establishing better relationships with families and communities. The intergenerational thread that connects Native children with elders and sustains cultural knowledge is an Indigenous principle that supports children's relationships with mentors and role models who are the culture bearers in tribal communities. Culture bearers are the tribe's educators and leaders with which mainstream education needs to have stronger connections and relationships.

Native Administrators in Schools

Educators interested in serving as school administrators need at least a master's degree for entry-level positions. For higher-level administrative positions, doctoral degrees are often preferred or required by school systems. As noted, Native Americans are less likely than other ethnic and racial groups to attain graduate degrees, thus the challenge is to fund and prepare more Native Americans with graduate degrees in education. Having more Native American school administrators in public schools with significant Native American populations also may reduce the high turnover rates among non-Native administrators, many who perhaps have no affinity for these communities and serve only in a titular capacity. They may provide no real leadership to faculty or students, may be nearing retirement, or may leave after serving a year or less. Often, this type of inconsistent leadership leaves these schools and districts in disorder, which affects faculty morale and reinforces the assumption that these schools are not worthy of much time and effort. However, given the mandates of the No Child Left Behind Act of 2001 (Public Law PL 107–110),[1] it is essential that these schools have steady, dependable leadership from individuals who actively demonstrate commitment to these communities, in addition to meeting federal requirements for academic achievement. Chance and Ristow (1990) suggest that administrator hopefuls need to develop cultural understanding of specific tribal customs, traditions, needs, and expectations before taking on a position in a school with a large Native American population. While professional development programs that foster such understanding could reduce this turnover rate among non-Native administrators, the most critical need is for Indigenous leadership in schools serving tribal children (Arizona State University, 1970).

Preparedness and Professional Development

Research suggests that not only do administrator preparation programs provide little training for the different learning needs of culturally and linguistically diverse populations (Herrity and Glasman, 1999) but school administrators also are not likely to participate in professional development that addresses these concerns (Christman, Guillory, Fairbanks and Gonzalez, 2008). Not surprisingly, then, we find one of the greatest barriers to positive learning experiences for Native American children is the lack of understanding by school administrators of the teaching and learning practices that are effective with these students (Murry and Herrera, 1999). Non-Native administrators in schools with significant Native American/Alaska Native populations appear to be woefully underprepared for leadership in such schools. The need for programs that provide professional development for administrators is especially acute in many tribal communities. Administrators in these areas often lack knowledge of the needs of their Native American students. While much educational leadership research stresses the critical role of the principal in supporting and achieving school success, very little research has focused on the role of school leadership in enhancing educational success with Native

American students. Only a few federally funded professional development programs have provided staff development to prepare Native educators who were already teaching in schools serving Native communities to be more effective. Few would argue that steps have been taken to prepare teachers to work with diverse students (NCLB, 2001; U.S. Department of Education, 2002); however, preparation that produces culturally competent administrators has failed to keep pace with that provided for classroom teachers in general.

NATIVE LEADERSHIP

Charleston (1994), Boloz and Foster (1980), and Cleary and Peacock (1998) posit that Native American students have unique needs that must be met if they are to be successful in schools. For such success to be reached, the leadership in schools must be viewed through a Native American paradigm, that is, one that defines leadership as fluid and dynamic (Charleston, 1994) and sees it as a practice that can only be defined in context (Boloz and Foster, 1980). As well, leadership should be seen as a responsibility performed by those who are willing and able to provide it (Charleston, 1994). Thus, Native American leaders must earn the trust and support not only of school personnel and students but also of that of the community (See also Barnhardt, this volume). Mills and Amiotte (1995–96) suggest that graduates of effective preparation programs must have the academic background, preliminary field experience, and professional dispositions necessary to succeed anywhere in instructional leadership positions—even in schools serving Native populations—and to significantly improve the quality of education for Native American children.

INDIGENOUS LENSES BY WHICH TO UNDERSTAND NATIVE LEADERSHIP

Culture involves issues of perspective and ownership. In the United States, we are rewarded with cultural complexity. And we have different perspectives and ownership of different cultural traditions; whether in this country or in any other culturally complex society, certain cultural aspects may not be shared by all groups. Decisions about who gets to decide which cultural elements survive and flourish become critical and fundamental issues, since in the United Sates, such decisions impact the way we educate our children, as well as the way we make our policies and write our laws (Miraglia, Law, and Collins, 2006).

Culture is often easier to explain as something that affects everyone in a country or nation. Mandates about "how life is lived" involve judgments to be made by the particular collectivity that possesses this culture and *by no one else* (Tomlinson, 1991, p. 6). This is an essential concept of Native American sovereignty. This concept simultaneously serves as a source of confusion for numbers of Americans as well as a source of clarity for most Native Americans. Such tension becomes problematic when there are nations within nations, that is, for example, when Native American or tribal nations exist within the U.S. boundaries. If we theorize that Western culture is valued over all others in the United States, then what we teach, how our policies are made, and how our laws are created may not readily reflect the values of these embedded sovereign nations.

In this study, then, we use an Indigenous lens to view the way in which Native American leaders are prepared at mainstream higher education institutions, which tend to reflect Western paradigms. Tribal Critical Race Theory (CRT) emerged from critical race studies that evolved in the 1970s in response to Critical Legal Studies (Brayboy, 2006; Delgado and Stefancic, 2001; Haynes Writer, 2002). Like Critical Legal Studies, CRT is a "form of opposition scholarship" (Calmore, 1992, p. 2161). Beginning in the 1990s, CRT was applied to studies of education to provide different ways of examining mainstream educational institutions and the problems that people of color face in these institutions (Ladson-Billings and Tate, 1995). Using CRT in education compels scholars to work toward elimination of racism, sexism, and poverty within our schools and within our students' very lives (Delgado Bernal and Villalpando, 2002; Solorzano and Yosso, 2001).

Yet, CRT does not completely address the needs of Native Americans, having been targeted primarily at a "black-white" duality. From CRT, offshoots of Latino Critical Race Theory and Asian Critical Race Theory emerged, both specifically geared toward meeting the needs of Latinas(os) and Asian Americans, and both relying on the premise that racism is endemic in our society (Brayboy, 2006). Tribal Critical Race Theory, however, furthers the concept of racism and relies on the premise that "colonization is endemic to society" (p. 429). We return, then, to the concept of sovereignty fairly quickly. Whereas sovereignty stresses appreciation for heritage, language, religion and spirituality, and the existence of inherently correct economic, political, social, and legal systems within a nation, the context for Native American education has been anything but respectful of sovereignty. Brayboy (2006) writes, "The goal, sometimes explicit, sometimes implicit, of interactions between the dominant U.S. society and American Indians has been to change ('colonize' or 'civilize') us to be more like those who hold power in the dominant society" (p. 430). The main drive of Native educators with the goal of becoming school administrators is to dramatically improve educational experiences in schools for Native students. Shifting power relations from dominant groups controlling schools serving tribal communities to Native leaders in administrative roles is in line with the self-determination goals of tribal communities.

CREATING AN INDIGENIZED
LEADERSHIP PROGRAM

Knowing that Native American students in schools need appropriate cultural support and culturally based education, and mentors and role models, the university in this case study noted the need for Native administrators to lead school districts or other educational systems with significant populations of Native American students. In 2006, university personnel sought funding for Native American administrators to serve in school districts or at the state, regional, or national level with large populations of Native American students. After a year-long search for funding, enough money became available to the program in January 2007.

Entry into the program was competitive, with far more students applying than could be accommodated in the limited number of spaces held for those chosen for the cohort. Informational meetings were held in various locations throughout the state, including on reservations, prior to the application deadline. Selection of participants was accomplished through a committee that reviewed and graded each completed application with regard to the applicant's stated philosophy in an essay on Native American education, application letter, critique of a selected article, and undergraduate and graduate grade point average. The committee then met as a whole and discussed each application until consensus was reached as to who would be selected. Chosen applicants and their families were invited to campus for an orientation meeting about the program before it started. At this meeting, selected applicants emerged as the new doctorate cohort members, became acquainted with each other, and received materials provided by the university—laptop computers, books, and other materials.

Cohort members began the program in January 2007. The program required sixty-six credit hours for which students would receive a doctorate of education. The program provided for courses to be offered at locations convenient to the students via face-to-face instruction from university faculty. In the summers during the program, students would enroll in internships, which would be scheduled to take place in the state capital one summer and in Washington, D.C., the next.

LEADERSHIP PROGRAM CURRICULUM

The premise of curriculum and instruction for this program was underscored by the concept of reciprocity. We understood that as professional educators, we needed to learn from our students and the students from each other. Faculty members could not be seen as sole dispensers of knowledge and expertise and the students as passive recipients of that knowledge and expertise (Kirkness and Barnhardt, 1991). Preparation for high-level educational administration positions and/or the professoriate included university coursework and field-based experiences throughout the program. Coursework revolved around four components: leadership in local, district, state, and national educational contexts; curriculum and instructional leadership using a Native American paradigm; culture and language; and assessment.

RESEARCH QUESTIONS

Given the needs and the desire of Native American students to become involved as administrators at higher levels and with greater influence in Indian education, the researchers became aware that they should view the accomplishments and deficits of the program with a critical lens. The following research questions guided this reflection.

1. What helped these Native American students prepare for and persist in their educational administration doctoral program?
2. In what ways did the program impact the students?
3. How did students perceive the effect of the program on their long-term goals?
4. What could others learn from the experiences of these students?

RESEARCH DESIGN AND METHODS

Since this case study was concerned with participant perspectives, a qualitative research design was chosen as the proper method. Giving voice to participants through qualitative research (Merriam, 1998; Patton, 1990) yielded multiple findings that directed us to participants' strengths and member relationships both inside and outside of the study (Brayboy and Deyhle, 2000; Nicholson, Evans, Tellier-Robinson, and Aviles, 2001). Data were collected through open-ended, structured questionnaires. The questionnaires were distributed electronically by a third party to the program, a trusted and valued faculty member to the students, but one who had no vested interest in the outcome of the research. Students were advised to return their questionnaires to this person, who then removed all identifiers and combined all responses into one large document. Therefore, we, as researchers, were not able to identify participants' responses to the questionnaires. We worked to crystallize (Janesick, 2000) the data to aid in the interpretation of meaning.

DATA ANALYSIS

Data from the questionnaires were analyzed in three stages of coding (Strauss and Corbin, 1990). Coding involved organizing data and breaking them into manageable units; synthesizing them and looking for exemplars within the data; and understanding what was important and what was to be learned (Bogdan and Biklen, 1998). The first stage, open coding, involved the breaking down, examining, comparing, and conceptualizing of data. The second stage, axial coding, involved sorting and defining data into categories and themes. Selective coding, the third stage of analysis, developed the story, revisited categories, and looked for interrelationships among categories. Selective coding also aided both in interpretation and meaning, helped to reduce and refine data for explanations, conclusions, inferences and linkages, and dealt with rival explanations (Strauss and Corbin, 1990). The data were then cast against the lens of Tribal Critical Race Theory (Brayboy, 2006).

STUDY PARTICIPANTS

Interview questionnaires were conducted electronically with a total of twelve male and female participants. Participants were from different Native American/Alaska Native tribes and Pueblos. Participants worked in rural or semirural, public or Bureau of Indian Education (BIE) preK–12 schools or school districts, or at the state level in an educational leadership capacity. Participants were administrators who:

- possessed a master's degree from an accredited institution,
- held membership/enrollment in a federally or state-recognized Native American tribe or Pueblo,
- experienced five years of prior educational service in a public, private, or federal educational institution,
- expressed commitment to complete a four-year program of study, and
- committed to serve Native American students following their completion of the doctoral program.

Consent was obtained from participants in the study by assuring their confidentiality and explaining that by completing the electronic questionnaire they were giving their consent for their information to be used in this study. Each participant also was provided with a copy of the informed consent letter. We explained further that failing to return the questionnaire would not result in any penalty or prejudicial actions from program personnel or those conducting the research. At the time of data collection, participants were approximately one-quarter of the way through their three-year educational leadership degree program.

DATA RESULTS

After the data had been coded, we noted six themes facilitating retention in graduate school that emerged from the analysis. They included (1) support from key people, (2) good fit with the program, (3) advocacy, (4) deepening comprehension, (5) concerns, and (6) confidence. All themes are best represented through the voices of the participants.

Support from Crucial People

One of the first themes to emerge was support from crucial people. Participants found that key people were involved in helping them weigh the advantages and disadvantages of the program and the degree, as well as in making the decision to apply for the program. One participant noted, "I was informed about the [program] after attending a conference with my director. She asked me what my professional plans were for the next few years. I shared with her my desire to obtain a degree in Educational Administration. A few weeks later she shared information she had received about a doctoral program at a local university."

Another participant explained that her supervisor had encouraged her to apply, indicating that she would increase her skills and continue learning throughout her life. This participant further explained that her supervisor wanted her to be able to take advantage of opportunities "like these."

Participants also discovered that the relationships with their fellow cohort members had gradually become more important in their own success. Relying on each other for support and motivation, one member noted about his colleagues, "They are my support and I am their support. We have a study group that meets during the week whether just to share our struggles or to talk through our assignments—to make sense of what we don't understand." Taking this thought a step further, another participant stated, "I look to my classmates as key supports in getting through the program. We have a *pact* to finish this program." Other members of the cohort were simply "people that I can count on," as another participant explained.

Thus, participants found the cohort design to be supportive. Indeed, all members found that they could depend on each other for help they needed. They gathered strength and motivation from the group. They learned new concepts with and from each other.

Another group of crucial people were family members. Most every cohort member clearly realized that his or her family was vital in sustaining them not only through the program but through the actual application process. One participant offered, "I told my family and they were very supportive. I had just gotten out of the hospital and they helped to do all the running around for me to get the application and recommendations to the post office on time."

A second participant plainly stated, "My family played a key role in encouraging me to apply for acceptance." Another participant explained that her husband and children had convinced her to apply as soon as she shared information about the doctoral program with them.

So, in the theme "support from crucial people" we find that cohort members were influenced both professionally and personally. We note that families were integral in providing support for these students to apply for the program. Some cohort members found that their family members had a kind of authority over whether they applied for the doctoral program or not. Participants actively sought their opinions and most received undeniable support to make the kinds of commitment that the program would entail. Indeed, support from their families and other people were coupled together for these students. Many times, the students spoke of both family members and key others who were influencing and supporting them in the same breath. Waters (2004) writes, "All our relations have a strong influence on the shaping of our identity" (p. 161). These were significant people who were identified as having influences on their lives particularly in supporting their educational leadership aspirations.

Good Fit

Another pattern materialized regarding how participants felt a certain "fit" with the program. They got a feeling that the time was appropriate or that the program was going to be suitable for them. One participant stated, "When I learned of the program, I knew that it was the opportunity that I was hoping for. I immediately applied. Even though I had just learned of the program and was afraid that I might miss the deadline, I still rushed to submit the paperwork."

Another participant reflected, "After I left the orientation session that evening, my wife and I made an almost immediate decision that this doctorate program was the best fit for me and the busy schedule I had." Yet another participant explained that she had worked as a mentor with another Native American student in a master's cohort at our institution and had seen for herself how the student had benefited considerably from the experience. She noted that she would not have been able to pursue a doctoral program elsewhere due to her time and work constraints as well as her family and community commitments.

Yet, some others were completely assured about getting a doctoral degree from the outset. One stated categorically, "I have ALWAYS thought about it." Another seemed to reflect on the decision she had made by saying, "I searched deep within myself and Yes, this is what I want, what I want for my family and what I need to do for Native People."

So, under this theme we discovered that most participants felt that this educational leadership program for Native educators would be the direction they would pursue. They seemed to feel that the doctoral degree was not a chimera but instead was the "right thing to do." The doctorate was tangible and participants seemed to have an innate sense of what it would feel like to be in a doctoral program, taking classes, studying, and ultimately completing the degree.

Advocacy

A clear theme to emerge from the data was the participants' desire to advocate for others, especially those in Indian education. We saw that time and again, participants were attracted to the educational leadership program not only because it had a focus on serving Native American graduate students and their communities but also because the participants themselves had a desire to serve Native American students and their communities. For instance, one participant said that once he had discovered that the program would target Native American students, he found "that was enough of an incentive for me to apply."

Another participant explained that she, along with others, had a "pact to finish this program and to become strong advocates for educational excellence in Indian Country." The idea of helping other Native Americans in education was very appealing and empowering. One participant stated that she wanted to "continue to work in precollege programming for [her tribe's] students. [She] also wanted to have an opportunity to create an effective bridge between secondary and post-secondary schools in [her] own community."

The goal of other participants was to be part of the change that needed to take place in Indian education. For example, one participant described advocacy as "mak[ing] it possible for others to make changes for our children."

Thus, we can see that participants in the cohort felt strongly about their need to advocate for Native American education and students. Though they admitted that having their expenses for the program covered was a good thing, it was more important that they would be working with other Native Americans in the program. This incentive was quite present in their responses; they reflected, "How can this program help me to help others?" Clearly, participants were in the doctoral program as a way to give back to their communities.

Deepening Comprehension

An additional theme was how participants' comprehension levels seemed to be deepening and evolving. Participants explained that they felt some transformation in the way they were thinking, especially in how they thought about Indigenous education. For example, one participant reflected, "I look more critically at the overall school environment. I question decisions and study the impact of many of the decisions that are made. I seem to see more than just the topical view of the goings-on in my school district. I know there must be more beneath the surface and I am curious to find out what is just beneath the surface."

In agreement with this participant, another commented, "I'm more in tune with the happenings in our school, the district, and the agency. My suggestions are meaningful because I see and know the underlying issues and agendas." Still another offered:

> The impact is greater than I expected. I believe the program has broadened my view considerably, particularly with regard to my school and the programs I believe our school should provide. I view many of our programs from a critical eye, with an eye toward research. I also know that unless there is data to support my statement, I can't make the statement with any conviction. My conversations with my supervisor have become more powerful as have my conversations with my peers.

Another cohort member acknowledged that he was more critical and analytical in his position as a result of his experiences in the doctoral program. He said that he read more professional articles and used the analytical skills he had learned. A different participant explained, "I often refer back to discussions and observations from class sessions. This causes me to sometimes question things I might not have ordinarily done or to support things more vigorously than I might have." When discussing the doctoral program, one participant reflected, "It [the program] has assisted me in thinking critically and obtaining ideas for making a lasting impact in the lives of students and staff that work around me."

What became evident was that the participants had sincerely considered how the program was affecting them. They found that what they had studied and the experiences they had up to that point in their program had altered the way they looked at many issues in education. It was evident that they found themselves having a more critical eye and ear than previously. As one expressed, they were "scratching beneath the surface to see what was actually there."

Concerns

Participants in the cohort were not without their concerns. Concerns about the program, the time required, and overall apprehension also was present. Some of the participants seemed to work through their concerns while they responded to the study questionnaire, while others seemed to need to list them as obvious. One participant expressed her concern about the process used to select applicants for the program. She explained that she felt there was a bias in the process and that some students, even at this point in the program, were experiencing preferential treatment. Another participant wrote that he was hoping for the course work to be a bit more "real world-like." Another expressed her concern that the technology she needed in order to do her coursework in the program was not available from home. Differences were found among students regarding online class sessions.[2] One student expressed dislike for online courses while another participant wanted more online class sessions.

The most serious concerns seemed to center on how the program required them to spend time away from their families. For instance, one participant explained that he felt the most serious impact of the program in the evenings "when I am usually helping my kids with homework or other activities. I do not help as much anymore, nor do I get to my kids' classrooms as much as I used to."

Several students expressed apprehension about the program because of competing priorities, most often those between the program and family, the program and their work, or all three. As an example, one student expressed: "I am torn between my family routine and my school expectations and my work duties. I have been stressed on many occasions throughout the past semester. Much of the stress is due to pressures in maintaining balance among all my personal commitments to work, home, and school."

Besides having "no social life," another participant indicated that she, at least in the beginning, had been discouraged by the seeming lack of understanding about the program she encountered from her supervisor and some of her colleagues at work. She maintained that being only "cautiously supported" was challenging, as she never really knew whether her supervisor would continue to support her involvement with the program or not.

Thus, while we can see that while some participants had concerns about how their commitment to their program would affect their families and their jobs, others had concerns about the program itself. Most participants appeared to feel comfortable with their colleagues in the cohort, but some apparently harbored concerns about bias in the selection process and favoritism. Some students had difficulties in navigating online class sessions due to technology problems at home or dislike for online courses. A few indicated concerns about the support they were experiencing from their supervisors or work colleagues, at least initially. As is readily evident, no matter what the concern was, the internal dissonance it created in some participants was noticeable.

Confidence

Participants also wrote extensively about developing more confidence as they progressed in the program. One participant explained, "I am gaining the confidence and skills to hold jobs that require responsibilities that impact many people." Another participant expressed that now she would like to see "how far I can go." She initially did not anticipate that she could "really make changes and challenge the system." However being in the cohort and expanding their knowledge seemed to affect participants in significant ways that were empowering to some. One way was in increasing their possibilities about what they could do. One participant offered: "I see myself getting a position at the State Department of Education. Being of Native American descent, I feel I will have more influence at the state level on Indian Education which will affect all students in a state. If I don't do that, then my other goal is to take over the Bureau of Indian Education which has been neglected for so long."

Still another participant noted that "teaching at [a tribal college] is something that is a solid possibility." One participant stated that the doctoral program provided him with "opportunities to evaluate his effectiveness as a leader" and caused him to "reconsider applying for a higher position," a position he had previously never thought he could reasonably apply for or obtain.

The confidence levels of participants increased during the program. While some participants indicated a general overall increase in confidence, others were more specific about the manner in which their increased confidence had affected them. One participant identified a specific leadership position for which he would now like to apply; another was interested in improving the Bureau of Indian Education. Such aspirations are noteworthy and merit attention. Increased confidence allowed participants to think about possibilities and to strive for positions heretofore thought unattainable.

EFFECTIVE COMPONENTS OF EDUCATIONAL LEADERSHIP PROGRAM WITH NATIVE STUDENTS

This study closely examined how Native American graduate students perceive their educational experiences in a mainstream education institution. As researchers, we were interested in how well this university program would serve the academic and leadership aspirations of Native American educators. Additional analysis was conducted using an Indigenous critical lens to further examine the earlier emerging themes—support from crucial people, good fit, advocacy, deepening comprehension, concerns, and confidence—to provide a deeper understanding of participants' experiences in the program. Several research questions were addressed. We wanted to know which components of the educational leadership program resonated with the participants' realities, how the program was influencing their leadership practice, and how the program might be facilitating "change agent" behavior among these Native educators. Patterns emerged from that analysis that informed these research questions.

Mentoring Relationships and Academic Persistence

Participants explored the nuances of their network and support systems that influenced their decision to apply for and encouraged them to continue in the educational leadership program. While all of the themes dealt in some way or another with other people, it was the ongoing support from crucial people that participants emphasized. They explored their relationships with people who influenced them to apply to the doctoral program and to persist in advancing their education and leadership roles. They wondered whether such relationships would be redefined or even changed over the course of the program. In no instance did a participant indicate that he or she alone had made the decision to apply.

Some participants described this support and encouragement as mentoring. Jackson, Smith, and Hill (2003) studied Native college student's perspectives on persistence and found that mentoring relationships and programmatic support were beneficial. Iris Heavyrunner-PrettyPaint (2009) developed a Family Education Model that reveals the relationship web that extends from Native students' families and home communities to their academic and social memberships in a new higher education community when they enter college. Mentoring and other supportive kinds of relationships at all these membership levels typically are a large influence with Native college students who have attained their educational goals (Willetto, 1999). Having such authentic and personal experiences with mentoring and support relationships as college students, these educators can bring these skills and knowledge to their leadership practice in schools.

Change Agency and Advocacy

This outward reflection to other people resonated with creating the kinds of change that could positively impact their tribal communities and the children and families they serve at their schools. Participants instinctively knew that they did not exist without being connected to others in relevant ways that revealed responsibility for commitments made. The doctoral program had to work in synchronization with the relationships in the participants' lives. Not only did the program have to work well with their relationships with their families and friends, the participants also had to be able to advocate for others, primarily children, teachers, and community members. The advocacy that participants showed went well beyond the relationships the participants already had with their families and colleagues. Advocacy became a larger part of their lives as they took on a more public leadership role advocating for others in their school communities in addition to their families. The Lakota concept of *Mit'ākuyē Oyāśin* (all my relations) came to the forefront in this theme for advocacy. Participants shared how they defined their leadership roles as relevant to real change in their school communities.

Leadership Knowledge and Practice

Tying theoretical ideas and concepts of leadership relevant to improving the experiences of children was a shared practice among these Native educators.

Participants felt that their capacity to understand difficult scholarly concepts about leadership had increased along with their ability and skill for identifying resolutions for complex educational problems. We noted how participants contextualized the knowledge and skills they were learning in the program to their school communities through dialogues among their cohort peers. Participants speculated how the knowledge they were gaining would help them to help others.

Participants looked outside of themselves for understanding their own places as emerging leaders within the context of their doctoral program and cohort. Participants explained how their relationships with each other, their families, and their communities were affected and impacted. They discussed how their increasing knowledge was empowering with regard to how they could affect positive change in the larger community, thereby lending credence to the notion of how the "concepts of culture, knowledge, and power take on new meaning when examined through an Indigenous lens" (Brayboy, 2006, p. 429).

Efficacy and Challenges

Confidence was layered with the ability to see how their own increased efficacy could help other people. Overall, the participants' foci were continually on other people, people they hoped would benefit from their work in the doctoral program. Respecting the participants' "philosophies, beliefs, traditions, and visions for the future" is essential in understanding what these lived realities of Indigenous peoples are (Brayboy, 2006, p. 429). The participants needed to continually reflect about how their experiences in the doctoral cohort program would affect others beyond themselves so they could help others. Within these discussions, participants expressed how they felt about challenges, both those challenges realized through a reflexive process and challenges they perceived from others. One of the most difficult situations for these students was that the doctoral program took them away from their priorities—families, communities, and schools—and that was the challenge that weighed most heavily on these graduate students' minds and hearts when they were away. This sense of commitment to family and community reveals not only the ties to Indigenous values but also the dedication that it takes to become a leader in schools.

Findings also indicated that there were real causes for the students' uneasiness. Some things in the program infrastructure did not work so well. For instance, because the students were considered distance education students, they were not automatically afforded the same rights and privileges that "main campus"[3] students had. For example, they had to learn how to use specific jargon to navigate the library system to get interlibrary loans. They had to repeatedly and assuredly self-identify as distance students, for example, so that they would not get messages that their interlibrary loan books could be picked up at the circulation desk on the main campus, which for most of these graduate students was approximately 425 miles away. They had to distinguish themselves clearly enough in their requests that library staff made specific notes of their status; they could then expect for the interlibrary loan books to be sent through postal mail to their homes or schools. Despite issues such as described here, these Native educators were able to navigate the university system to attain the scholarly materials necessary for their doctoral courses. Such practices seem to support the conceptual idea that "educational policies toward Indigenous peoples are intimately linked around the problematic goal of assimilation" (Brayboy, 2006, p. 429). Taking their experiences with them back into the schools where they served Native children no doubt informed how they resolved institutional challenges that came into play in their leadership roles.

We are also reminded that stories, such as the one regarding interlibrary loan services and how these cohort students had to self-identify as being different, reflect human realities that exist among a unique student group, one that is often invisible amid the traditional college students at a mainstream university. Brayboy (2006) explains, "Stories are not separate from theory; they make up theory and are, therefore, real and legitimate sources of data and ways of being" (p. 430). This story is one of being treated differently because of an instructional modality (distance education) that defined these Native students as different; a status that the university system could not easily identify within its current categories, realm of knowledge, or structure.

Specifically, Brayboy (2006) discusses that colonization is endemic to society. In viewing this tenet through the experiences of these Native American doctoral students, we may not readily note any overt signs of attempts to colonize (Pewewardy and Frey, 2004). We do, however, note that "European American thought, knowledge, and power structures dominate present-day society in the United States" (Brayboy, 2006, p. 430). If such is the case, then, indeed, we note attempts to colonize. As Waters (2004) asserts, "Failure to recognize full nationhood of Indigenous peoples creates an active agency that denies our survival" (p. 168).

We must take a broader view of the context in which the participants were having the experiences they had and perceptions of what it meant to be Native students in a hegemonic higher education setting. The context they experienced was that of a major research university, which was comparable to most others in the United States, and whose employees, including researchers, operate in a meritocratic system that is vested in perpetuating the status quo (Christman et al., 2008). The participants were graded using a system set up through Western thought and had to fit coursework around the traditional semesters the university used. And their professors assuredly had graduated with doctoral degrees from similar universities.

Participants in our study examined leadership roles in their schools. By using an Indigenous framework, they explored and exposed discrepancies in the cultural infrastructure of the United States, such as with schools and universities; and used their growing understanding to improve on their own experiences in a higher education institution along with creating change for other Indigenous people. They saw that their theory and practice *had* to connect in ways that they could make meaning, as well as with the urgent need for creating change in American Indian education and especially in their schools. They described themselves as agents of social change. They reflected about social justice throughout their responses and often focused on a plan for real change as a way to make things better for their communities. Educational politics must be reframed for social justice (Marshall and Gerstl-Pepin, 2004), and educational leadership roles are perhaps the most relevant to make those changes that impact equity for nondominant groups.

IMPLICATIONS AND CONCLUSIONS

There are a number of implications that arise from this study that indicate what we can learn as program faculty and as graduate students in mainstream educational leadership programs. Participants in the study most certainly felt an affinity, an obligation, to those outside the mainstream institution, especially their families, students, and communities. Native graduate students felt strongly that their communities must benefit from the program, too. To do so required the participants to have sufficient time to reflect on their experiences and to hold them up to those "back home." Thus, we still see a wide gap between Western academe and the Indigenous worldview and culture-based education with Native graduate students trying to narrow that gap. Although Western ways of thinking may not necessarily have been compatible with their own, students were change agents working for social change within the system, hoping that they could take useful parts of the Western university system and program and put a Native American focus on them. Thus, one implication is that we must carefully consider how mainstream academic programs that truly serve Native American students should be structured. We must traverse that area between what can be accepted by mainstream university administration and what can be accepted by Indigenous peoples (Yosso, 2005). We must learn to navigate "living on barbed wire" (Christman and McClellan, 2008, p. 18), a reality experienced by many diverse students in leadership programs in Western academe (Myerson and Ely, 2003). We must purposefully craft higher education programs so that Native American students can maintain their cultural identities, knowledge, and languages intact. In many Indigenous stories, we find lessons to be learned from Coyote: "Coyote has forgotten the simple things. He has forgotten his relations. He has forgotten what is behind him and at his feet. When Coyote behaves in this way, he always finds trouble" (Burkhart, 2004, p. 16). It is this lesson about maintaining relationships that Coyote teaches that mainstream higher education institutions especially should recognize when serving Native American students.

Still, our study is a cautionary tale in several ways. Western institutions of higher education in the United States operate in ways that reflect the dominant society. We, as researchers, must not forget that we are part of a larger societal system that rewards those who work to maintain dominant social, legal, political, economic, and religious structures. We must make certain that our work and our research acts to serve Indigenous peoples in ways that allows them to maintain their identities and ways of knowing. We must feel compelled to do what Waters (2004) proposed, "Because individuals are used to carrying out colonizing enterprises, whether consciously or not, one of my selves stays busy educating those who have the power to dislodge or interrupt the harmful hegemonic thinking about 'what America is'" (p. 170).

Western higher education systems continue to interrupt the social, cultural, and academic development of Indigenous students. Such impediments usually serve to set students apart rather than invite them into the collectivity. In this study, Indigenous students experienced confrontations to their Indigenous worldviews through Western epistemologies about what and whose knowledge is relevant. Doing so made for convoluted logic at best. In a worse scenario, doing so contradicted both Indigenous worldviews and self-identity. Cordova (2004) indicates that "Indigenous Americans . . . [find] their codes of conduct on the premise that humans are naturally social beings, . . . [where] humans exist in the state of 'we'" (p. 175). Asking Native students to identify as separate individuals confounds basic notions of existence according to Indigenous knowledge and ways of living.

By examining the context of Native educators and their approaches to learning in a mainstream university, we see that an Indigenous lens was prevalent as they shared their perspectives and experiences. Leadership skills were evident across these Native educators' discussions as they related stories about how they maintained mentoring relationships and extended and created support networks including with program and workplace peers. These educators strived to express a deeper understanding as emerging leaders in the field and in their school communities and especially in relation to their sense of leaders as change agents. Participants recognized the knowledge they gained. They saw that by applying these newly acquired analytic reasoning skills with real issues regarding education in their respective communities, they increased their confidence and understanding for creating the kinds of change that can have real impact on Native children's learning experiences and outcomes. These skills are essential for when they become leaders in schools.

Recommendations for Native leadership programs are summarized as:

1. Recognize and honor mentoring relationships as a priority for serving Native students.
2. Support and respect cultural knowledge and language rather than assimilate and displace Native students' cultural identities, relationships, and sense of connectedness.
3. Address program challenges with students and empower them to make changes most relevant to the cohort.
4. Establish peer support processes and encourage graduate students to continue meeting as a cohort of emerging leaders.
5. Provide professional development opportunities for Native educators to practice leadership skills in authentic ways that reflect the realities of schools and the Native children they serve.
6. Create a balance between theoretical-abstract and practice-based literature to teach problem solving in schools.

NOTES

1. The No Child Left Behind Act of 2001, Public Law PL 107–110 (NCLB), which was signed into law by President Bush on January 8, 2002, was a reauthorization of the Elementary and Secondary Education Act, the central federal law in precollegiate education. See more at http://www.edweek.org/ew/issues /no-child-left-behind/.

2. Four-fifths of each class is delivered in a face-to-face format, but about one-fifth of classes are provided online in an asynchronous mode.

3. Main campus student is our term for students who are not distance students or branch campus students. The term, "student," names those who take classes on the main campus in the traditional face-to-face manner. The term is so institutionalized that there is not another term to differentiate types of students, other than those who are not main campus ones. Although the modern university makes great use of distance technologies and offers classes at other campuses, it is up to the student who is not on the main campus to self-identify as being different, a notion we hope to interrupt here by referring to "students" as main campus students.

REFERENCES

Aguilera, D. E. (2003). Who defines success: An analysis of competing models of education for American Indian and Alaskan Native students (Doctoral dissertation). University of Colorado–Boulder.

Aguilera, D. E., Lipka, J., Demmert, W., and Tippeconnic, J., III. (Eds., 2007). Culturally responsive schools serving American Indian, Alaska Native and

Native Hawaiian students. Special Issue. *Journal of American Indian Education, 46*(3).

Arizona State University. (1970). Report on all Indian Upward Bound Project at Arizona State University. *Journal of American Indian Education, 10*(1), p. 5–7. Retrieved November 18, 2011, from http://jaie.asu.edu/v10/V10S1com.html.

Bogdan, R. C., and Biklen, S. K. (1998). *Qualitative research for education: An introduction to theory and methods.* Boston: Allyn and Bacon.

Boloz, S. A., and Foster, C. G. (1980). A guide to effective leadership for the reservation administrator. *Journal of Native American Education, 19*(2), 24–28.

Brayboy, B. M. J. (2006). Toward a tribal critical race theory in education. *Urban Review, 37*(5), 425–46.

Brayboy, B. M., and Deyhle, D. (2000, Summer). Insider-outsider: Researchers in Native American communities. *Theory into Practice, 39*(3), 163–69.

Burkhart, B. Y. (2004). What Coyote and Thales can teach us: An outline of American Indian epistemology. In A. Waters (Ed.), *American Indian thought* (pp. 15–26). Malden, MA: Blackwell Publishing.

Calmore, J. (1992). Critical race theory, Archie Shepp, and fire music: Securing an authentic intellectual life in a multicultural world. *Southern California Law Review, 65,* 2129–231.

Chance, E., and Ristow, R. (1990, October). Incorporating alternative assessment measures in an educational leadership preparation program: Portfolios and educational platforms. Paper presented to the Annual Meeting of the University Council for Educational Administration, Baltimore, Maryland.

Charleston, G. M. (1994). Toward true Native education: A treaty of 1992. Final report of the Indian Nations at Risk Task Force. Draft 3. *Journal of Native American Education, 33*(2), 1–23.

Christman, D. E., Guillory, R. M., Fairbanks, A. R., and Gonzalez, M. L. (2008). A model of American Indian school administrators: Completing the circle of knowledge in Native schools. *Journal of American Indian Education, 47*(3), 53–72.

Christman, D. E., and McClellan, R. (2008, February). "Living on barbed wire": Resilient women administrators in educational leadership programs. *Education Administration Quarterly, 44*(1), 3–29.

Cleary, L., and Peacock, T. (1998).*Collected wisdom: Native American education.* Needham Heights, MA: Allyn and Bacon.

Cordova, V. F. (2004). Ethics: The we and the I. In A. Waters (Ed.), *American Indian thought* (pp. 173–81). Malden, MA: Blackwell Publishing.

Delgado, R., and Stefancic, J. (2001).*Critical race theory: An introduction.* New York: New York University Press.

Delgado Bernal, D., and Villalpando, O. (2002). An apartheid of knowledge in academia: The struggle over "legitimate" knowledge of faculty of color. *Journal of Equity and Excellence in Education, 35*(2), 169–80.

DeMarrais, K. B., Nelson, P. A. and Baker, J. H. (1992). Meaning in mud: Yup'ik Eskimo girls at play. *Anthropology and Educational Quarterly, 23*(2), 120–44.

Demmert, W. G., Towner, J. C., and Yap, K. O. (2003). A review of the research literature on the influences of culturally based education on the academic performance of Native American students. (ED-01-CO-0048/0002). Northwest Regional Educational Laboratory. Portland, OR: U.S. Department of Education.

DuBray, W. H. (1993). Native American values. In W. Dubray (Ed.), *Mental health interventions with people of color* (pp. 33–59). St. Paul, MN: West.

Haynes Writer, J. (2002). Terrorism in Native America: Interrogating the past, examining the present, and constructing a liberatory future. *Anthropology and Education Quarterly, 33*(3), 317–30.

HeavyRunner, I., and DeCelles, R. (2002). Family education model: Meeting the student retention challenge. In M. Benham, Special Issue, *Journal of American Indian Education, 41*(2), 29–37.

HeavyRunner-PrettyPaint, I. (2009). Miracle survivor (*Pisatsikamotaan*): An Indigenous theory on educational persistence grounded in the stories of tribal college students (Doctoral dissertation). University of Minnesota–Minneapolis.

Herrity, V. A., and Glasman, N. S. (1999). Training administrators for culturally and linguistically diverse school populations: Opinions of expert practitioners. *Journal of School Leadership, 9*, 235–53.

Jackson, A. P., Smith, S. A., and Hill, C. L. (2003, July–August). Academic persistence among Native American college students. *Journal of College Student Development, 44*(4), 548–65. doi: 10.1353/csd.2003.0039.

Janesick, V. J. (2000). The choreography of qualitative research design: Minuets, improvisations, and crystallization. In N. K. Denzin and Y. S. Lincoln (Eds.), *Handbook of qualitative research* (2nd ed., pp. 379–99). Thousand Oaks, CA: Sage.

Kirkness, V. J., and Barnhardt, R. (1991, May). First Nations and higher education: The four Rs—Respect, relevance, reciprocity, responsibility. *Journal of Native American Education, 30*(3), 1–15.

Ladson-Billings, G., and Tate, W. F., IV. (1995). Toward a critical race theory of education. *Teachers College Record, 97*(1), 47–68.

MacIvor, M. (1999). Redefining science education for Aboriginal students. In M. Battiste and J. Barman (Eds.), *First Nations' education in Canada: The circle unfolds* (pp. 73–98). Vancouver: University of British Columbia Press.

Marshall, C., and Gerstl-Pepin, C. (2004). *Reframing educational politics for social justice*. Boston: Allyn and Bacon.

McCarty, T. L., Lynch, R. H., Wallace, S., Benally, A. C. (1991, March). Classroom inquiry and Navajo learning styles: A call for reassessment. *Anthropology and Education Quarterly, 22*(1), 42–59.

Merriam, S. B. (1998). *Qualitative research and case study applications in education*. San Francisco: Jossey-Bass.

Mills, E., and Amiotte, L. (1995–96, Winter). Native American administrator preparation: A program analysis. *Tribal College: Journal of Native American Higher Education, 7*(3), 27–41.

Miraglia, E., Law, R., and Collins, P. (2006). *The culture debate in the U.S.: Whose culture is this, anyway?* Pullman, WA: Washington State University. Retrieved October 11, 2006, from http://www.wsu.edu:8001/vcwsu/commons /topics/culture/culture-definitions/whose-text.html.

Murry, K. G., and Herrera, S. G. (1999, Spring). CLASSIC impacts: A qualitative study of ESL/BLED programming. *Educational Considerations, 26*(2), 19–24.

Myerson, D. and Ely, R. (2003). Using difference to make a difference. In D. Rhode (Ed.), *The difference "difference" makes: Women and leadership*. Redwood City, CA: Stanford University Press.

National Center for Educational Statistics. (2007, September). Number and percentage distribution of degrees conferred by degree-granting institutions, by level of degree, race/ethnicity, and sex: 2003–04. In *Status and Trends in the Education of Racial and Ethnic Minorities*. Retrieved July 24, 2009, from http://nces.ed.gov/pubs2007/2007039.pdf.

National Center of Educational Statistics. (2007). Status dropout rates of 16- through 24-year-olds, by race/ethnicity and nativity: Current Population Survey October 1980–2007. In *Student Effort and Educational Progress*. Retrieved July 23, 2009, from http://nces.ed.gov/programs/coe/2009/section3 /table-sde-2.asp.

National Center of Educational Statistics. (2008). Size of the American Indian/ Alaska Native population and percentage distribution of the total population, by race and states with the largest American Indian/Alaska Native populations: 2006. In *Status and trends in the education of American Indians and Alaska Natives: 2008*. Retrieved July 23, 2009, from http://nces .ed.gov/pubs2008/2008084_1.pdf.

New Mexico Higher Education Department. (2006). Certificate and degree recipients in New Mexico: Statewide numbers of graduates at each degree level and number of recipients by racial/ethnic and gender clusters. In *The condition of higher education in New Mexico, 2005–2006*. Retrieved July 23, 2009, from http://hed.state.nm.us/cms/kunde/rts/hedstatenmus/docs/649408–12 –21–2006–13–46–59.pdf.

New Mexico Public Education Department. (2007). *Personnel by ethnicity and gender, 2006–2007*. Retrieved October 26, 2007, from http://www.ped.state .nm.us/div/is/data/fs/23/06.07.pers.eth.gen.pdf.

Nicholson, K., Evans, J. F., Tellier-Robinson, D., and Aviles, L. (2001). Allowing the voices of parents to help shape teaching and learning. *Educational Forum, 65*(2). Indianapolis, IN: Kappa Delta Pi.

No Child Left Behind Act (NCLB) of 2001. (2001). H.R. 1, 107th Congress 1st Session, sec. 3122 (b) (1).

Patton, M. Q. (1990). *Qualitative evaluation methods* (2nd ed.). Thousand Oaks, CA: Sage.

Pavel, M., Swisher, K., and Ward, M. (1995, March). Special focus: American Indian and Alaska Native demographic and educational trends." In D. J. Carter and R. Wilson, *Minorities in higher education 1994: Thirteenth annual status report* (pp. 35–56).Washington, DC: American Council on Education.

Pewewardy, C. (2002). Learning styles of Native American/Alaskan Native students: A review of the literature and implications for practice. *Journal of Native American Education, 41*(1), 22–56.

Pewewardy, C., and Frey, B. (2004). American Indian students' perspectives of racial, multicultural support services, and ethnic fraud at a predominantly white university. *Journal of American Indian Education, 43*(1), 32–60.

Radda, H. T., Iwamoto, D., and Patrick, C. (1998). Collaboration, research and change: Motivational influences on American Indian students. *Journal of American Indian Education, 37*(2): 2–20.

Reyhner, J. (2001). Family, community, and school impacts on American Indian and Alaska Native students' success. A literature review prepared under contract from Westat as part of U.S. Government's American Indian/Alaska Native Education Research Initiative. Flagstaff, AZ: Northern Arizona University. Retrieved on January 9, 2014, from http://jan.ucc.nau.edu/~jar/AIE/Family.html.

Silverman, R. J., and Demmert, W. G., Jr. (1986). *Characteristics of successful Native leaders.* ERIC Document Reproduction Service, No. ED 269 208.

Solorzano, D. (1997). Images and words that wound: Critical race theory, racial stereotyping, and teacher education. *Teacher Education Quarterly, 24*(3), 5–9.

Solorzano, D. G., and Yosso, T. J. (2001). Critical race theory and LatCrit theory and method: Counter storytelling Chicana and Chicano graduate school experiences. *International Journal of Qualitative Studies in Education, 14*(4), 471–95.

St. Germaine, R. (2000). *Drop-outs rates among Native American and Alaska Native students: Beyond cultural discontinuity.* ERIC Document Reproduction Service, No. ED 388 492.

Strauss, A., and Corbin, J. (1990). *Basics of qualitative research: Grounded theory procedures and techniques.* Newbury Park, CA: Sage.

Swisher, K. G., and Tippeconnic, J. W., III. (1999). Next steps: Research and practice to advance Indian education. Charleston, WV: ERIC/CRESS, ERIC Reproduction Service, No. 427 902.

Tharp, R. G., Dalton, S., and Yamauchi, L. A. (1994). Principles for culturally compatible Native American education. *Journal of Navajo Education, 11,* 33–39.

Tomlinson, J. (1991). *Cultural imperialism: A critical introduction.* Baltimore, MD: Johns Hopkins University Press.

U.S. Census Bureau. (2005). *U.S. Census Bureau state and quick facts: New Mexico.* Retrieved October 21, 2007, from http://quickfacts.census.gov/qfd/states/35000.html.

U.S. Department of Education (2002). *No Child Left Behind Act of 2001.* Washington, DC: Author, Office of the Secretary, Office of Public Affairs.

Waters, A. (2004). Ontology of identity and interstitial being. In A. Waters (Ed.), *American Indian thought* (pp. 153–70). Malden, MA: Blackwell Publishing.

Weaver, H. N. (2000). Balancing culture and professional education: Native American/Alaska Natives and the helping professions. *Journal of Native American Education, 39*(3), 1–18.

Willetto, A. (1999). Navajo culture and family influences on academic success: Traditionalism is not a significant predictor of achievement among young Navajos. *Journal of American Indian Education, 38*(2), 1–33.

Worthley, K. M. E. (1987). Learning style factors of field dependence/field independence and problem solving strategies of Hmong refugee students (Master's thesis). University of Wisconsin–Stout.

Yosso, T. J. (2005, March). Whose culture has capital? A critical race theory discussion of community cultural wealth. *Race, Ethnicity, and Education, 8*(1), 69–91.

7

Getting the Right Leadership

*Ten Things We Learned about
Being a First-Year Principal*

JOSEPH MARTIN

The importance of effective school leadership for reservation-based schools serving large populations of Native students is getting long-overdue attention, along with the accompanying need for Native leaders to understand and define leadership in their practices. Teachers are generally considered to have the most immediate in-school effect on Native student success. However, with the national imperative for every Native student to pass the high-stakes exams for graduation, and the urgency from tribes for schools to be more responsive to their needs, more professionals agree that school principals are best positioned to ensure successful teaching and learning, especially among reservation-based schools with the highest needs (Bartlett and Brayboy, 2005). No documented instances exist of "high need schools" being turned around without intervention by powerful leaders. Many other factors may play a role in such turnarounds, but leadership is the catalyst.

Building on this foundation, Northern Arizona University (NAU) through its Department of Educational Leadership, has administered two professional development grants from the U.S. Office of Indian Education. Since 2002, the Diné-Hopi Cohort Leadership Program (DHCLP) has trained Native teachers employed in reservation schools with the stipulation that they become principals in Indian-serving schools upon their graduation. This chapter presents findings from an empirical study about Native principals' practices and their goals of blending mainstream (Western) paradigms of leadership with Indigenous concepts of leadership. Additionally, strategies are identified that educators can consider regarding high-quality leadership in reservation schools. Also discussed are key issues regarding the challenges that exist in creating educational leadership programs that adequately prepare Native principals to serve in reservation-based schools.

The chapter begins with a discussion of the conditions and circumstances surrounding reservation schools and how the DHCLP leadership program was organized to address them. Then, the ten most important lessons learned during the first year of their principalships—as reported by the program participants—are examined. Finally, the chapter sums up the basic qualities essential to reservation school leadership and emphasizes the importance of developing a leadership quality that meets the particular demands of the situation, the requirements of the people involved and the challenges facing the schools.

RESEARCH DESIGN AND METHODS

A total of fifty Native teachers who completed the educational leadership program were involved in the two grants awarded to NAU for its DHCLP program. The research design and methods used to study them were qualitative. Findings were based on analysis from data collected over an eight-year period from student course evaluations, site visits with students, their mentors, and administrators at the schools, student focus groups, analysis of survey questionnaires sent to students and school officials, and interviews with school board members and superintendents who were involved in hiring the students after graduation. The study design also used secondary data from an evaluation conducted on the program.

PARAMETERS OF THIS STUDY

As with any federally funded project, an evaluation plan was included in the initial applications for funding for the DHCLP. The external evaluation data findings report provided descriptions of project activities and evaluation of project accomplishments, including impact indicators. These data were used in this study.

THE STUDY POPULATION

The students' tribal backgrounds included Acoma, Apache (San Carlos and White Mountain), Blackfoot, Cayuga, Cherokee, Colorado River, Diné (Navajo), Fort McDowell, Gila River, Hopi, Onondaga, Pine Ridge Sioux, Tlingit, Tohono O'odham, Tuscarora, Yavapai-Apache, and Zuni. The majority of DHCLP students were Diné and Hopi.

CONDITIONS AND ISSUES IN
RESERVATION-BASED SCHOOLING

Reservation schools in the Southwest are a division unto themselves. Their degree of remoteness, the cross-cultural priorities they must address, the range of expectations they must attend to, their limited resources, the differences in governance (tribal, state, and federal) that they face, their high rate of turnover among key staff, and the enormous need for their continuing service, combine to make Hopi and Navajo schools some of the most challenging (and rewarding) places in which to provide a meaningful educational experience.

CHALLENGES

Though reservation schools share with their urban and suburban counterparts many challenges as a result of the No Child Left Behind legislation, they are particularly hamstrung by its demands in the areas of school accountability and teacher qualifications (National Indian Education Association, 2005). Many once-homogeneous reservation communities also are becoming increasingly diverse, which means that not only are reservation schools different from urban and suburban schools but they also differ markedly from one another. Because each tribal reservation community is unique, there can be no one-size-fits-all approach, either to reservation education or to the preparation of principals for reservation schools.

EDUCATIONAL GOALS

When asked what was needed to improve the quality of educational services of reservation schools, many of the participants agreed that what was needed was radically decentralized school governance and thus increased responsiveness to the needs, aspiration, and wishes of a given community of parents and students. For example, real opportunities where parents have a real say in the education of their children—including long-range planning for effective language and culture instruction, intergovernmental coordination, effective school leadership and teaching, and changes in school governance—would make responsive parental and community involvement more likely. However, when asked about the role of tribes, states, and the Bureau of Indian Education in these changes, participants agreed that their roles should be facilitative, not coercive, in bringing the changes about (Martin, 2008, p. 5). The situation where individual reservation schools are subordinate to either the state or the Bureau of Indian Education is made more complex by the lack of fit between the reservation schools and the tribal communities. This situation is markedly different from the situation in most of the rest of America.

In addition, because of the dynamics of the language and cultural issues and the diversity of expectations held by tribal members, as well as difficulty of filling principal positions in these often remote locations, few people are innately skilled at creating the types of inclusive conversations that lead to effective leadership in these schools. Fortunately, those leadership qualities and characteristics are readily learned when directly taught (Begaye, 2006; Bergstrom, Cleary, and Peacock, 2003). The position of principal in a reservation school setting differs from that of the urban school administrator, often requiring more sacrifice to adjust to the demanding day-to-day involvement in every aspect of school activity. Additional barriers involve geographic isolation, hard-to-staff reservation school conditions, cultural differences between the home and school, and economic challenges brought on by poverty (Rural School-Community Trust, 2007).

Principals who serve children living in high-poverty reservation communities have the unique responsibility of developing learning communities capable of meeting the specific needs of large numbers of school children living in difficult situations brought on by poverty. Student achievement cannot increase unless the barriers created by poverty are addressed first. To address the barriers created by poverty, principals in high-poverty tribal communities must lead staff to go beyond traditional job expectations by making sure they have the necessary skills to develop deep commitments to meeting the challenges of all students and making decisions in their best interests (Barnhardt, 2008; Rural School-Community Trust, 2007). All these above concerns and conditions in reservation schools reveal the importance of school leadership with the skills to create safe and supportive school environments.

ADMINISTRATOR STANDARDS

In the 1990s, administrator standards were developed that identified important principal leadership responsibilities. However, the scope of the standards does not distinguish between what is essential for being a reservation school principal and a school principal in any other place. For example, while there are 184 indicators for the six Interstate School Leaders Licensure Council (ISLLC) standards, none offer guidance on which responsibilities and practices should take primacy—or what is essential—for Indian school principalship (Waters and Grubb, 2005). Some of them "even are culturally inappropriate or counter constructive to the communities we serve" was one principal's take on the subject of standards (Martin, 2008, p. 7). In summary, Castagno (2009), the project evaluator, elaborated: "Another challenge some participants expressed was how best to negotiate the tension between preparing them for the unique issues they would face in rural schools serving Native youth and preparing them according to the standardized curriculum and expectations developed by the state and university" (p. 9).

DINÉ-HOPI COHORT LEADERSHIP PROGRAM (DHCLP)

The DHCLP projects were funded through the U.S. Department of Education's Office of Indian Education between 2000 and 2008 as a partnership between Northern Arizona University, Navajo Technical College (now Navajo

Technical University), the Diné Nation, and the Hopi Nation. The overall goal was to graduate and credential Native educators who would become principals in schools with a high enrollment of Native students. The program grew out of awareness that there existed not only a lack of well-trained Native principals but also a lack of culturally responsive training for Native administrators. The DHCLP program attempted to fill this gap by providing culturally responsive leadership training to those Native educators who were committed to serving schools in their tribal communities (Castagno, 2009; Sciacca, 2005).

Indian tribal leaders have long advocated adopting a culturally responsive curriculum to strengthen the training of Native principals. Such an approach uses skills training that links cultural knowledge originating in reservation communities to the curriculum of the institution. Some of the topics the DHCLP program included in its training were:

- the role of education in tribal nation building,
- tribal leadership beliefs,
- the communication and leadership styles of Indian school boards and tribal leaders,
- appropriate communication with parents and elders,
- school-tribal community development,
- tribal education codes, particularly for managing language and culture programs,
- policies of Indian and tribal preference in hiring practices,
- tribal labor relations and cultural decision making,
- Diné education standards,
- the attributes of power structures found in tribal communities, and
- institutional racism and issues of social justice and inequality from a tribal perspective.

In terms of leadership skills, DHCLP students were taught a variety of leadership strategies and approaches primarily to capitalize on tribal and school-community cultural backgrounds, rather than attempting to override or negate them.

ESSENTIAL KNOWLEDGE AND SKILLS

The ideal principal for opening a new school or improving an already high-performing school may not necessarily possess the qualities needed to move the school in a direction desired by the tribe and/or to turn around a persistently low-performing school. The DHCLP operates on the premise it needs to equip students with a set of skills that comprise a road map of how to accomplish their mission, instead of a recipe that prescribes a set of preordained steps they must follow to achieve desired results. A good road map displays the nature of the terrain and any obstacles that might interfere with travel. While recipes require relatively little judgment, sound judgment is essential if principals are to help teachers and students to complete their journey (Duke, 2004). The DHCLP aims to prepare students who are "at home" interpreting the needs of a school and tribal community, while at the same time preparing them to be adept at applying effective school leadership for addressing whatever challenges they face and achieving the desired results from and for all stakeholders.

FINDINGS

The students interviewed for the research were highly reflective and talked openly about using a variety of strategies to examine school improvement planning and the decisions they took into account to affect change. Some talked about reversing the downward spiral of a struggling school while others worked on implementing evidence-based, shared, or common insights—not magic bullets, not single programs, and not final solutions but effective practices that for some are culturally responsive approaches to address reservation education.

Forsaking academic recipes for school leaders, the students' version of being a good principal in a reservation-based school was about developing a deep understanding of how to support teachers and staff throughout the school. This goal included coordinating responsibilities with central office personnel, school board members, and parents; managing the curriculum in ways that promote not just state and Bureau of Indian Education Standards but also local tribal-community education priorities; and developing the ability to transform schools into more effective organizations that foster culturally appropriate and powerful teaching and learning for all students. Students placed a high premium on personal values and focused on cultural rather than structural change (NAU/EDL USOE Grant Proposal, 2005).

The reasons given by participants for joining the program included wanting to effect change in their communities, to address the constant turnover in leaders within their local schools, to integrate language and culture into leadership positions, to acquire skills and the necessary degrees to become educational leaders, and to attending a leadership preparation program that focused on Navajo and Hopi educational issues. Many of the participants referenced the notion of "change" in their reflections about why they joined the program; one said, "There are some changes that need to be made." Other participants were keenly aware of the challenges facing reservation schools related to high turnover rates, political issues, and the tensions between culturally responsive education and standards-based education. They viewed this program as an opportunity to play a role in improving the education of Native youth in their communities. As one participant explained, "Many educational issues unique to reservation schools were examined and explored that may not be addressed by programs targeting [the] general population. Of all the things we did in the program, the topics about being a principal in a reservation school made the most sense and I'm realizing how valuable they are in my current job" (Castagno, 2009. p. 3).

GETTING THE RIGHT LEADERSHIP

The most important learning takes place on the job, not in university classrooms. A principal offers this view: "I learned I could spew the answers in class and knew the theory well, but I struggled with implementing what I knew successfully" (Martin, 2008, p. 9).

Native principals and other school leaders will undoubtedly have moments when they feel overwhelmed or question their chosen professions. In times such as these, Robert Ramsey's book, *What Matters Most for School Leaders*, proves to be a life-line for these budding principals, helping "school leaders to stay the course and stay on course" (Ramsey, 2005, p. viii). The rest of this chapter explains the ten leadership lessons identified by participants and researchers as the most important to beginning principals, presented in reverse order with number one, the most important, at the end of the chapter.

10. Sensible Risk Taking

The tenth leadership skill most often mentioned as being critical for this group of beginning principals was the importance of taking risks. Howard Gardner identifies risk taking as among the qualities found in exemplary leaders (1995). He writes: "The capacity to take risks speaks to a confidence that one will at least sometimes attain success" (p. 33). Leaders must accept the fact that they might fail, which is why beginning reservation principals are possibly reluctant to take risks.

Some have defined risk taking as a negative concept—an idea that has traditionally been rampant in reservation schools (Boloz and Foster, 1980). Nothing speaks this message clearer than the simple statement made by one principal: "Risk taking is similar to a conversation that is abrupt and direct. Many Indian people are very uncomfortable with that type of conversation. I think that is why there is a negative view of it and people who use it" (Martin, 2008, p. 10). This negative perception stems, perhaps, from the historical financial emphasis on accountability. Times have changed, and this group of beginning principals recommends that others facing similar situations adopt a more forward-looking and positive attitude toward both risk taking and accountability.

The rapid changes in accountability systems for all schools, but particularly for reservation schools, have placed a strong focus on standardized achievement results. These increasingly are being demanded by governing agencies through the emphasis on high-stakes tests, accreditation standards, and sanctions for inadequate yearly progress. They provide the possibility for putting the spotlight on sensible risk taking and accountability as central elements of best practice. Hence, the principals interviewed for this study submit that an increased emphasis should be placed on "results assurance," in which the focus is on results versus the more traditional reliance on "process assurance," or compliance-focused strategies (Schlenker and Weigold, 1991). Such an attitude would demand an explicit acceptance of risk in the sense that risk is viewed as a choice or opportunity rather than a fate or something to be avoided. Seen in this light, sensible risk taking becomes something that first-year principals in reservation settings may look forward to as a means to get better results (Schlenker and Weigold, 1991, p. 25–29).

According to Tony Wagner (2006), author of, *Change Leadership: A Practical Guide to Transforming Our Schools*, successful leaders make sure they get to know the skills and motivators of their constituents. They raise the bar gradually, offer coaching to build skills, and they encourage risk taking so that leaders can step out into an area that may not be their usual safe haven (Wagner, 2006). Risk taking for this group of principals meant they had an opportunity to establish the kinds of relationships in which their leadership views could be best expressed.

9. Distributing Leadership through Delegation

The ninth leadership skill learned by this group of beginning principals is the art of delegation. Delegation was identified as a difficult area for a majority of the beginning principals. It was clear from everything said by this group of beginning principals that they originally felt that delegation meant they were shirking their own duties by foisting them off on others or feeling that they were imposing additional tasks on already overburdened staff members (Martin 2008, p. 4). Instead, they had to learn to view delegation as involving or empowering staff members.

Principals have to be confident about their leadership to be able to delegate. They must adopt strategic goals, which must come in the form of collaborative achievement. More to the point, a number of the principals in this group felt people were more receptive to their delegation when they knew that they placed human needs above organizational needs and that their best interests were taken into consideration.

As Boloz and Foster (1980) state in their article about effective reservation school administration, principals can retain the policy-making role by "outlining the limits within which delegated authority is to be exercised" (p. 2). Yet, as some of the principals shared, there will always be people who delegate and then micromanage every aspect of a project. Several principals expressed this concern: "We think micromanaging is something Native leaders have to work hard at avoiding" (Martin, 2008, p. 7). Others expressed their views on delegation in this way: "When I first came to the school, my predecessor was considered to be the head, everyone else opted out. With the formulation of teams with clear targets, I've been able to delegate leadership and to energize teachers to take responsibility for change and development" (Martin, 2008, p. 8).

8. Create a Climate of Personal Attention to a Win/Win Culture

Our eighth leadership lesson learned is to think and believe in a "win/win" culture. Steven Covey (1989) authored an outstanding book entitled *The Seven Habits of Highly Effective People*, with win/win as one of the effective habits. Win/win is a philosophy of human interaction, a frame of mind that is constantly looking for mutual benefits. Teamwork and collaboration are the basis for bringing together the knowledge, experience, and skills of multiple team members in support of a win/win philosophy (Covey, 1989).

Many of the principals in this beginning phase of their experience realized their schools already housed several major issues that needed to be dealt with. For instance, in some cases an air of selfishness existed, an unwillingness to cooperate, along with defensive communication at the schools, and a sense of being jaded by the constant turnover of administrators. Consequently, the issue was not that the people at the schools were simply not cooperating. The problem was the paradigm they were operating under. Covey (1989) states, "Often the problem is in the system, not in the people. . . . If you put good people in bad systems, you get bad results" (p. 263). When some of the students did background research on their schools, they learned that funds in the emotional bank account were pretty low when each of them came into the picture; they then learned they had to start depositing funds a little at a time.

The principals realized they needed to establish a sense of community and build relationships. Many of the new principals were values driven, optimistic, and developed a consistent instructional climate at all levels of the schools. Some of them started with faculty lunches and thank you cards with lottery or game tickets inside, coffees at the door during the winter months, birthday cards, and a parent of the month recognition program, to name just a few. As one principal commented, "It was hard to find a work place that exemplified teamwork. In our tribal community and school, our pastimes, especially with sports and politics, emphasize winning and coming out on top. Workers are rarely raised in environments that emphasize true tribal teamwork and collaboration" (Martin, 2008, p. 5).

One important practice, often mentioned as a learned skill in regards to implementing a win/win school culture, was needing to be careful not to "overpromise" and "underdeliver." "Do the opposite" was a commonly mentioned strategy from this group (Martin, 2008, p. 6).

7. Focusing on Building Consensus

The seventh leadership skill, one that is closely related to building a win/win culture, concerns building consensus, or agreement and support, among stakeholders. Some of the previous principals were loners during their first year, and it was easy to see why they were unable to build consensus within the staff, an issue partly attributable to their lack of communication with staff. Basically, they were hiding out behind closed doors. Communication is crucial, and it will take place whether principals take the time to engage in it or not. If not, the message becomes whatever the angriest person on staff makes it. For example, if a principal contacts the faculty only on matters of organizational procedures, teachers will see these as the school's major concern and may give less attention to teaching and learning.

When these new principals stepped into their roles, they had no idea that 85 percent of the people who came to them would have a complaint they wanted resolved. At first, the principals felt overwhelmed but quickly learned that the frequency of these occurrences was not unusual and that, when people are complaining, sometimes they just want someone to listen to them. It helped to remember that good leadership is 85 percent listening.

To counter this challenge, these principals started from day one promoting a type of consensus leadership. The approach these principals utilized combined a moral purpose with a willingness to be collaborative and to promote collaboration among teachers, whether through teamwork or extending the boundaries of participation in decision making. They worked hard at making sure that the communication dynamics were culturally appropriate but managerially flexible. They addressed complaints on a group level and tried to avoid being seen as a principal who led out of fear or demands for loyalty. They listened to the concerns of the teachers, staff and, students, and they and their staffs, as a group, decided what the best solution for the problem was.

6. Build Broad Commitment to Change

The sixth leadership lesson involves recognizing that implementing changes takes time. Putting in the work to fully understand the circumstances of that change is required to make it happen successfully. The need to place a high premium on personal values and to focus on school culture rather than structural change was an important lesson each of the principals learned while implementing and managing change in their schools. Participants expressed belief that leadership style is an important consideration for building commitment for change. Depending on the followers, some styles may result in building greater levels of commitment. The use of rewards and punishments can be compelling in some instances, but participation, collaboration, and a compelling altruistic vision may resonate with workers and generate greater levels of commitment.

Change often is accompanied by uncertainty and anxiety, conditions that are certain to lead to conflict. For example, if the goal is to strengthen instructional practices, the principal cannot possibly affect the school's instructional culture without spending time in the classroom to observe instruction. Staff will begin to listen more, become more self-reflective, and be more open to revising how they teach if they see the principal modeling these skills.

This lesson of leadership is rewarding, but also time consuming, because the principal needs to speak with everyone involved at the school. For some of the principals, it was not enough to just put a good instructional leadership team in place and expect that team to lead. "The principal must truly be an instructional leader who also talks about and gives presentations on instructional issues as well as actively observing and coaching teachers on instructional practice" (Martin, 2008, p. 8).

Another important lesson learned by these principals was that the bigger the change, the longer it takes. If the goal is to accomplish a big change in record time, it helps to break it into many small changes that can be punched out one after the other. For example, changing negative behavior, especially if people believe there is nothing wrong, is a case in which seeking small increments of change is always the best approach.

Effective reservation school leadership involves not just knowing what to do but also when, how, and why to do it. What has made the difference in the successes of this group is that they focused on the right change in their schools, and, more importantly, understood the most effective order of the change they were proposing. A principal who is well informed about the details and undercurrents in managing a reservation school and who uses that information to bring about change will show positive results.

5. Making Ownership a Priority

The fifth leadership skill participants learned was to make everyone a part owner of the school's success. Rick DeFour's (2002) article, "Leading Edge: Bring the Whole Staff on Board" is an excellent source. This group of principals utilized DeFour's techniques, including insisting that staff work together in collaborative teams focused on student learning and providing the time and support to promote team success.

Gordon (2006) recommends targeting the "talent and engagement levels of the people within an individual school" and honing in on those teachers and principals who understand the strengths of students and who understand and care about students. Gordon purports moving beyond the assumptions that are barriers to students learning and teachers being effective, namely standards and increased testing, weakness foci, educator knowledge foci, perfect curriculum, and ignoring workplace climate and parent engagement (pp. 9–22).

An obstacle encountered by several of the principals was the unwillingness of certain staff members to accept responsibility for student learning and most especially student conduct. As leaders for their schools, the principals needed to acknowledge responsibility for student learning and student behavior, as well as build a collective sense of responsibility among the entire staff. Teachers met in teams and were asked to work together to identify areas of concern regarding student performance and classroom management. Teams were then asked to develop strategies for addressing those concerns. Encouraging ownership is not a formal administrative position exercised from above; it starts with expanding the teachers' professional roles in small everyday actions that make their jobs more fulfilling and less difficult.

4. Ongoing Site-Based Mentorship Support

The fourth leadership approach the participants found most helpful was having a mentor (Villani, 2005). From the first day on the job, new principals are expected to perform the same tasks as experienced principals. Mentors offer support and insight in real-life problem solving and enhancing acquisition of the right perspective.

Increasing evidence shows that throughout the stages of their careers, Native principals can benefit from a mentoring system in which a seasoned leader helps them place theory and praxis in the context of experience (Vogel and Rude, 2007). *Entry: The Hiring, Start-Up, and Supervision of Administrators* (Jentz, Cheever, Fisher, Howe Jones, Kelleher, and Wofford, 1983) can assist first year principals in working with a mentor to organize the first few months on the job. The authors suggest that skilled mentors help leaders calibrate future action with emerging insights. "Attention is given to a hands-on, interactive training format that focuses on authentic learning and establishes the right relationships needed for effective leadership" (p. 84).

This group of principals felt lucky because each of them had at least one mentor. For some, their mentor was a principal of the school next door, and, for others, the mentor was a previous principal of their school who was able to assist in many areas. Ideally, especially for this group of beginning Native principals, most of them had the services of a mentor that had experiences in an Indian-serving school, both hardship and success, that they deemed very helpful.

3. Mastering the Dimensions of Responsive Leadership

The third leadership skill these principals learned was to be responsive not reactive. Many times they felt pressured to give an answer to a problem right away, and the stress of a new and overwhelming situation often encourage unconscientious reaction. A former superintendent at the school where one of the candidates first obtained a principalship position taught the new principal that "knee jerk" reactions were inappropriate, and the best way to make a good decision is to give it some time.

The biggest concern expressed by some of the principals was the increased amount of mandatory administrative and compliance work arriving from district, state, federal, and sometimes tribal governments (Martin, 2008, p. 5). Principals expressed anger and frustration with the ever-increasing workload and challenges in the following ways:

- I'm running the whole day. . . . I find it very hard to close the door when someone wants to see me—because who else would they see? It's getting worse the longer I'm in the job.
- It's the horrendous hours you put in to do things well. . . . So it's huge. . . . You've still got to get it done. (Martin, 2008, p. 4; Sciacca, 2005, p. 9)

Though the workload may seem proliferating, any time administrators avoid being responsible, they automatically limit themselves. The more they react to stress by avoiding responsibility, the more they allow themselves to be controlled by things and circumstances "out there" and the greater is their sense of being powerless. They wind up acting like victims and become ineffective complainers. The more personal responsibility administrators assume for their actions, the more potential they have available to direct toward achieving what they truly want. When reactive, they are neither flexible nor creative. However, by simply walking around and talking to a few key individuals, one can get a sense of what people are thinking and avoid being reactive (Martin, 2008, p. 6).

In reference to leadership, Covey (1992) expands on a quality that is crucial to the success of any leader but particularly for a beginning Indian principal: leadership quality and characteristics. Reservation school principals have to be generalists. These leaders must be prepared to do many things, and their training program must be multifaceted. The quality and characteristic a person adopts in her leadership role is born from her core ideas and feelings about the nature of humans. "Whatever someone has at the center of his life, work or pleasure, friend or enemy, family or possessions, principles or passions, will affect his perceptions, and perception governs beliefs, attitudes, and behaviors" (p. 69).

Another important item to consider about being responsive is that administrators are only as good as the people they surround themselves with. Some of the best advice for those in any supervisory role is that if it is possible to do so, hire people with heart and passion. Specifically, school administrators need to hire people who genuinely like children, are enthusiastic about coming to the school, realize they still have a lot to learn, and, of course, are competent to teach Indian children and understand the challenges and opportunities of working in a reservation school. If a principal knows her teachers are dedicated and enthusiastic, she can expect them to be responsive and not reactive.

2. Doing the "Right Things"

The second leadership skill is learning to deal with tough issues by doing what is right by all stakeholders, including teachers, parents, school board members, and especially, the children. The group of principals interviewed in the study took the stance that it is far more important to do the right things than it is to do things right. The actual quotation is: "Management is doing things right; leadership is doing the right things" (Drucker, 2001, p. 157). Leadership implies a social construct, and doing the right thing organizationally requires having the right timing and involving the right people for the right reasons.

Each of the principals talked openly about seeing good Indian and non-Indian leaders with high aspirations who were undone by weak relations with their boards, staff, parents, and the general community. Nothing undermines the credibility of a leader more than one who has no idea why they are doing what they are doing and what their own preferred leadership quality might be and why. It is therefore important for leaders of reservation schools to have a conceptual framework for determining what is right. Without a framework or philosophy, principals are susceptible to accepting any new fads or canned approaches in education that emerge.

Native principals of a reservation school assume a myriad of responsibilities important to running a school, but many of the duties are not essential to improving student achievement. For example, issues such as facilities maintenance, finance, law and public relations are important but not necessarily essential in these terms. In an era of accountability when student performance is critical and outcomes of the effects of principal leadership regarding student achievement continue to amass, it is not enough to just know what is important; Native principals must also know what is essential in order to do the right thing for the right reason.

Schools serving tribal communities need a critical mass of high-quality managers who do things right, but they probably do not belong in a struggling school that requires the leadership of a principal who can reverse the downward spiral of a low-performing school or turn a troubled school around. In rapidly advancing times, technical-rational approaches may be beguilingly attractive, yet, in reality, they are unlikely to result in improved schooling for Indian students unless accompanied by an understanding of the difference between being an effective Native school principal in a tribal community and being a leader that is merely concerned with high-stakes tests, school performance report cards, accreditation standards, or sanctions for inadequate yearly progress. In addition to being results driven, they must have a vision that is greater than simply improving test scores; they must also have a vision that is targeted toward promoting tribal sovereignty, self-determination, and nation-building.

The first year on the job, this group of beginning principals all had to deal with a profusion of personnel issues, including student, staff, and parent complaints. They believed they could not go wrong if their leadership philosophy was "people-centered." Being a principal of a school located in a reservation context is clearly not a "desk job," but, rather, it is about displaying people-centered qualities and skills. One of the most profound assertions in the text by Ramsey (2005) is: "As a school leader, you have a multitude of decisions, great and small to make every day. But you have only one standard or criteria to apply: What's best for kids?" (p. 20). By keeping children first and creating a climate of hope on campuses, leaders truly set the stage for both school and student successes.

In terms of handling difficult personnel issues, the need to know school board policy and the tribes' Indian preference hiring policies and sticking to them was heavily emphasized by participants. They found that making the right decision was not always popular with stakeholders. In smaller tribal communities, good relationships and family ties can be an asset, but even the slightest misinformation can result in a horrendous experience. In hindsight, participants realized that they could never document the reasons for their decisions sufficiently, despite documenting extensively.

When dealing with an angry parent, principals should always follow the same process: pay attention, treat them with respect, and make evident that their concerns are understood—as the parents see them. Awareness of personal habits like eye contact, emotional behavior, and body gestures will help determine communication effectiveness. For an assertive type administrator, it will be helpful to know what the local cultural beliefs are regarding personal "qualities of leadership" " and to work within the acceptable parameters.

At times, other staff members with more insight might be in a better position to handle particularly difficult or politically sensitive issues. A principal's knowledge will help him decide how to proceed in handling a complaint. Building relationships and acquiring a network of support to call upon during difficult moments is essential. There will be times when the situation will dictate that the principal act as a firm leader (in relation to values, expectations, standards, and policies) and, on occasions, even be uncompromising. Simple reminders such as "model integrity, honesty, and dignity on and off the job" to more serious suggestions, including the notion to "become visible in community activities" and "let people in on what you do and deal with every day" (Ramsey, 2005, pp. 6–8), will help to minimize the need to resort to such practices.

Finally, in this litigious society and the overlapping of jurisdictional issues on education between state, tribal, and federal policies, principals must be careful to cover themselves legally.

1. Define Your Job with an Entry Plan

According to this group of principals, the most important leadership lesson they learned as a principal was the importance of having an entry plan. Whether as a veteran principal entering an unfamiliar school or an assistant principal who has been promoted to the principalship, entering without a plan and consideration of new circumstances will inevitably result in a rough start. A good beginning is crucial, and first impressions happen only once. Leaders, regardless of their level, are most vulnerable in their first few months in a new position because they lack detailed knowledge of the challenges they will face and what it will take to succeed in meeting them and they have not yet developed a network of relationships to sustain them.

A principal's entry plan sketches out how he will get to know the school and let it get to know him. The plan describes the interviews, visits, observations, and readings she should do and lists the activities that enable assessment of the school's basic strengths and weaknesses and how to be most effective in the new role. The plan can be elaborate, with charts, graphs, and schedules, or something less formal. Once the strengths and weaknesses of the school are defined, principals can set concise goals and communicate them to the superintendent, the school board, and the school community.

Transitions are times when small differences in a new principal's actions can have disproportionate impacts on results. Failure to create momentum during the first few months guarantees an uphill battle for the rest of their tenure in the job. The result is that it is imperative to make better decisions that are genuinely understood and acted upon by the people who must implement them (Jentz, 2006, p. 16).

SETTLING INTO A NEW ROLE AS PRINCIPAL

Our group of beginning principals learned countless other leadership skills during their first year. Developing as a Native principal, particularly in a reservation community, takes time, skill, and mentoring. During their experiences as first-year principals working in tribal communities, people wanted to know if there exists a difference between Indigenous styles of leadership versus a non-Indigenous style of leadership. Especially valuable for them as they attempted to differentiate between the two is the idea that, to achieve anything worthwhile, they all had to struggle to develop a consensus-oriented organization. The one thing that they all agreed upon is that "great leadership works through the emotions" (Goleman, Boyatzis, and McKee, 2002, p. 3).

Simplistically put, they all learned that groups look toward their leaders for emotional support and in turn the leaders can affect these emotions either positively or negatively (Goleman, et al., 2002, p.5).

To arrive at an explanation regarding leadership style, then, we believe it is necessary to discuss Burns's (1978) transactional and transformation leadership terminology. Transactional leadership concerns those skills necessary for ensuring completed transactions within an institution and for storing up political credits and debits (Burns, 1978). Transformative leadership (Burns, 1978), on the other hand, is defined as those leadership skills necessary for transforming perceived ways for doing things within an organization and for promoting intrinsic motivation within the organization's participants.

The author who coined these thoughts back in the 1960s, Douglas James MacGregor (2000), would take exception to the either/or, good guy/bad guy dichotomy in the way some might view leadership, for example, using Western thought processes versus Indian cultural values. We, therefore, take the position that the terms represent two distinct sets of procedures for choosing a leadership style. The key here is difference, not necessarily good or bad, as some might indicate. All leaders, Indian or non-Indian, will need to use both types of procedures in their leadership roles but will approach them in different ways. For instance, Indian school administrators will use cultural background knowledge and attributes of power found in tribal communities (Martin, 2008, p. 9).

By their own admissions, as the principals in this study look back and thoughtfully observe the things they learned about leadership, they have come to understand the particular leadership qualities one must have to be an effective leader. They are, in no particular order of importance, as follows: integrity, humor, respect, love, faith, hope, service, selflessness, determination, cooperation, understanding, wisdom, and concern for the advancement of others.

As new principals seek to bring these qualities into their life and persona, they will enhance their leadership capacity in all aspects of life. However, additional skills must be developed as extensions of these qualities for a leader to be productive in a school serving large numbers of Indian children situated in a tribal community, including the abilities to:

- listen for understanding,
- work in partnership not only as education leader but as community leader,
- gather, distribute, and utilize the collective wisdom of an organization and its constituent parts and people,
- act as a peacemaker and a coordinator of compromise,
- bring disparate people and teams together into cooperative activities in respectful settings for communication and work,

- work through unexpected problems positively and productively, and
- bring to the table a solid knowledge base of how best to teach Indian children with diverse learning needs in a reservation school environment.

While this chapter is not a complete analysis of what these groups of beginning principals gained in their first year combined with the years of experience each has amassed as a teacher and teacher-leader, it is a core sampling of the learned wisdom taken from experience and ongoing inquiry. In conclusion, this study points to the need for additional research in the area of Native educational leadership in schools serving tribal communities in order to inform and shape the leadership programs that prepare teachers to lead schools.

REFERENCES

Barnhardt, R. (2008). Theory Z + N: The role of Alaska Natives in administration. *Democracy and Education, 17*(2).

Bartlett, L. and Brayboy, B. (2005). Race and schooling: Theories and ethnographies. *Urban Review, 37*(5), 361–74.

Begaye, T. (2006). Defining the context and understanding behind language and culture in Native communities. In D. Beaulieu and A. M. Figueira (Eds.), *The power of Native teachers* (pp. 1–4). Tempe, AZ: Center for Indian Education.

Bergstrom, A., Cleary, L., and Peacock, T. (2003). *The seventh generation*. Charleston, WV: ERIC, Clearinghouse on Rural Education and Small Schools.

Boloz, S. A., and C. G. Foster. (1980). A guide to effective leadership for the reservation administrator. *Journal of American Indian Education*, Arizona State University, Center for American Indian Education, 19(2), 2–3.

Burns, J. M. (1978). *Leadership*. New York: Harper and Row.

Castagno, A. E. (2009). A final evaluative discussion of the Diné-Hopi Cohort Leadership Program. Northern Arizona University.

Covey, S. R. (1989). *The seven habits of highly effective people*. New York: Fireside Publishing.

Covey, S. R. (1992). *Principle centered leadership*. New York: Fireside Publishing.

Drucker, Peter F. (2001). *The essential Drucker*. New York: Harper Collins Publisher.

DuFour, R. (2002). Leading edge: Bring the whole staff on board. *Journal of Staff Development, 23*(3), 76–77.

Duke, D. L. (2004, September/October). The turnaround principal: High stakes leadership. *National Association of Elementary School Principals*, 12–23.

Gardner, H. (1995). *Leading minds: An anatomy of leadership*. New York: Basic Books.

Goleman, D., Boyatzis, R. E., and McKee, A. (2002). *Primal leadership: Realizing the power of emotional intelligence.* Boston: Harvard University Business School Publishing.

Gordon, G. (2006). Building engaged schools: Getting the most out of America's classrooms. New York: Gallup Publishing.

Jentz, B. (2006). *The entry plan handbook: How to begin a leadership position successfully.* Newton, MA: Leadership and Learning.

Jentz, B., Cheever, D. S., Jr., Fisher, S. B., Howe Jones, M., Kelleher, P., and Wofford, J. W. (1983, April). *Entry: The hiring, start-up, and supervision of administrators.* New York: McGraw-Hill. *NASSP Bulletin, 67,* 118–19.

Martin, J. (2005). Northern Arizona University educational leadership USOE grant proposal. Administrator Professional Development Grant Proposal to the U.S. Department of Education, Office of Indian Education, Washington, DC.

Martin, J. (2008). Analysis of the beginning principals perception in selected Navajo and Hopi schools regarding leadership practices. Flagstaff: Northern Arizona University.

MacGregor, D. (2000). *Douglas MacGregor on management: The human side of enterprise.* New York: John Wiley and Sons.

National Indian Education Association. (2005). Preliminary report on No Child Left Behind in Indian country. Washington, DC: NIEA.

Ramsey, R. D. (2005). *What matters most for school leaders.* Thousand Oaks, CA: Corwin Press.

Rural School and Community (2007). Rural School Community Trust 2007 Annual Report. Washington, DC.

Schlenker, B. R., and Weigold, M. F. (1991). Accountability and risk taking. *Personality and Social Psychology Bulletin, 17*(1), 25–29.

Sciacca, J. (2005). Final evaluation report of the Dinè-Hopi Cohort Leadership Program. Northern Arizona University, Flagstaff.

Villani, S. (2005). *Induction programs that support new principals.* Thousand Oaks, CA: Corwin Press.

Vogel, L., and Rude, H. (2007, October 26). Analysis of Native American administrator candidates' motivation to support culturally sensitive schools. Paper presented at the National Indian Education Association Conference, Honolulu, Hawaii.

Wagner, T. (2006).*Change leadership: A practical guide to transforming our schools.* San Francisco: Jossey-Bass.

Walters, T., and Grubb, S. (2005). *Leading schools: Distinguishing the essential from the important.* Aurora, CO: Mid-Continent Research for Education and Learning.

8

Native American Innovative Leadership

Motivations and Perspectives on Educational Change

LINDA R. VOGEL AND HARVEY A. RUDE

Culturally responsive leadership that effectively supports development of learning communities in schools serving American Indian communities is the key to achieving positive student outcomes. There is a great need in tribal community schools for comprehensive research and evidence-based practices that support the best educational policies for these learners (Faircloth, 2006). Begaye (2006) delineates the multiple understandings that contribute to the current view of Native culture, tracing influences from anthropology, psychology, and linguistics. American Indian culture is constantly changing through the interrelated nature of cognitive codes and individually drawn assumptions about Native American values (Duran and Duran, 1995; Wilkins, 2002). Knowledge of the language and culture of Native American students and educators is an asset that can be accentuated, rather than discounted, in promoting leadership that supports the highest level of learning for students who may experience challenges from the prevailing Western society in their local communities. Many Native American teachers and students speak with conviction about the need for community outreach and involvement of tribal community members, elders, and other representatives who are outside the formal education process to integrate Native culture and values with the curriculum taught within the public schools (Cummins, 2000; Reyhner, Martin, Lockard, and Gilbert, 2003).

Many Native American educators can vividly recall their own childhood experiences in which parents were either hostile toward public education as a result of the boarding school era or consciously suppressed information about cultural heritage and beliefs. Shreve (2007) reported that cultural heritage for Native American students is often viewed as a potential deficit within the non–Native American dominant culture. A number of Native scholars (Cajete 2000; Deloria and Wildcat, 2001; Hale, 2002; Swisher and Tippeconnic,

1999) have provided recommendations to enhance the cultural recognition and integration of learner experiences into the academic program for these students. It is imperative to apply these understandings in professional development programs for educational leadership in order to achieve appropriate academic, interpersonal, and societal outcomes in Indigenous school communities.

The purpose of this chapter is to describe the perspectives of Native American educators participating in a graduate licensing program for administrative leadership in preK–12 schools. Research participants were queried about their epistemological views on leadership and motivations to lead Native American schools. Key questions guiding this research were:

1. What educational leadership knowledge and skill sets best support Native children's learning and outcomes as described by Native teachers in the Native American Innovative Leadership (NAIL) program?
2. What nuances of epistemologies and motivations for educational leadership are voiced by Native graduate students?

THE NATIVE AMERICAN INNOVATIVE LEADERSHIP PROGRAM

Another recent investigation into the preparation of culturally responsive administrators centered on the views and beliefs of Native American educators working toward their administrative license in a graduate program sponsored by the U.S. Department of Education through the Office of Indian Education. This project was developed specifically to address and support the needs and challenges of Native American educational leaders in both content and delivery. The project, named the NAIL project at the University of Northern Colorado consisted of a thirty-nine credit hour course of study, culminating in an interdisciplinary master of arts degree and principal and special education director licensure. Open to educators from all Native American tribes, the program was delivered primarily through distance technology so participants could continue their current full-time employment and remain with their families and communities while earning an advanced degree and licenses to serve in an educational leadership capacity in schools serving predominantly Native American students. Combining leadership and administration courses already offered by the university in the areas of educational leadership and special education, the NAIL project specifically included culturally relevant readings, discussions that encouraged sharing of cultural experiences and perspectives, and assignments that gave voice to aspiring Native American educational leaders.

RESEARCH METHODS

This grounded theory study was conducted with twenty-nine Native American graduate students who were currently teaching in schools and who aspired to lead schools serving their tribal communities. Both qualitative and quantitative methods were used in the study, including document analysis and statistical testing (descriptive/ frequency scores). The primary data source for this study were graduate student papers based on two course assignments that asked students to describe their personal educational platform (philosophy) and the epistemologies that guided their educational philosophies and practice. These student papers were used to examine research constructs including the motivational basis of the students' aspirations to become educational leaders and the epistemologies they brought to the role of educational leader in schools serving tribal communities.

DATA ANALYSIS METHODS

Analysis of participants' motivations for aspiring to become school leaders was based on grounded qualitative data analysis theory, using the primary category of motivation in axial coding. Constant comparative analysis of participant responses among participant responses was conducted, with the identification of themes emerging from the coding categories related to motivation.

Themes were developed based on the individual contexts of the participants using codes that were both objective and subjective in nature. The researchers presented constructed meanings as these emerged through the analysis of Native graduate students' discourses and ideas about leadership and motivations (goals) for becoming leaders in schools and creating change to better serve Native children's learning opportunities. To avoid a possible bias in findings by the researchers as they espoused the hermeneutic epistemology in structuring the analysis of data, two graduate assistants also coded the data. Inter-rater agreement of 97 percent among the three sets of coding for participant epistemologies confirmed the reliability of the findings.

THE STUDY POPULATION

The twenty-nine participants in this study represent twelve tribal nations. The majority of students are Diné (Navajo) and the remaining students are Oglala Lakota, Pawnee, Crow, Northern Arapaho, Old Harbor, Chemehuevi, Ponca, Arapaho, and the three affiliated tribes of the Salish Kootenai. At the time of this study all participants were practicing teachers at schools with high percentages of Native American students, many located in tribal nation communities.

BACKGROUND OF STUDY

Participants were exposed to a variety of epistemologies and theoretical ideas on educational leadership in their graduate coursework. Discussion points included specific practices and structures currently in place at the participants' schools, the relationship between school leadership and the school climate, and the instructional techniques and the academic outcomes of these practices and structures. In the development of their own personal educational platforms, participants also shared perspectives about the major aims of education, including the academic and social significance of student learning as these intersect with family and community aspirations for their children.

FINDINGS

Study findings were organized by themes that emerged from the analysis of participants' discourses about educational leadership knowledge and skill sets relevant to children's learning and the development of culturally relevant education systems. Native graduate students were asked to reflect about educational issues that influence both the learning of children and leadership action in the context of the schools where they were working at the time of this study. Participants' discourses highlighted the blending of Indigenous and Western epistemologies as these informed and shaped their leadership platforms (approaches) to educational issues as they are preparing for leadership roles in educational institutions serving their communities.

ESSENTIAL LEADERSHIP SKILL
AND KNOWLEDGE SETS

Knowledge and skill sets for educational leaders serving Native communities were identified by participants as relationship building, including understanding the sociocultural backgrounds of students and knowledge of local communities and families, as collaborative instructional leadership, as communication driven, and as data-driven decision making. These also are discussed in the final section of this chapter, which addresses implications and recommendations for educational leadership preparation programs and Native educators.

Relationship Development

Participants stressed the need for leaders to develop relationships with children to understand the unique situational factors of each individual child in order to best respond to particular dilemmas. Respondents focused much of their discussion and reflection on the need for educational leaders to understand students' home lives and cultures well enough for the leader to support instructional leadership with teachers so that the most appropriate instructional decisions—ones that positively influence student learning and outcomes—could be made.

Collaborative Instructional Leadership

Participants described a preference for a collaborative leadership style and the need to listen and ask for input from others—skills sets viewed as critical for educator and leadership success. A respondent stated: "I am willing to listen and ask for input . . . [because] other people might have a better solution or ideas that would be best for solving a problem facing our schools or students. . . . I always look at the past and then rely on my knowledge base to help define what I need to do." Another participant explained: "Teaching requires us to make sense of experiences so we can relay that understanding to our students. We must keep track of past and current knowledge because learning depends on it."

Participants identified the importance of leadership having the knowledge and skills to understand and influence action plans that inform students' learning environments and outcomes. A respondent explained: "Even in dealing with classroom management or if a student is having difficulty learning, I like to see documented intervention [by the teacher] that was implemented to improve performance and then review why it did not work and draw up an action plan to use practices that have some research basis."

Effective Communication

Leaders need to have effective communication skills and to be flexible in responding to new ideas. Understanding multiple ways of viewing the world and approaches to resolving educational issues that exist in schools today were identified as essential skills in educational leadership by respondents. A respondent explained: "I don't think an effective leader is one who sticks with one epistemology or one way of viewing the world. I think when one does that they are setting themselves up for failure, because they become rigid." This participant described leadership as involving skills needed to interact with others in ways that support healthy relationship building. He elaborated: "We must be able to communicate and compromise. We must be able to realize when we are wrong and we have to be open to new ideas. . . . After all, leadership is the process of guiding people in the right direction."

A participant shared:

> People are not the same. We have different backgrounds. We do not all have the same beliefs nor do we have the same value system. It is vital to

understand and respect views that are different from our own. People look for leadership that is understanding and patient. I have so much more respect for my principal when he treats me like a professional and listens to my point of view. We don't have to agree, but he understands and respects where I am coming from. To be an effective leader, we have to possess that skill. We have to understand all the differences in people so that we can resolve issues. Never should an individual feel disappointed or let down because they were not heard or understood. To be an effective leader, that skill must be honed to perfection. We all have to remember that we are human. We have flaws and imperfections, but those are the weaknesses that can make us stronger leaders for tomorrow.

Data-Informed Decision Making

Participants indicated the importance of understanding and being able to interpret student data with teachers and create action plans that positively impact academic and social development outcomes. Some respondents stated that they also had a focus on the utility of data-driven decision making in their school environments as a necessary skill set for improving student learning.

Respondents also described the necessity of leadership to have the ability to proactively respond to the current demands of state and federal testing and accountability systems for preK–12 schools. One wrote, "Especially with the No Child Left Behind mandates that all stem from quantitative data, the [school leader's] ability to understand and interpret these facts can help satisfy the governmental regulations and policies."

LEADERSHIP AND CHANGE

Many participants (40 percent) identified a need to change the current reality in schools. Within their discourses, all participants expressed the desire to affect positive learning outcomes through their new educational leadership roles where they would practice their newly acquired skills and knowledge to effectively lead schools. Education was emphasized as an instrument of broader social change, including the program that they were currently enrolled in. One participant said, "I believe education is the key to opening doors to success and experience. . . . All children, regardless of their background or situation, should be given the same chance to learn." Another described the positive impact of a former tribal leader's message about the function of education for his community: "Chief Manuelito counseled his people to climb upon the ladder of an education. His words in support of education have sustained many Navajos and have lifted them out of the dust of poverty and ignorance."

Epistemological Perspectives and Leadership

Respondents emphasized the need to listen to others to develop their own understandings about each person's unique life journey, how they are connected to those who have come before them and to a sense of place (Indigenous). Several participants drew from their Indigenous knowledge of connectedness and a sense of place. One explained: "I believe that Mother Earth has a distinct connectedness to me. I believe that an effective leader must know who he is and where he comes from in order to put his current situation into perspective."

Reflecting on an Indigenous worldview of developing one's knowledge, a participant wrote:

Knowing where people are coming from and why they view things as they do is an important piece in understanding human dynamics and building relationships. . . . The culture's whole way of discovering truth and knowledge is that you're doing so because of a sense of being "incomplete" and, through your quest, you're subject to uncertainty, change, and growth. You exist in a wide open universe, awaiting your own personal enlightenment—yours and yours alone.

Educational Leadership for Social Justice

Respondents indicated they felt strongly about an educational leadership platform informed both by a critical theory and an Indigenous epistemology, a platform by which school leaders have a social justice responsibility for improving Native children's education experiences and outcomes. However, no matter what epistemological preferences participants shared in their discourses, they all expressed a desire to make positive change that largely impacts children's lives. Many of the study participants spoke about "fighting for the rights of those people who don't have a voice" and enacting change. One respondent powerfully wrote: "I have a passion for speaking up for our Native American Nations and the injustices that have been and continue to be done to them. I have a real conviction that education, along with renewed spirituality, is the Native American's salvation."

Participants' discourses focused on a key goal of changing the historically negative outcomes experienced by Native children through exercising educational leadership roles. One educator shared how her desire to become a leader stemmed from her father's influence and her teaching experiences:

Because we all have been born into various social and economic groups and have different life experiences, we are not all the same. After I was six years old, my parents placed me in a boarding school. My parents managed to attain their eighth grade education. My parents struggled from paycheck to paycheck, but my father encouraged his children to go to school and become doctors and lawyers. I decided at an early age that I was going to go to college. Thinking back on my life, I have come to realize that, if you can just encourage a child to set high goals, such as telling them, "You can go to college or you can become a doctor or a nurse," a child will make it happen.

Participants used critical theory sources to identify conceptual ideas that resonated with their leadership platforms, which they hoped to carry out in the school communities they were serving. A respondent shared reflections:

Paulo Freire (1970) said to the peasants, "You can farm on your own and run your own business," but the Chilean peasants said they were only farm workers, not business people. So Paulo Freire had to show them how they could do it. The peasants realized that they could do many things through discourse and dialogue. I have given the children in my classes, through my teaching, the ability to discuss, write about things, and express their ideas. . . . They become full of positive self-esteem. I was especially impressed with a student I had this year. Throughout the year, he felt that the other children were picking on him, and he and his family thought they should move him to another school. But, as he became a more able speaker and writer, his outlook on his surroundings became more positive. He even wanted to stay in during recess to work on his writing drafts and became more vocal and participated in classroom discussions.

This participant elaborated on the critical theory framework of the NAIL project: "This Native American leadership program is a form of critical theory. We are being given the tools to become educational leaders, principals, and administrators. Some of us are struggling to internalize whether we are capable of it. Some of us have been put down many times, but we believe we can help many generations of Native Americans and others through our examples as educational leaders."

Other examples of blended epistemological influences emerged in these participants' discourses. Although leaning toward a social justice perspective with an interest in politics and economics, one Native educator explained that his worldview is shaped by his experiences of growing up in a small, isolated village in Alaska. However, he also recognized the relevance of facts and data gathered through a scientific approach related to a given situation. He wrote: "I don't think that I am one or the other [epistemology] but rather a mixture of them. My environment has shaped my thought and I believe that my compromise was an acceptance of a little of each [epistemology]."

Women in Educational Leadership Roles

The need for increased female leadership in a historically matrilineal culture was cited by many participants (all female), who also expressed the desire to encourage and inspire other Native American girls and women to become actively involved and vocal within their tribal communities.

Female respondents in the study identified nurturing, relationship building, and an explicit ethic of caring as essential to their leadership for social and educational change. Greater empowerment of women was intrinsic in the traditional matrilineal structure of many Native American tribes. While most respondents discussed the need for more leadership roles for women, one-third saw their role as continuing a tradition of female leadership. As one explained:

> I am continuing the legacy of powerful women in my family. I have vowed to continue to influence Native education and stand up for the rights of our tribe, families, women, and children. . . . As a native woman, I feel like the world always wants to put Native people in a box and categorize us into one category, such as spiritual or artistic. The reality is that we do have some of these characteristics, but there are also some of us that are very logical and mathematical in our thinking. These stereotypes sometimes lead to the conclusion of educational institutions that Native students can't excel in math and science, which is completely untrue.

Another participant indicated that she strongly believes in encouraging Native girls to set goals and high standards, but she also felt that Native youth of both genders need active advocates to create greater educational, social, and economic opportunities for them. These perspectives reveal a blend of feminist and Indigenous epistemologies useful in understanding the embedded conceptual ideas that shape their leadership goals in schools.

Cultural Traditions

How cultural traditions and knowledge shaped their approaches to educational leadership was evident in respondents' discourses. A participant shared:

> I also carry within me my traditional and cultural teachings. I find myself going back to those teachings before I make any decisions as a teacher, a mother, a student, a sister, and a wife. I think that, as a Native American, one cannot just take one and say I am this . . . when in all actuality we all in some way go back to our own cultural teachings and traditions to overcome and be a part of today's world as a leader and as an individual who is striving to make it in today's world.

Participants highlighted their perspectives about Native holistic worldviews—views of reality that directly contradict the assumption that intellectual understanding of one's reality is divided into discrete categories of ideologies (Hale, 2002, p. 81). As Cajete (2000) explains, "Coming-to-know is the best translation for education in Native traditions. . . . But, a coming-to-know, a coming-to-understand, metaphorically entails a journey, a process, a quest for knowledge, and understanding" (p. 80).

One participant described her own "way of knowing" as rooted in her culture and encompassing many seemingly contradictory elements. She explained that in her Native system of acquiring knowledge, "There is always some type of method in learning that creates a natural order to things." She described her blend of epistemological influences as humanism (Pulliam 1991), as knowledge focusing on mankind, and as rooted in the "basic moral, ethical, aesthetic, and religious principles drawn from the collective experience of culture" (p. 179). Realism and idealism were also combined in this participant's epistemology toolkit as examining objects through reason but "taking it one step further" to involve the mental, spiritual, and physical experiences of a person. The term she used for her epistemology was "holism" which she described as the development of oneself as a creative learner and independent thinker (Herring, 1996). "My belief system is that, if you are honest and have respect for all living elements, then your actions will be in harmony with you and the universe." This educator's response resonates with the tenets of Indigenous philosophy described by Cajete (2000).

Epistemologies are also seen as tools that can be applied in particular situations to best interpret the individual's experiences. "We cannot mis-experience anything; we can only mis-interpret what we experience" (Cajete, 2000, p. 76). Respondents noted the value of understanding a variety of epistemologies in order to better understand how other people view the world and interpret their experiences and how this skill is valuable to an educational leader. The process of intellectualizing about epistemologies in the NAIL program promoted leadership skills for examining their direct experiences with ideological ideas that bridged Western and Native knowledge acquisition (Barnhardt and Kawagley, 2005).

The fact that Native educators in this study identified Indigenous and other epistemological ideas as dynamic influences on their educational leadership platforms, enabling them to imagine effective action plans that can impact student learning in positive ways, is not surprising. Des Jarlais (2008) explains that Indigenous knowledge acquisition is a process through which "the particulars come to be understood in relations to the whole, and the 'laws' are continually tested in the context of everyday survival" (p. 43).

Kirkness and Barnhardt (2001) further explain the salient features of Native knowledge "are that its meaning, value, and use are bound to the cultural context in which it is situated; it is thoroughly integrated into everyday life, and it is generally acquired through direct experience and participation in real-world activities" (p. 7). Participants in this study emphasized social construction and integration of cultural knowledge, contextualization, and experience as a means of gaining knowledge, identifying these as relevant theoretical and conceptual ideas for understanding how epistemological ideas can be used to inform and shape their leadership platform and practice.

NATIVE AMERICAN EDUCATIONAL LEADERSHIP MOTIVATIONS: COMMUNITY SERVICE AND PRESERVATION OF CULTURAL INTEGRITY

Participants' motivations (goals) to become educational leaders emerged from the analysis of their epistemological frameworks discourses. One respondent stated, "Native American students have been the victims of poor teaching as well as poor planning on the part of the Federal government and school administrators. Someway, somehow, this trend needs to be reversed. It is my personal belief that this reversal needs to come from within the Indian Nations."

Educators' motivations to make positive changes in educational outcomes with their communities were described in the context of what changes were most relevant to their communities' goals. These were:

1. *Increased community involvement*—73 percent of the respondents cited the need for greater community involvement in the education of Native American students, which they felt could be best developed by a Native American educational leader.
2. *Increased cultural curriculum integration*—73 percent of the respondents felt that the success of Native American students in an academic setting relied on appropriate integration of culture into curriculum and pedagogy. Increased student self-esteem and motivation were described as the potential results of cultural understanding and integration.
3. *The existence of role models*—62 percent of the respondents described the need for positive Native American role models as vital to Native American students' academic success. Participants said that Native American educational leaders could best demonstrate to Native American youth that they can successfully "bridge two worlds" by mastering skills and contents presented in mainstream schools and yet continue to embrace their Native American cultural values and language.
4. *Mentoring*—41 percent of the respondents said that they would like to increase the mentoring of Native educators and youth to set high achievement and career goals, as well as mentoring non-Native

teachers regarding the integration of Native cultural values in educational settings as they assume educational leadership roles.

COMMUNITY INVOLVEMENT

The essential role of parents in their children's education was described by respondents as the first step in building the necessary level of community involvement in Native American schools. The need to support the relationship between parents and teachers as partners in the educational process was stressed. "Community involvement begins with parental understanding of students' learning attributes, deficiencies, and methods of instruction [that] dictate flexibility." A respondent explained, "The team will include the student, the parent, and the teacher. When the student and the parent have the input on what is to come out of their education, this will instill confidence and the pride of ownership." Another participant wrote, "We need to share responsibility and resources to benefit all students, working with and respecting parents as partners in the educational process. We need to recognize that education of our students is a responsibility for the whole community."

Using extracurricular and tribal activities held at schools was viewed as a starting point. "In reservation towns and tribal communities, a school serves as a community gathering place for basketball games and powwows. We need to use these events to connect with the families and then encourage them to participate in other activities that directly affect their child."

Keeping communication lines open and making parents feel welcome as a part of the students' education was viewed as essential. One respondent elaborated, "I have realized that, if I reach out to the parents, they are more than happy to be involved. Some parents (especially Native parents) are very timid when it comes to talking to teachers and often feel unwelcome in schools. I encourage them to be a part of their child's education by keeping the communication lines open. Even simple things like talking to them in the store or at a basketball game are valuable." This respondent went on to encourage the offering of classes at schools to parents in order to "build a community of positive parenting which would benefit the students."

Grandparents were also identified as valuable sources of cultural reinforcement and academic support. One respondent cited a program implemented in her community that "helps ensure that the culture is being passed on to the younger generation . . . [and] also provides students with additional one-on-one tutoring in math and reading." "The Elders should be actively involved with the students in order to share their experiences and knowledge," another educator in the study explained. The extended family structure of the tribal community was discussed by several participants, often citing that "it takes a village to raise a child."

The resources available among community tribal members were also identified as essential for Native American student success. A respondent wrote, "I feel that educators find their greatest resources many times in their community . . . from the people to the land. A teacher should seek out resources within the community before implementing resources outside of the community. Such resources include the tribal community college, tribal programs. . . . and Elders." Another participant explained, "The Elders should be actively involved with the students in order to share their experiences and knowledge. . . . The language program could be enhanced by these Elders."

Several respondents also viewed increased communication between the school and tribal political representatives as another form of community involvement that needed to be strengthened. "The educational system would need to pressure the political representatives to present what the community needs." However, as one educator noted, "We [educators] emphasize empowerment of community, parents, and students, but all is forgotten in the entire process of meeting better scores on state mandated tests."

A participant summarized: "Community involvement is essential to all schools, because the connection with the community either lifts up student education or brings it down. When a community rallies behind a school and supports the teachers and other school administrators, it creates a healthy environment for students."

CULTURAL CURRICULA INTEGRATION

Nearly three-fourths of Native American educators in this study identified the need to increase the integration of tribal culture into the academic curriculum as a motivation for their desire to become school leaders. Cultural education was viewed as essential "to promote and foster lifelong learning." One educator explained the vision she would use to lead a school:

> Each teacher at my school would be required to know the students' background[s] through home visits throughout the school year. This would be part of their evaluation. In seeking educational and support personnel, I would include in the [teaching] position [job] description as a preferred qualification a knowledge of and familiarity with the language, culture, and people. The curriculum will be based on the needs of the students served, the cultural values and the individual interests of Native students.

Many respondents stressed the fostering of tribal language skills (citing research supporting bilingual and immersion programs) and the integration of tribal values in curriculum, as well. The positive impact of cultural integration in a school's curriculum on students' self-esteem and motivation was also identified by respondents. A participant explained,

> When teaching the Native American students, we have to connect with their cultural background so we can increase their self-esteem and build up enough skills so they can make it in the mainstream of society. The integration of the tribal language and culture is one of the components being used by the Family and Child Education Program (FACE) on the reservations and it is proven to be very successful as a model of family literacy. . . . Using the cultural background approach on the Native students helps them to keep their bodies, minds, and spirits strong by learning the history and traditions which connects them with their ancient tradition.

Several respondents identified the positive effects on student behavior that can also result from the explicit teaching and modeling of tribal values. One educator explained,

> In the days of the teepee (Ni-toy-is), our people gave everything that the child needed to be a real person (Nii-tsit-ta-pii), which is what helped them to strive for success in their lives. The classroom will be treated in the same way [in my school]. Our success was accomplished and measured by the values that we lived by. Our people lived to take care of each other. The tribe was the responsibility of everyone.

Pedagogy is another area respondents identified as requiring greater cultural understanding to support instructional leadership. Active, hands-on, concrete experiences, coupled with collaborative and cooperative learning, were described as the most culturally appropriate methods of instruction. These techniques promote learning by encouraging the development of communication skills within a nonthreatening environment.

> In Native aspects of education, most students will not speak until directed and they tend to sit in the back of the room, hoping to go unnoticed. They don't like confrontations, meaning they do not like to be pointed out or spoken to. They want to make a quick exit before the class is dismissed because they do not want to be confronted, which means they will have to respond orally. I have found that most Native students will behave in this manner without really knowing what they are doing.

Cooperative or collaborative learning situations, however, exemplify the value of listening to peers in order to come up with the best possible solutions.

"This includes validating every one's contributions and including everyone that wants to participate," one teacher explained. Regarding social skills, one respondent stated, "I believe that if students get exposed to realistic social experiences, then they will begin to understand why effective social skills are crucial. This again leads to allowing students to be able to function and socialize in both worlds—Western and Navajo, for example."

POSITIVE MENTORING AND ROLE MODELS

A majority (62 percent) of the Native American educators in this study described the need to have positive cultural role models as another motivating factor in their pursuit of leadership positions. As Native Americans in educational leadership positions, they expressed the belief that they could mentor other Natives to enter and excel in the educational field. This mentoring role also applied to non-Native educators working in predominantly Native American schools, as well as to Native American students. Respondents discussed the need to include non-Native teachers in appropriate tribal celebrations in order to further the non-Native teachers' understandings of the students' cultures. An understanding and appreciation of tribal culture was viewed as an element in retaining good non-Native educators, particularly in reservation schools.

Several respondents gave examples that, with the assistance of tribal elders, have worked successfully in their current schools. Such mentoring was also identified as crucial to have teachers as positive role models in the classroom. Giving students the opportunity to explore and ask questions in order to become confident in their own learning was a salient theme in identifying teachers as role models. "Engagement of students is enhanced when there is a strong positive relationship between the student and the teacher," observed one educator. The need for strong, positive relationships based on mutual respect among faculty and staff to model a healthy working environment that supports student learning was also discussed by several educators in this study.

Role models and mentors are particularly important in Native American culture because humility is highly valued. Self-identification as a leader might make it appear as though an individual thinks that he or she is better than others and is attempting to set themselves above others. This aversion to power for the sake of control or dominance over others is indicated by the fact that most Indigenous languages do not have a word that is a direct equivalent of "leadership" (Simms, 2000). Leaders in Native communities emerge in differentiated roles based upon the usefulness of their expertise to the community—as identified by other members of the tribe (Edmunds, 1980).

Motivation for giving back to community was evidenced by these Native educators throughout this study by their perspectives and personal goals to attain educational leadership roles with which to proactively create change in schools. For these educators motivation (goal) is not in a leader title but having the desire to make a difference in the lives of Native children and their communities. Identification as a potential leader requires a justification of one's abilities and usefulness in bettering the life conditions of others in the group. Encouragement and support by those already in positions of respect is necessary so that those who aspire to leadership are not viewed as selfish or prideful but, rather, as sincerely desiring to improve the life conditions of the group.

CONCLUSION: INDIGENOUS PRINCIPLES FOR EFFECTIVE EDUCATIONAL LEADERSHIP

Principles that highlight values common among many Indigenous groups emerged as findings from the analysis of participants' perspectives about education services with Native communities. Principles that the participants described as informing the essential knowledge and skill sets of educational leaders are:

1. importance of relationships,
2. support for individual growth,
3. personal responsibility to serve the community,
4. mentoring and role models,
5. experiential learning,
6. contextualizing knowledge,
7. collaboration,
8. community involvement, and
9. understanding and preservation of local cultural beliefs, traditions, and languages.

IMPLICATIONS FOR EDUCATIONAL LEADERSHIP PREPARATION PROGRAMS

Recommendations for educational leadership programs serving Native American educators emerged from the study findings. These include the following:

- Collaboration and the inclusion of all voices in discussion and decision-making processes should be emphasized throughout the leadership preparation program, both implicitly and explicitly.
- Learning activities and assignments should be structured to ensure that all program participants contribute, as well as to ensure that administrators seek out opinions from school and tribal leaders to inform their critical thinking processes.

- Respectful participatory action as a methodology for involvement of parents, community members, and students in the learning process should be a part of the leadership program curriculum, as well as focused discussions about proactively responding to and involving those who are resistant.

Finally, it should be the goal of educational leadership programs, as perhaps with all educational programs serving Natives, to strike a respectful and harmonious balance between Western theories and attempts to objectify and categorize the human experience and the Indigenous theories that promote the holistic, unifying, and subjective knowledge of humans. As the participants so amply intellectualized in their discourses, Native American educators utilize a blend of Indigenous and Western worldviews (epistemologies) to understand both the complexity of educational issues and to guide their leadership for change. A key expectation of Native educators is that the higher education institutions preparing them for leadership in schools must provide knowledge about Western concepts and skills without compromising the cultural integrity of Native educators knowledge and traditions. Given the goal of these Native American educators to serve their communities, it is the responsibility of those administrating higher education programs to ensure that such opportunities are provided, so that Native students have the experiences and tools that will enable them to effectively enact the positive changes their communities envision. To realize self-determination goals, Indigenous communities strive to have an educated population that supports the sociocultural, educational, and economic needs of a sovereign tribal nation. It is within the context of such tribal nation goals that Native leadership programs should be developed.

REFERENCES

Barnhardt, R., and Kawagley, A. O. (2005). Indigenous knowledge systems/Alaska Native ways of knowing. *Anthropology and Education Quarterly, 36*(1), 8–23.

Begaye, T. (2006). Defining the context and understanding behind language and culture in Native communities. In D. Beaulieu and A. M. Figueira (Eds.), *The power of Native teachers.* Tempe, AZ: Center for Indian Education.

Cajete, G. (2000). *Native science: Natural laws of interdependence.* Santa Fe, NM: Clear Light Publishers.

Cummins, J. (2000). *Language, power and pedagogy: Bilingual children in the crossfire.* Clevedon, UK: Multilingual Matters.

Deloria, V., and Wildcat, D. R. (2001). *Power and place: Indian education in America.* Golden, CO: Fulcrum Resources.

Des Jarlais, C. W. (2008). *Western structures meet Native traditions: The interfaces of educational cultures.* Charlotte, NC: Information Age Publishing.

Duran, E., and Duran, B. (1995). *Native American postcolonial psychology*. Albany, NY: State University of New York Press.

Edmunds, R. D. (Ed.). (1980). *American Indian leaders*. Lincoln: University of Nebraska Press.

Faircloth, S. C. (2006). Early childhood education among American Indian/Alaskan Native children with disabilities: Implications for research and practice. *Rural Special Education Quarterly, 25*(1), 25–31.

Freire, P. (1970). *Pedagogy of the oppressed*. New York: Continuum International Publishing Group.

Garrett, J. T., and Garrett, M. T. (2002).*The Cherokee full circle: A practical guide to ceremonies and traditions*. Rochester, VT: Bear and Company.

Hale, L. (2002). *Native American education: A reference handbook*. Santa Barbara, CA: ABC-CLIO.

Herring, R. D. (1996).The unrecognized gifted: A more humanistic perspective for Indigenous students. *Journal of Humanistic Education and Development, 35*(1), 4–11.

Kirkness, V. J., and Barnhardt, R. (2001). First Nations and higher education: The four R's-respect, relevance, reciprocity, responsibility. In R. Hayoe and J. Pan (Eds.), *Knowledge across cultures: A contribution to dialogue among civilizations* (pp. 1–18). Hong Kong: Comparative Education Research Centre.

Reyhner, J., Martin, J., Lockard, L., and Gilbert, W. S. (Eds.). (2003). *Learn in beauty: Indigenous education for a new century*. Flagstaff: Northern Arizona University.

Pulliam, J. D. (1991). *History of education in America*. Upper Saddle River, NJ: Prentice-Hall.

Shreve, B. G. (2007). Of gods and broken rainbows: Native American religions, western rationalism, and the problem of sacred lands. *New Mexico Historical Review, 82*(3), 369–90.

Simms, M. (2000). Impressions of leadership through a Native woman's eyes. *Urban Education, 35*(5), p. 637–44.

Swisher, K. C., and Tippeconnic, J. W., III, (Eds.). (1999). *Next steps: Research and practice to advance Indian education*. Charleston, WV: Clearinghouse on Rural Education and Small Schools.

Wilkins, D. E. (2002). *American Indian politics and the American political system*. Lanham, MD: Rowman and Littlefield Publishers, Inc.

9

Indigenous Knowledge and Culture-Based Pedagogy

What Educators Serving Native Children in Mainstream Educational Institutions Must Know

LISA GRAYSHIELD, DENNY HURTADO, AND AMILEAH DAVIS

Pedagogy in public education is grounded in Western European ontological thought and discourse, providing little room for traditional systems of Indigenous-centered expression and identity to be realized. Both past and recent literature supports the critical importance of incorporating Indigenous/tribal culture into state and federal education programs that provide high-quality education for American Indian and Alaska Native (AI/AN) children. Executive Order 13336 (2004) is one of the most recent in a series of presidential executive orders urging those who serve AI/AN students in our nation to "recognize the unique educational and culturally related academic needs of American Indian and Alaska Native students consistent with the unique political and legal relationship of the Federal Government with tribal governments in a manner that is consistent with tribal traditions, languages and cultures."

As a result of numerous efforts and collaborations among Native educators, researchers, community members, tribal education departments, and non-Native allies, the literature clearly provides definitive procedures to be used by those interested in addressing the cultural incongruity of public school education for Native children (Aguilera, Lipka, Demmert, and Tippeconnic, 2007, p. 5–6). However, many of these efforts are focused on tribal grant or Bureau of Indian Education funded schools. Little information is available to address the vast majority of Native American children who attend public schools. Today, more than 90 percent of AI/AN children attend predominantly non-Native public schools, though in most instances they represent a fraction of the student body (Hoffman, Sable, Naum, and Gray, 2005). It is unlikely that the vast majority will attend schools where their unique tribal cultures will take precedence over mainstream text book depictions of American Indian culture. It is even more unlikely that educators will receive appropriate training to effectively engage Native students in a manner that values the differences inherent among tribal people. Additionally, when generic (i.e., pan-Indian) training is offered to educators in the form of best practices in "Indian education"—without the involvement of students' respective tribes— commonly held stereotypes about "Indians" are further reinforced.

While the initial intent of culture-based professional development (CBPD) was aimed at increasing academic functioning for Native students in schools, the implications will have far greater impact if *all* children are beneficiaries of Indigenous knowledge. The primary purpose of this chapter is to provide a brief overview of literature on Indigenous ways of knowing in educational discourse. Then a theoretical construct can be established that informs the framework of a model for culture-based professional development in educational leadership and teacher education.

Indigenous forms of knowledge serve to offer new ways of addressing the declining trends in educational attainment. They can do so by offering a new view of intellectualism that promotes the conscious sensitizing of individuals to the critical impact they have on the world for future generations to come. There is no more urgent time in history than now to incorporate past lessons into current educational data bases so as to promote an intellectually stimulating educational environment, committed to high-quality education for *all* children.

INDIGENOUS WAYS OF KNOWING

Indigenous knowledge is defined as a multidimensional body of lived experiences that informs and sustains people who make their homes in a local area. In response to the U.S. government's demand for ownership of land in the 1850 treaty negotiations, Chief Seattle stated the basic philosophical stance underlying Indigenous ways of knowing: "This we know, that all things are connected like the blood that unites us. We did not weave the web of life; we are merely a strand in it—whatever we do to the web, we do to ourselves" (Kaiser, 1987).[1] This statement acknowledges a key tenet of Indigenous ways of knowing (IWOK): the interconnectedness of all things. IWOK also always take into account the current sociopolitical colonial power dimensions of the Western world (Denzin, Lincoln, and Tuhiwai Smith, 2008). Many educators have demonstrated their desire to better meet the needs of their Native students but have been limited in their training and ability to do so. Indigenous ways of knowing can assist them in helping students to recognize three forms of knowledge critical to the success of a transcultural education: cultural knowledge, survival knowledge, and academic knowledge (Brayboy, 2005). It is the firm belief of the authors that American schooling practices must go beyond their limited emphasis on objective school content to a more relevant subjective form of education with a primary focus on the development of human potential through creative transformation.

Three central ideas of IWOK emphasize (a) the use of cultural knowledge so that Indigenous communities can relate harmoniously to their environment, (b) survival knowledge to overcome the damage caused by the experience of colonization, and (c) academic knowledge, which provides an alternative perspective on human experience and learning that differs from or extends Western empirical science (Denzin et al., 2008, p. 144). Western education paradigms teach skill sets in isolated academic subject matters, while Indigenous paradigms place emphasis on natural processes of holistic learning at deep intellectual and spiritual levels. They emphasize creative acts of perception and cultural roots (Cajete, 1994). Kincheloe and Steinberg (1993) describe the educational and epistemological values of Indigenous knowledge in terms of its multilogicality, that is, how it blends perspectives in cognition that are reflected back through the cues received from the physical surroundings. When applied at a school-wide level, the underlying assumptions of IWOK can promote awareness of fluid contextual processes across curriculum. The underlying pedagogical assumptions of IWOK are conducive to creative intellectual pursuit, as opposed to simply acquiring objective conclusive perceptions. Fixico (2003) states that "Indian thinking is based on inquiry into relationships and community, and it bears reminding us that community extends beyond human relationships" (p. 7). Applying the philosophical foundations of IWOK to the methodological constructs of the schooling community has the potential for transformative sustainable changes in human behavior on a wide scale.

INDIGENOUS CULTURAL KNOWLEDGE

The authors of this chapter argue that the original goals for meeting the "unique needs of American Indian children," as outlined in government legislation, numerous reports, and in a growing body of professional literature, are critical in transforming the way knowledge and intellectualism is defined, promoted, and assessed for all children, whether American Indian or not. In this chapter, we argue that the fundamental difference between Indigenous and Western forms of knowledge lies in the alteration of the nature of education from one involving a natural process of holistic learning at a deep intellectual and spiritual level (the Indigenous), to one that limits creative acts of perception and seeks to pull school children "away from their cultural roots" (the Western) (Cajete, 1994). We also believe that localized Indigenous knowledge should become a pedagogical approach appropriate for all children. However, concerted efforts by educators and tribal communities alike must be made to validate the need for such an approach. If both Native and non-Native children are to benefit fully from public school education, all educators must themselves become students of life processes, challenging themselves and their students to think critically, not simply regurgitating information from textbooks.

Freire (1970) insists that without learning the processes of "inquiry and praxis" through the curricula, students cannot be "truly human"—able to pursue knowledge in the world, with the world, and with each other. To this end, it seems as though Indigenous ways of knowing have broad implications and the potential to benefit all students by helping them realize their connection and relationship with the world around them. Cajete (1994) outlines the key elements of a modern education founded on Indigenous epistemologies in his book *Look to the Mountain: An Ecology of Indigenous Education*. Cajete (1994) describes an *indigenized* public school education as follows:

> Education at the human level would be the conscious sensitizing of humans to the profound communications made by the universe about us, by the sun, the moon, and the stars, the clouds, the rain, the contours of the earth and all its living forms. All music and poetry of the universe would flow into the student; the revelatory presence of the divine, as well as insights into the architectural structures of the continents and the engineering skills whereby the great hydrological cycle functions in moderating the temperature of the earth in providing habitat for aquatic life, in nourishing the multitude of living creatures would be as natural to the educational process. The earth would also be our primary teacher of sciences, especially biological sciences, and of industry and economics. It would teach us a system in which we would create a minimum of entropy, a system in which there is no unusable or unfruitful junk. (p. 22–23)

INDIGENOUS SURVIVAL KNOWLEDGE

Extending the ideas of Critical Race Theory to the experiences of Indigenous people, Brayboy (2005) outlines the salient roots of Tribal Critical Race Theory and its use within American Indian education and scholarship. Using an Indigenous lens for examining phenomena seeks to meet the specific needs of tribal peoples and students by recognizing the profound impact of colonization and other oppressive U.S. policies that have removed tribal groups from their land, language, and culture. Duran and Duran (1995) use the term "soul wound" to identify the deep spiritual trauma left in the wake of white settlement, greed, and colonization. Brayboy (2005) maintains that colonization is endemic in society and within the microcosm of most (if not all) Westernized public schools. This critical lens works to reject both the conscious and unconscious assimilation practices in educational institutions in favor of more integrative, culturally sensitive, Indigenous, and community-centered learning (Brayboy, 2005). In this chapter, we are posing an even more radical stance than previously taken in earlier Indian education reform efforts—articulated by those who survived the rhetoric of assimilation policies in American schooling practices. In short, we suggest that Tribal Critical Race Theory stands to offer much in the way of CBPD and how education is appropriately delivered to Native students; like Cajete (1994), we also ardently support the idea of looking at American education through an Indigenous lens.

INDIGENOUS ACADEMIC KNOWLEDGE AND CULTURE-BASED PROFESSIONAL DEVELOPMENT

Culture-based professional development is a model of educator professional development based on building the relationships necessary in promoting mutual respect and friendship. It is intended to facilitate a process of growth specifically aimed at increasing the teaching/learning capacity of educators, administrators, and students in mainstream education institutions through the incorporation of Indigenous knowledge. Both Native and non-Native teachers must be fully committed to becoming students of IWOK for the specific purpose of embracing a "humanizing pedagogy that values the students' background knowledge, culture, and life experiences, and in creating learning contexts where power is shared by parents, communities, students and teachers" (Villegas, Neugebauer, and Vanegas, 2008, p.142).

For currently established mainstream public school institutions, CBPD is an important bridge toward the promotion of an education based on Indigenous/tribal knowledge for *all* Native and non-Native children. CBPD calls for attention to educational reform efforts at the local, school, and tribal level. These efforts should systematically address school functioning by engaging in a process of relationship building that shifts the current educational paradigm toward one that includes local Indigenous knowledge. Active engagement in CBPD requires educators (teachers, counselors, administrators, school board members, policy makers) to recognize the local tribal community as a valuable resource in producing sustainable changes for all children in schools. Therefore, it is important to understand the philosophy underlying the incorporation of IWOK into the professional development of teachers.

CBPD is not presented in this chapter as a new idea per se. Tribes, tribal education departments, parents of tribal children, and advocates for culture-based education (CBE) have readily offered their knowledge and expertise to educational institutions for generations. In fact, the theoretical roots for ideas like CBPD and CBE include other more humanizing paradigms from disciplines outside education. Duran, Firehammer, and Gonzalez (2008) explored applications for Barro's (1996) liberation psychology principles in addressing the soul wound present in many AI/AN families and individuals as a result of the shared colonization experience. With the obvious acknowledgment that Western schooling has been a divisive tool of colonization, such a theory lends clear insight into how to overcome histories of systemic oppression. Adams, Fryberg, Garcia, and Delgado-Torres (2006) put this simply: "If people do not identify instances of oppression, they are unlikely to mobilize resources to defend themselves against it." Here, then, we see that without an understanding of the Western education system's role in oppression of AI/AN's and other historically and/or socially marginalized groups, we cannot begin to fully address the needs of Native and non-Native youth or validate the vital constructs that make up their epistemological and ontological worldviews. CBPD, CBE, liberation psychology, and other paradigms embedded in Indigenous ways of knowing demonstrate such an understanding.

CBPD defines culture as fluid and inextricably linked to the establishment of relationships that serve to promote or demote culturally established norms. In the case of AI/AN as recipients of mainstream schooling practices, the relationships that have been established are foundationally weak and essentially confrontational. The confrontational nature of these relationships is best explained through a paradox of intention informing the conflicts between mainstream educational institutions and tribal/Indigenous communities. The child is literally caught between two worlds of conflicting intentions—those of mainstream Western paradigms, which inform educational standards and define academic success with achieving Adequate Yearly Progress as mandated by No Child Left Behind (2001), and those that emphasize maintaining a *unique* tribal/Indigenous identity as reflected in the culture, language, and traditions of their respective communities, traditions that also are the sovereign right of tribal children (Aguilera and LeCompte, 2008).

FOUR LEVELS OF RELATIONSHIP

Central to this model is a thorough examination of the patterns that connect constituents to established relationships (both past and present) so as to provide pertinent information in eliciting a responsive partnership based on mutual respect and friendship. CBPD includes four levels of relationship building informed by critical inquiry.

FIRST-LEVEL RELATIONSHIPS are characterized by patterns of knowledge unique to a particular tribe—for example, the history of schooling related to their experiences of assimilation practices, which interfere with the natural development of a healthy tribal/Indigenous identity. An active process of transformation is proposed through which tribal members themselves engage in dialogue designed to deconstruct an imposed reality and educators seek to more fully understand and appreciate tribal/Indigenous culture. Numerous resources are available for how to engage in this dialogue; however, the primary resource is the historical memory of the local tribal members.

Second-level relationships are categorized by the patterns of knowledge, attitudes and skills related to the surrounding non-Native community, such as perceptions of school, law enforcement, social and political issues of resource development, and access. These relationships are often established as a result of discord that has historical roots in colonization and oppression. In order to provide multicultural competency education and address concerns as they arise, community-wide efforts with a specific intention to improve these relationships must be engaged on a regular basis between community members, governing bodies, and other stakeholders (see Brayboy, 2005).

Third-level relationships are categorized by an in-depth assessment of first- and second-level [past and present] patterns in determining an appropriate plan of action for the establishment of a relationship based on mutual respect and friendship. Past relationships are intrinsically related to the present status of Indian education today. While some tribal/Indigenous people have fared well in school, the degree to which their identities are compromised is of equal concern in determining success from a tribal/Indigenous perspective. Again, the purpose of CBPD is to begin a process of transformation in school functioning that will allow tribal/Indigenous intellectualism to flourish in a meaningful and respectful way, one that is equal to the intellectualism of nontribal/Indigenous children Such a transformation will simultaneously foster mutual respect and friendship between the tribe and the school. This model is conceptual; it is dependent on both parties' courage to reflect honestly and their willingness to engage as equals in meaningful dialogue and action.

Fourth-level relationships are fully valued by both the tribe and the school and marked by equal drive and valuation in pursuit of ways to incorporate Indigenous ways of knowing into public school culture. While some transformational gains will be made if first-, second-, and third-level relationships are established, once fourth-level relationships are reached in any endeavor, change will occur. It is necessary to recognize that while the work of a few does not necessarily represent the views of all, and numerous challenges will arise in gaining consensus among parties, the one overarching shared goal of CBPD is to build a foundation of mutual respect and friendship. Therefore, the process is neither static nor definitively measurable; rather, it is fluid and intentional.

Facilitator Role

A neutral facilitator is critical in the process. Such a person should possess special knowledge in Indian education practices and policies, should be recognized as an advocate for CBE, should seek to provide educational services that promote IWOK, should have a clearly defined role within education networking systems, and should be committed to facilitating positive relationships designed to promote mutual respect and friendship. The facilitator is instrumental in maintaining open and respectful communication, providing credibility to the process—such as securing funding and offering professional development credits—maintaining the CBPD historical record in collaboration with the tribe and school, and assisting with identifying sustainable processes from which to build on. The facilitator will work closely with key persons from both the tribe and school communities to promote the collaborations necessary in building these relationships. Many of the processes proposed in this model will require that Indian education committees and boards, along with school persons currently engaged in increased academic achievement, be reestablished as CBPD learning communities. The tribe provides the primary knowledge base for learning, determines what information is important for educators to be "culturally sensitive" to tribal children in school, shares their knowledge, assists in the development of relevant curriculum, and provides a safe learning environment on tribal grounds for welcoming educators from the local school. The primary role of public school persons in the CBPD model is as students and collaborators in the promotion of Indigenous forms of knowledge for practical use in the classroom as well as in identifying systemic processes that denote the building of an Indigenous school community. While these roles are not "new" in the promotion of American Indian education endeavors, it may be necessary for those currently engaged to reevaluate the pretexts for which they serve in their prescribed roles toward the development of a new vision for advocacy.

ESSENTIAL RESOURCES LIST

The dedication of numerous researchers, authors, community members, and collaborators has gone into the development of resources that promote the basic tenets for which this model is based. The CBPD model has a resource list, which is essentially a compilation of scholarly materials deemed important to the development of educators serving tribal communities. The following will summarize only a few resources recognized by the authors as critical information in the formation of a CBPD-learning community; there are many more resources that are not listed here.

Northwest Native American Reading Curriculum
(Costantino and Hurtado, 2002)

This culturally appropriate reading curriculum was developed as a collaborative project between the Evergreen Center for Educational Improvement at the Evergreen State College and Office of Indian Education at the Office of Superintendent of Public Instruction in Olympia, Washington.

A Manual for Chief State School Officers and
State Education Agencies (CSSO manual)

The CSSO manual is a primary source for gaining critical knowledge on the political/social aspects of American Indian education in general. The CSSO manual was prepared by the Tribal Education Department National Association (TEDNA), with assistance from the Native American Rights Fund (NARF) in 2006. It is a compilation of pertinent information including historical Indian education law and policy beginning in 1776, a description of current federal Indian education programs, an overview of tribal sovereignty and elementary and secondary education including state public schools, suggested guiding principles for government-to-government relationships and suggested steps for resolution of issues, and a model protocol for state education agencies to address education issues on a government-to-government basis with tribal governments and tribal education departments. The model protocol of the manual is available online at www.narf.org.

Indigenous Culture Based Education Continuum
(Demmert, Hilberg, and Rawlins, 2008)

This instrument was developed to report on the influences of culturally based education on academic performance where the use and teaching of an Indigenous language in a culturally based education environment is currently taking place. The main purposes of the instrument are to provide a measure of culturally based education level in programs from which to identify and set goals for further learning and to identify relationships between the level of CBE to student academic performance and general well-being of students. Levels of CBE are determined on six identified critical elements. These include (1) recognition and use of Native American languages, (2) pedagogy that stresses traditional cultural characteristics and adult-child interactions as the starting place for education, (3) pedagogy in which teaching strategies are congruent with the traditional culture as well as contemporary ways of knowing and learning, (4) curriculum that is based on traditional culture and recognizes the importance of Native spirituality and places the education of young children in a contemporary context, (5) strong Native community participation in educating children and in the planning and operation of school activities, and (6) knowledge and use of the social and political mores of the community. This instrument, "Learn-Ed Nations Inventory: A Tool for Improving Schools with American Indian and Alaska Native students" is available from the Northwest Regional Educational Laboratory (NWREL) website at http://educationnorthwest.org/resource/562.

The Journal of American Indian Education (JAIE)

This publication was founded in 1961 and continues to publish papers directly related to the education of American Indian/Alaska Natives (AI/AN). The *JAIE* encourages dialogue between researchers and teachers through research-based scholarship and practitioner articles elucidating current innovations in the classroom. The goal of *JAIE* is to improve Native education through knowledge generation and transmission to classrooms and other educational settings. Information and special editions can be obtained via web at http://jaie .asu.edu.

American Multicultural Counseling Division's
Multicultural Competencies

The American Multicultural Counseling Division (AMCD) standards provide the critical knowledge needed to establish sincere and honest relationships based on mutual understanding and trust. The American Multicultural Counseling Division, a division of the American Counseling Association (ACA), provides standards to understand one's own preconceived values and judgments that may hinder the ability to relate to differences. They are intended to guide a process of self-awareness toward a better appreciation of the differences that exist among diverse groups. Information can be obtained online at www.counseling.org/. Numerous other forms of multicultural competency standards have been developed. The "Native American Awareness for Educators and School Psychologists" website (http://www.minotstateu.edu /schpsych/ndasp/Native.htm) provides a nice overview of Native American values, attitudes, and behaviors, together with educational considerations.

A list of other American Indian literature resources that can provide additional understanding of Indigenous education in the United States includes:

1. Deloria, V., and Wildcat, D. (2001). *Power and place: Indian education in America.* Golden, CO: Fulcrum Resources.
2. Cajete, G. (1994). *Look to the mountain: An ecology of Indigenous education.* Durango, CO: Kivaki Press.
3. Villegas, M., Neugebauer, S. R., and Venegas, K. R. (2008). *Indigenous knowledge and education: Sites of struggle, strength, and survivance.* Cambridge, MA: Harvard Education Press.
4. Mendoza, J., and Reese, D. (2001, Fall). Examining multicultural picture books for the early childhood classroom: Possibilities and pitfalls. *Journal of Early Childhood Research and Practice, 3*(2). University of Illinois–Urbana-Champaign. Available at http://ecrp .uiuc.edu/v3n2/mendoza.html.

5. Lomawaima, T. K., and McCarty, T. L. (2006). *To remain an Indian: Lessons in democracy from a century of Native American education.* New York: Teachers College Press.

SUMMARY AND CONCLUSION

It should be stated that if the specific tribal community is not involved in the professional development planning and training offered to educators, whether the training is provided by a consultant group, a mainstream college or university, or by the school, it is a generic "pan-Indian" training and *not* culture based or place based. It is also important to note that some states have adopted culturally informed standards as a collaborative effort with tribes to incorporate into the state curriculum standards. This effort must continue and local schools should educate teachers as to the importance of building relevance into the curriculum for Native children and in establishing a common bond. Native children need to see themselves in the curriculum, and non-Native children should be afforded the opportunity to learn and respect the Indigenous history and ways of knowing of the people in whose homelands they reside.

NOTE

1. Kaiser writes about the numerous versions of Chief Seattle's speech including Ted Perry's in 1978; see "Chief Seattle's Speech(es): American Origins and European Reception," published in Swann and Krupat, 1987, *Recovering the Word: Essays on Native American Literature*, pp. 497–536. Another source is David Buerge's article "Seattle's King Arthur: How Chief Seattle Continues to Inspire His Many Admirers to Put Words in His Mouth," appearing in the July 17, 1991, *Seattle Weekly*.

REFERENCES

Adams, D. W. (1995). *Education for extinction: American Indians and the boarding school experience 1875–1928.* Lawrence: University Press of Kansas.

Adams, G., Fryberg, S. A., Garcia, D. M., and Delgado-Torres, E. U. (2006). The psychology of engagement with Indigenous identities: A cultural perspective. *Cultural Diversity and Ethnic Minority Psychology, 12*(3), 493–508.

Aguilera, D. E., and LeCompte, M. D., (2008). Restore my language and treat me justly: Indigenous students' rights to their tribal languages. In J. C. Scott, D. Y. Straker, and L. Katz (Eds.), *Affirming students' right to their own language: Bridging educational policies to language/ language arts teaching practices* (pp. 130–72). London: Routledge and Taylor and Frances Group.

Aguilera, D. E., Lipka, J., Demmert, W. and Tippeconnic, J., III (Eds.). (2007). Culturally responsive schools serving American Indian, Alaska Native and Native Hawaiian Students. [Special Issue] *Journal of American Indian Education, 46*(3), 5–6.

Borman, G., Stringfield, S., and Rachuba, L. (2000). *Advancing minority high achievement: National trends and promising programs and practices.* College Entrance Examination Board, National Task Force on Minority High Achievement.

Bowman, N. R. (2005). *A critical, cultural, and contextual analysis of NCLB's impact on early childhood and elementary students.* Madison: Department of Educational Leadership and Policy Analysis, University of Wisconsin–Madison.

Brayboy, B. M. (2005). Toward a tribal critical race theory in education. *Urban Review, 37*(5), 425–46.

Cajete, G. (1994). *Look to the mountain: An ecology of Indigenous education.* Skyland, NC: Kivaki Press.

Constantino, M., and St. Charles, J. (2000). *Reading and the Native American learner research report.* State of Washington, Office of Superintendent of Public Instruction, Office of Indian Education.

Deloria, V., and Wildcat, D., (2001). *Power and place: Indian education in America.* Golden, CO: Fulcrum Resources.

Demmert, W., Jr., and Towner, J. (2003). *A review of the research literature on the influences of culturally-based education on the academic performance of Native American students.* Portland, OR: Northwest Regional Educational Laboratory.

Denzin, N. K., Lincoln, Y. S., Tuhiwai Smith, L. (2008). *Handbook of critical and Indigenous methodologies.* Los Angeles: Sage.

Duran, E., and Duran, B. (1995). *Native American postcolonial psychology.* Albany: State University of New York Press.

Duran, E., Firehammer, J., Gonzalez, J. (2008). Liberation psychology as the path toward healing cultural soul wounds: Expanding cultural considerations. *Journal of Counseling and Development, 86*(3), 288–95.

Everson, H., and Millsap, R. (2005). *Everyone gains: Extracurricular activities in high school and higher SAT scores.* College Board Research Rep. No. 2005–2. New York: College Entrance Examination Board.

Executive Order No. 13336, 3 C.F.R. (2004). Retrieved February 18, 2015, from the U.S. Government Publications Office website, www.gpo.gov/fdsys/pkg/CFR-2005-title3-vol1/html/CFR-2005-title3-vol1-eo13336.htm.

Fixico, D. (2003). *The American Indian mind in a linear world.* New York: Routledge.

Freeman, C., and Fox, M. (2005). *Status and trends in the education of American Indians and Alaska Natives.* NCES 2005–108. U.S. Department of Education, National Center for Education Statistics. Washington, DC: U.S. Government Printing Office.

Freire, P. (1970). *Pedagogy of the oppressed.* New York: Seabury Press.

Gilbert, W. S. (2010). Developing culturally based science curriculum for Native American classrooms. In J. Reyhner, W. S. Gilbert, and L. Lockard (Eds), *Honoring our heritage: Culturally appropriate approaches to teaching Indigenous students* (pp. 43–55). Flagstaff: Northern Arizona University. Retrieved January 7, 2014, from Northern Arizona University website, http://jan.ucc.nau.edu/~jar/HOH/.

Hall, D. (2005, June). Getting honest about grad rates: How states play the numbers and students lose. *The Education Trust.* Retrieved January 18, 2015, from www2.edtrust.org/NR/rdonlyres/C5A6974D-6C04-4FB1-A9FC-05938CB0744D/0/GettingHonest.pdf.

Hoffman, L., Sable, J., Naum, J., and Gray, D. (2005). Public elementary and secondary students, staff, schools, and school districts: School year 2002–03. Retrieved March 12, 2012, from National Center for Education Statistics website http://nces.ed.gov/pubsearch/pubsinfo.asp?pubid=2005314.

Jackson, H. H. (1885). *A century of dishonor: A sketch of the United States government's dealings with some of the Indian tribes.* Norman: University of Oklahoma Press.

Jalomo, R., Jr. (2000). Assessing minority student performance. In S. R. Aragon (Ed.), *Beyond access: Methods and models for increasing retention and learning among minority students: No. 112 (Winter 2000), New directions for community colleges* (pp. 7–18). San Francisco: Jossey-Bass.

Johnson, J, and Strange, M. (2007). *Why rural matters: The realities of rural education growth.* Rural School Community Trust. Retrieved December 10, 2011, from website http://www.ruraledu.org/articles.php?id=1954.

Kaiser, R. (1987). Chief Seattle's speech(es): American origins and European conceptions. In B. Swann and A. Krupat (Eds.), *Recovering the word: Essays in Native American literature* (pp. 497–536). Berkeley: University of California Press.

Kincheloe, J., and Steinberg, S. (1993). A tentative description of post-formal thinking: The critical confrontation with cognitive theory. *Harvard Educational Review, 63,* 296–320.

Louis, W., and Taylor, D. (2001).When the survival of language is at stake: The future of Inuttitut in Arctic Quebec. *Journal of Language and Social Psychology, 20*(1–2), 111–43.

Martín-Baró, I. (1996). In A. Aron and S. Corne (Eds.), *Writings for a liberation psychology.* Cambridge, MA: Harvard University Press.

McCoy, M. L. (2005). *Compilation of state Indian education laws.* Boulder, CO: Native American Rights Fund.

National Indian Education Association. (2005). *Preliminary report on No Child Left Behind in Indian country.* Washington, DC: Author. (Available at http://www.niea.org.)

Nichols, S., Glass, G. and Berliner, D. (2005). *High-stakes testing and student achievement: Problems for the No Child Left Behind Act.* EPSL-0509–105-EPRU. Tempe: Arizona State University, College of Education, Educational Policy Studies Laboratory, Education Policy Research Unit. Retrieved January 16, 2015, from http://edpolicylab.org.

No Child Left Behind Act. (2001). Public Law 107–110, § 1, Jan. 8, 2002, 115 Stat. 1425. Codified at 20 U.S.C. §§ 6301 et seq. Retrieved January 23, 2015, from the U.S. Department of Education website, www2.ed.gov/policy/elsec/guid/states/index.html#nclb.

Northwest Regional Educational Laboratory. (2002). Learn-Ed nations inventory: A tool for improving schools with American Indian and Alaska Native students. Retrieved January 27, 2014, from http://educationnorthwest.org/resource/562.

Reyhner, J. (2006). American Indian/Alaska Native education: An overview. Flagstaff: Northern Arizona University. Retrieved January 7, 2014, from http://jan.ucc.nau.edu/~jar/AIE/Ind_Ed.html.

Smith, G. A., and Tober, E. E. (2005, September). *Washington update.* Poster session presented at the annual conference of the National Indian Education Association, Denver, CO.

St. Charles, J., and Costantino, M. (2000). *Reading and the Native American learner research report.* Olympia, WA: Evergreen Center for Educational Improvement.

Utter, J. (1993). *American Indians: Answers to today's questions.* Lake Ann, MI: National Woodlands Publishing.

Villegas, M., Neugebauer, S., and Venegas, K. R. (Eds.). (2008). *Indigenous knowledge and education: Sites of struggle, strength and survivance.* Cambridge, MA: Harvard Education Press.

Williams, C. L., and Berry, J. W. (1991). Primary prevention of acculturative stress among refugees: Application of psychological theory and practice. *American Psychologist, 46,* 632–41.

10

Concluding Remarks

Exploring Indigenous Leadership in the Journey to Self-Determination

DOROTHY AGUILERA–BLACK BEAR

Decolonizing educational systems requires us to develop a critical consciousness about the function of remedial (a deficit model) education in stripping sovereignty and nation status away from tribal nations by systematically miseducating Indigenous populations. The educational system also miseducates others about tribal nations and Indigenous peoples and justifies the ongoing miseducation based on a racist dialogue about the achievement gap, lack of motivation, and lack of parent and community involvement among Indigenous people. Society as a whole has become more apathetic about the disparity in education between the "haves and the have nots" for millions of children.

My earlier research (Aguilera, 2003) revealed the relationship between leadership and reform in schools serving Native children.[1] It illuminated the critical contribution of collective action in our journey to self-determination that transpired in schools that implemented Indigenous controlled models of reform prioritizing culture-based education.

Culturally responsive education (CRE) is a right of Indigenous children, but indigenized leadership is imperative to achieving reform in schools that can both decolonize education and support cultural sovereignty. At the same time, mainstream higher educational institutions can establish community-based teacher and school leadership preparation programs that emphasize and provide the skills and experiences of place-based practice targeting the academic and social development of Native children and other educational goals as determined by the Indigenous community with whom they are serving.

INDIGENOUS LEADERSHIP FOUNDATIONS AND ROLES IN EDUCATION

Consider how the body of research summarized in this volume informs self-determination in education. It demonstrates the positive effects that ensue when Indigenous communities control, lead, and teach knowledge in their own educational systems, based on their own principles and standards. These scholars provide many examples of Indigenous leadership that are aligned with goals and needs of the local community, established within the community, and created, shaped, and facilitated by the community. This book provides both empirical and theoretical research with anecdotal evidence that adds to the sparse literature examining Indigenous leadership in communities and educational institutions, particularly highlighting the dynamics of leadership that necessarily must intersect complex social contexts. These scholars illuminate how educational leadership and teacher education programs in many ways support and extend the positive impacts these educators have had within their school communities and in higher education institutions. Their stories depict how Indigenous leaders build bridges between their communities and educational institutions in ways that are important to local efforts for achieving self-determination and shaping an education that serves tribal nations and Indigenous peoples. Several strands of the research and practice of Indigenous leadership highlighted by scholars in this book address community-based leadership, place-based leadership, administrative leadership, teacher education and professional development, all targeting the improvement of educational services and overall the learning experiences of Indigenous students. This research indicates the extent to which leadership drives processes that involve relationship building, collaboration, collective action, and alignment of academic, sociocultural, and human development goals across Indigenous communities and education institutions. Understanding how relationships are created and practiced and how these evolve over time within Indigenous communities is imperative to the fundamentals of Indigenous leadership. Acquisition of such knowledge, epistemologies, traditions, languages and how these are interrelated with practice and action occurs within the local context of Indigenous communities rather than solely from textbooks, literature, lectures, or conferences. In this book, multiple perspectives are shared on the principles and practices of leadership, including research participants' perspectives, experiences, and worldviews about leadership within both community and education institutional contexts. Several authors discussed the priority for shifting the dominance of Western knowledge within the mainstream academy because decolonizing education and self-determination in education involve a journey to reclaim Indigenous knowledge, languages, and cultural traditions. This book calls for a distinct shift from the dominance in the curricula of higher education professional development programs by Western paradigms for understanding leadership in schools. This shift represents respect for, and prioritization of, Indigenous knowledge, particularly in the localized educational programs implemented with Indigenous students in higher education institutions. This journey to self-determination and educational sovereignty has been the key focus of Indigenous scholars and community leaders for several centuries.

ELDERS AS LEADERS/MENTORS

The intellectual contribution offered in this book illustrates how several Indigenous communities have collectively decolonized education by creating a set of localized, culturally relevant processes involving educators and leaders from within the community and the higher education institution. The core of Indigenous knowledge systems to decolonize education and gain self-determination requires involving elders as leaders/mentors within the intergenerational relationship contexts of our communities. Leadership involves the proactive participation and collective action of an intergenerational community of elders, families, and children. The essence of a culturally strong and dynamic nation is to build its educational institutions on a foundation of knowledge—ideally its own knowledge is at the center. Elders should be acknowledged as educational leaders, whether in the context of family, community, or the educational institution. Understanding that deeply engrained and long-lived Indigenous epistemological ideas are localized knowledge systems spanning social structures and recognizing how these are essential domains in the daily lives of Native people is imperative to building the relationships with Indigenous leaders that support self-determination goals. Acknowledging the role and expertise of community leaders is important to those Western institutional leaders embarking on relationship building with Indigenous communities—particularly when seeking institutional funding that targets educational services to Indigenous populations. Power relations often undermine self-determination in education in these partnerships especially when programs are heavily informed by Western paradigms rather than Indigenous. The emphases on Indigenous frameworks that shape the educational programs, described by scholars in this book, reveal the dynamic leadership in Indigenous communities that is forging the frameworks for change and self-determination in education.

The authors of this book present contrasts between indigenized programs that emerge from communities and mainstream educational leadership programs that reflect different approaches to serving Native educators seeking advanced degrees in educational leadership. They also described differences between programs that are grounded in the local context rather than solely in a curriculum that provides the history, politics, social, and economic conditions of the American Indian population. While background information about Indian legislation and policies that either impede or mitigate educational sovereignty of Indigenous peoples is useful and the paradigms and educational theories informing the education of Indigenous populations are plentiful, these chapters, which are contextualized locally in teacher preparation programs and home grown with Native educators, begin to fill a void.

These studies point to how Indigenous communities and leaders have successfully prioritized localized Indigenous knowledge in leadership and teacher preparation programs for higher education. Community leadership is embedded in localized Indigenous knowledge, including historical and sociocultural contexts that are unique in the world. As argued by scholars in this book, leadership authority comes through the support and empowerment of the community and is awarded based on generosity, honesty, reciprocity, relationships, mentoring, and cultural knowledge. However, in considering how a leader from outside the community should respond to Indigenous values and belief systems, it is of substantial importance for the leader to have the skills and knowledge to value and respect how to engage in a community shaped by an Indigenous epistemology, such as the relationship of people to place. Such place- based leadership involves always keeping in the forefront an understanding of the relationship of people to place (McCarty, 2002).[2]

Familiarity with localized Indigenous knowledge is essential to this work. Often, Indigenous leadership scholars who professionally reside in mainstream academia also maintain close community ties, participating across varied sociocultural contexts. Through the processes of collaboration in community-based leadership contexts, they can hold leadership roles across both in their communities and their institutions. In these contemporary times, sustaining knowledge of cultural traditions and language requires equitable power relations among the community leaders and the institution's educational leaders. Decolonizing education involves building a leadership bridge by which community leadership has a leadership role in educational institutions as well as in the community. This is a fundamental principle that must not be overlooked in educational leadership; it is the foundation of building collaborative leadership and partnerships between Indigenous nation leaders, who represent the tribal institutions, and the educational leaders, who represent the Western institutions. Tenorio (2011) writes:

> The participation of tribal leadership in public school education requires a paradigm shift by those involved in the local schools and in state education agencies which oversee them. At a minimum, it requires the latter to recognize that tribal member involvement in policy and decision-making is not merely fundamental to equitable delivery of services, but also to the establishment of cultural respect; this in turn creates the authentic partnerships needed to build a pluralistic society. In its full manifestation, it would empower Indigenous community-based leadership for self-determination and the transformation of schools into more community-based institutions.[3] (pp. 2–3)

Tenorio reminds us that the most dynamic function of building culturally strong leadership in schools is not only the impact on student and family engagement in action but also the potential for broad social and economic development and change across the community.

INDIGENOUS LEADERSHIP
IN EDUCATION INSTITUTIONS

This book contributes to the literature on Indigenous leadership and education, especially with regard to decolonizing education. By garnering the political and cultural capital needed in higher education to create leadership models that encompass the tenets of self-determination, Native leaders are able to serve the interests of Indigenous communities. This research has provided examples of leadership models that are embedded in a blend of epistemologies informing curriculum, pedagogy, and research within higher education institutions, teacher education, and educational leadership programs. Battiste (2008) describes this blending of paradigms as "transsystemic" knowledge, a futuristic education evolving from within the contexts of community-based and institutional leadership visionaries. She elaborates:

> In those few exceptional places, communities, schools, colleges, universities, workplaces that have acknowledged the IK [Indigenous knowledge] issue, the struggle becomes developing "transsystemic" analyses and methods, of reaching beyond the distinct systems of knowledge of Eurocentrism, Indigenous and Africanisms, etc., to create fair and just educational systems and experiences. This is part of the ultimate educational struggle—the future horizon of education—a regeneration of new relationships among and between knowledge systems, as scholars competent in both knowledge systems seek to converge and reconcile them.[4] (p. 10)

As Battiste points out, competency in multiple knowledge systems is fundamental to creating new relationships among these epistemologies, especially with regard to transforming human thought and behavior. Learning additional epistemological knowledge enhances one's ability to navigate across diverse social worlds, which is historically what Indigenous peoples have accomplished in their journeys to survive extreme situations. Examining the research literature to identify successful language and cultural knowledge revitalization projects and the leaders behind these educational sovereignty movements provides clear lessons about leadership. Among the many studied are the Native Hawaiian, Diné (Navajo), and Alaska Native communities, all whose leaders were diligent in their decades of commitment to establish language immersion programs in schools that continue today. These case studies describe how those leaders created the structures and processes by which elders—the carriers/teachers of language and cultural knowledge— could focus on developing the curriculum materials and pedagogy needed to create processes for developing and implementing standards and assessments.[5] Additionally, these community leaders created the higher education

Native teacher preparation programs that have begun to establish a "pipeline of Native educators," where streams of language fluent students from immersion schools choose to serve their communities by earning education degrees and becoming teachers in the same school systems they attended as children. Leadership emerged from within these Indigenous communities to establish schools that provide effective education programs for children (Aguilera and LeCompte, 2007).[6] Key components of successful reclamation and restoration models include shared leadership visions and strategic plans to establish a culturally responsive educational system and standards, professional development programs to establish and support the preparation of teachers and leaders, and resource development.

Leadership in educational institutions involves maintaining a consciousness of the goals of self-determination and decolonization of education through culturally responsive education; this, in turn, must be developed within a localized community context. Indigenous intellectual knowledge is fundamental to leadership that serves community needs. Indigenous leadership implies spiritual significance, as described in oral and historical narratives, especially as it pertains to localized contexts. Implicit in the literature is the fact that Indigenous leadership is shared and community based for the purposes of serving specific needs of the community. Individuals are asked to serve as leaders by their community. Shared leadership represents holistic systems of leadership in which community members share in community development, safety, education, economic development, governance, and sustainability.

CONTRADICTIONS AND TENSIONS

This research also illustrates inroads made in accessing educational leadership and teacher education programs in higher education institutions, inroads that are the result of decades of efforts by Native parents, educators, and leaders from Indigenous communities.[7] While these efforts also represent federal funding efforts devoted to professional development grants in the U.S. and Canadian education institutions, Native leaders are the catalysts for self-determination in academia and within their local communities.

However, this progress is overshadowed by the reality that a disproportionately high number of Native children and youth do not experience the same opportunities to learn their cultural knowledge, languages, and histories in their tertiary education as white students do. The root of this inequity is the overwhelming tendency of Eurocentric dispositions among school administrators, who serve state and federal mandates by the widespread use of assimilationist models of education. These non-Indigenous dispositions of administrators are in response to the notion that Indigenous culture is a problem rather than strength in children. These dispositions also frame the knowledge that is taught in schools serving Indigenous populations. The severity of this situation requires a closer look at making available Indigenously framed professional development programs and resources not currently existing in school communities and establishing coalitions among educational systems that can share resources with partner schools.

This issue emphasizes the importance of culturally responsive education in the schools serving high numbers of Native children. While professional development programs in higher education have led to increases in the numbers of Native educators in preK–12 schools, the No Child Left Behind era, with its accountability mandates and the priority it gives to English-Only and Western knowledge, continues to deplete the cultural knowledge and language education that Native children deserve and to which they have legal rights. Native educators who have the knowledge to establish culturally responsive education are confronted by the national education system's fixation on assimilation and high stakes testing, neither of which contribute to the healthy development of Native children. The accountability system has severely limited equitable educational services for Indigenous communities.

ACCOUNTABILITY OF EDUCATION INSTITUTIONS IN DECOLONIZING EDUCATION

This compilation of research also reveals the asymmetrical power relations and resulting tensions that continue to exist within higher education and preK–12 education with regard to the education of Native children. These must subside in order for Indigenous communities to fully realize the benefits of decolonizing education and self-determination efforts. While equity in education is included as an educational leadership initiative in some states, misinterpretation is widespread on what equity means and what access to an equitable education involves with regards to tribal nation communities.

Furthermore, misinterpretation of self-determination and language rights legislation adds to the inequities in educational programs and services that undermine self-determination and Native children's rights to their cultural knowledge systems. Schools providing educational services to tribes receive educational funding for No Child Left Behind entitlement programs, which have guidelines that support Indigenous language, cultural knowledge, and history. However, federal and state administrators of education policies and programs often ignore Indigenous students' rights and misapply the funds to English only and Eurocentric educational mandates, even when those policies contradict federal legislation for self-determination and legal rights to language and culturally relevant education (Aguilera and LeCompte, 2008).[8] These anti-Indigenous practices and policies in education have gone on far too long with devastating outcomes to Indigenous communities. It is a moral imperative for leadership at all levels of educational institutions and government to be accountable for cultural knowledge standards set by Indigenous communities. It is time to end all federal mandates for Eurocentric education services to tribal nation communities and to honor the rights of Indigenous peoples to their Indigenous knowledge systems in education institutions.

Tribes have access to a government-to-government system described as state compacts that often include a seat at the table with department of education administrators. These compacts provide an arena in which to address educational issues, community conditions, and resources to improve educational services to tribes. In some states the government-to-government structure involves cluster meetings between tribal nation leaders and directors with state administrators in education and health and human services branches. Oregon's nine confederated tribes participate in the government-to-government structure to address and resolve educational issues. These include higher education and preK–12 education clusters, which are essential to the tribal nations' efforts not only to decolonize education and exercise their rights of self-determination within educational systems but also to ensure that these systems serve the interests of Indigenous populations and tribal nations. An example is when mainstream higher education institutions apply for professional development grants to fund educational leadership and teacher education programs for Native graduate students. In these cases, institutions often request tribal nation leaders to write a partnership agreement, usually a memorandum of agreement (MOA), supporting the grant application. However, that exchange of signatures on the MOA document may be the extent of the relationship, rather than a truly equitable partnership between the tribal nation and its governing structure, education departments, schools, and higher education institutions. The majority of states (forty-four) have responded to efforts by Native leaders to create the structure and process of sovereignty at the state level for their tribal communities to enact goals that are established by federal self-determination legislation. State commissions and committees on Indian Affairs are forums that exist in many states. They were created, according to the National Conference of State Legislatures (NCSL), for the purpose of improving state-tribal relations.[9] Often both the stability and the impact of these efforts have been adversely influenced by priorities set by the state's elected legislators and leaders, who do not understand tribal sovereignty, particularly as it relates to education and self-determination for tribal nations.[10]

In an initiative to further the tribal nations' goals of self-determination in education in the early 1990s, the Native American Rights Fund partnered with Carnegie Corporation of New York to develop legal resources for tribal nations to establish their own education departments. The project primarily involved developing tribal education laws and reforming state and national Indian education legislation. Essential to a tribe defining its rights and goals along with its ability to effectively control education, tribal education laws have been nonexistent, except for a few tribes. However, they are critical to "delineating the forum and process for establishing tribal and non-tribal government-to-government relationships and working agreements on common education issues and goals" (McCoy, 1997, p. 6).[11] McCoy (1997) elaborates on tribal nations' roles in educational sovereignty:

> Indian tribes are sovereign governments just as are their state and federal counterparts. Many federal reports and some federal and state laws have focused on Indian education problems. Some reports and laws have pointed out the need to increase the role of tribal governments to address the problems. But instead of requiring active tribal government involvement, most federal and state education programs and processes circumvent tribal governments and maintain non-Indian federal and state government control over the intent, goals, approaches, funding, staffing, and curriculum for Indian education. And there are no effective programs to establish tribal education codes or operate tribal education departments. (p. 4)

At the National Indian Education Association (NIEA) Leadership Forum, issues such as these were discussed by tribal leaders, faculty/administrators, community leaders, and Native school leaders. Shifting power relations between state and federal governments by addressing self-determination and equity issues with these institutional leaders was a key point made by these attendees, noting that doing so is necessary to impact educational outcomes. Another shared need is a stronger commitment by state departments of education to work with the tribal and community leaders to use the already established Indigenous educational principles to decolonize education for Native populations. McCoy (1993) argues:

> The three sovereign governments in this country have a major stake in Indian education. Common sense dictates that tribal governments have the most interest because it is their children at stake, their most precious resource, and their future for perpetuating the tribe. Some progress has been made because of Indian education programs, Indian parent committees, Indian school boards, and tribally-controlled colleges. Some progress has been made through a measured amount of tribal control and input under laws that include the Indian Education Act of 1988, the Indian Self-Determination and Education Assistance Act of 1975, the Elementary and Secondary Act of 1965, and the Impact Aid Laws of 1950.[12] (p. 1)

The forum attendees noted that legislators and administrators of education continue to perpetuate state and federal control of education, despite legislation supporting tribal self-determination. State education institutions must be held accountable for their ethical responsibility to understand what it means to enter into a partnership (an MOA is a legal contract) with a tribal nation and receive federal funds to provide educational services to its tribal members. Several chapters in this volume described the community protocols and collaborative processes by which higher education should conduct partnerships with Indigenous communities. This body of research suggests it is imperative for tribal nation leaders to hold accountable institutions of higher education for establishing equitable partnerships with tribes and schools in support of decolonizing education in schools serving Indigenous communities. The same accountability should be expected of state and federal government agencies that continue to maintain authority and control of funds dictating what and how human, health, and education services are distributed to Indigenous communities. Addressing accountability issues in the context of mainstream education institutions and government entities exposes both limited literature and lack of understanding about Indigenous issues among government-funded institutions. Previous leadership forums with tribal leaders and scholars identified the need for mainstream higher education to provide accurate accounts of tribal nations to dispel misinformation about Indigenous peoples, as well as a need for self-education among government officials at local, state, and federal levels about the history, culture, and values of tribal nations and communities.[13] This book will help to educate those individuals who have an interest in Indigenous education and those who are accountable to the tribal nations for which they administer educational programs.

CONCLUSION

This book reveals how alliances are important to the work of mainstream institutions of education. Just as essential are collaborations with leaders in tribal colleges and universities. Building capacity for decolonizing education can be achieved by developing partnerships and coalitions that are grounded within the localized Indigenous knowledge systems across tribal higher education, agencies, and preK–12 education institutions. These can be achieved with institutional leaders who have already begun those efforts or expressed the desire to do so.

Higher education institutions should create opportunities for community-based leaders, particularly elders, to join in establishing Indigenous education programs that will provide access to culturally responsive education for Native students. Tribal community leadership roles in education institutions must initiate a shift in hegemonic power structures that represents true accountability for decolonizing education and providing institutional support for Indigenous self-determination. Involving elders in the decision-making processes as legitimate leaders in these institutional processes for equitable education systems is important, as they are the cornerstones of sovereignty in tribal nation communities. Continuing to encourage intergenerational leadership mentoring of younger tribal members by elders so as to sustain traditional leadership roles and practices is essential to Indigenous sovereignty. Accountability reaches beyond institutions into Indigenous communities, where leadership and other cultural resources are critical to sustaining Indigenous knowledge systems across generations. This is the mark of truly investing in educational sovereignty, and it has been initiated with the tribal college higher education system. However, funding inequities, as compared to mainstream and other land-grant institutions of higher education, have limited the impact tribal colleges can have in developing a cadre of highly skilled Native educators and leaders for local schools. Native educators must define their purpose and methods by Indigenous, not Western, standards and be accountable to their communities for sustaining cultural traditions and Indigenous knowledge systems. Tribal colleges have led the way in decolonizing education by establishing standards fundamentally relevant to the tribal nation communities they serve. They provide greater economic value through an educated populace from which is emerging new generations of tribal leaders. Mainstream institutions interested in supporting the educational sovereignty and self-determination goals of tribal nations should partner with tribal colleges to better understand how and where they can make the most positive contributions.

NOTES

1. See more on this topic in Aguilera, D. E. (2003). Who Defines Success: An Analysis of Competing Models of Education for American Indian and Alaskan Native Students (Doctoral dissertation). University of Colorado–Boulder.

2. Read more on this topic with Teresa McCarty's book *A Place to Be Navajo: Rough Rock and the Struggle for Self-determination in Indigenous Schooling"* (2002).

3. See more on community-based leadership in Tenorio, M. (2011), "Community-Based Leadership Praxis: Re-Defining Self-Determination in a Native Early College High School" (Doctoral dissertation). Lewis and Clark College, Department of Educational Leadership, Portland, Oregon.

4. Battiste, M. (2008). Animating Indigenous knowledge in education: From resilience to renaissance. Keynote presentation at the World Indigenous People's Conference (WIPCE), December 2008, Australia.

5. See the Alaska Native Knowledge Network's cultural standards and guidelines for each of the dimensions of revitalizing and sustaining Indigenous languages. Retrieved on December 2, 2011, from http://ankn.uaf.edu/publications /index.html#standards.

6. See more in Aguilera, D. E., and LeCompte, M. D. (2007). Resiliency in native languages: The tale of three Indigenous communities' successes with language

revitalization and preservation. In Aguilera, Lipka, Demmert, and Tippeconnic (Eds.) [Special Issue], *Journal of American Indian Education, 46*(3), 11–37.

7. Native American community is a term used here because it is inclusive of Native Hawaiian peoples, who are not yet recognized as federal tribal nations but are state recognized as Native people with sociocultural, political, and linguistic rights enforced by state legislation.

8. See more in Aguilera, D. E., and LeCompte, M. D. (2008). Restore my language and treat me justly: Indigenous students' rights to their Tribal languages. In Scott, Straker, and Katz (Eds.), *Affirming students' right to their own language: Bridging educational policies to language/language arts teaching practices* (pp. 130–72). London: Routledge.

9. State commissions and committees contact information are listed on the NCSL website. Retrieved December 6, 2011, www.ncsl.org/issues-research/tribe /state-tribe-relations-state-committees-and-commi.aspx.

10. See the Native American Rights Fund publication, "A manual for chief state school officers and state education agencies" (2006) at http://www.narf.org/pubs /misc/csso.htm.

11. Read more on this topic and the issues in McCoy, M. (1997, p. 4-6), "Tribalizing Indian education" at http://www.narf.org/pubs/edu/yellow.pdf.

12. McCoy, M. (1993; 1997). Tribalizing Indian education. Boulder, CO: The Native American Rights Fund. Retrieved June 17, 2015, from http://www.narf.org /wordpress/wp-content/uploads/2015/01/yellow.pdf.

13. Klopotek, B. (1997). Focusing our vision: American Indian urban higher education initiative. Symposium Report. St. Paul, MN: University of Minnesota, The American Indian Research and Policy Institute. Retrieved June 17, 2015, from http://www.cura.umn.edu/sites/cura.advantagelabs.com/files/publications /PUBS_M9704.pdf.

Index

Figures and tables are indicated with *italicized* page numbers.

aboriginal epistemology, 6
Aboriginal, use of term, 95n2
academic knowledge, 131–32, 180–81, 183–84
academic success. *See* student success
accountability: for cultural knowledge, 200; decolonization and, 199–202; doing the "right things" and, 155; higher education, 202; NCLB standards, 144, 199; standardized testing and, 148–49; tribal colleges and universities (TCUs), 45–46
Adequate Yearly Progress measures, 184
administrative framework: administrator standards, 145; for American schools, 105; explicit institutional routines, 109; government-to-government structure, 200; implicit behavioral routines, 109; Indigenized leadership program creation, 122; institutional ownership, 11; Native administrator qualifications, 118–19; Native administrator roles, 111–14; Native participation in decision making, 110–11; non-Indigenous dispositions of administrators, 198–99; preparedness and professional development, 119–20; reducing institutional barriers, 109; regional school districts, 106; Theory Z + N, 108–10; Theory Z, 106–108, *107*; turnover among non-Native administrators, 119; Type A, *107*, *107t*
advocates for Native concerns, 112–13; all my relations, 131; choice of graduate programs, 127; community, 131; in educational leadership graduate programs, 127, 131
Alabama, 23–24
Alaska: Native participation in decision making, 110–11; regional school districts, 106
Alaska Native Claims Settlement Act (1971), 108
Alaska Natives: epistemological perspectives, 168; State Operated School System, 106. *See also* Tlingit people
American Counseling Association (ACA), 188
American Indian Higher Education Consortium (AIHEC), 36–37; archives, 38; membership, 36
American Indian literature resources, 188
American Indian Movement, 38
American Indian Religious Freedom Act (1978), 19, 22, 31n6
American Indian Sites of Conscience project, 27
American Multicultural Counseling Division (AMCD), 188
antipoverty programs, 38
Asian Critical Race Theory, 121
Assembly of First Nations, 77
assimilation: early history, 18; higher education and, 35–36; schools and, 4; survival knowledge and, 183
Association of British Columbia Deans of Education, 90

bicultural skills, 113
boarding schools, 18, 26–27
Bordeaux, Lionel, 39, 43
British Columbia, 76; Indigenous
    teachers in, 78; regional Indian
    education conferences, 87
British Columbia Native Indian
    Teachers' Association, 77
Bull, Adam B., Jr., 24–25
Bureau of Indian Education: Effective
    Schools Team, 31n13; school
    governance, 144; schools funded, 179

Canada: failure of public education, 77;
    Indigenous rights, 77. See also British
    Columbia; Native Indian Teacher
    Education Program (NITEP)
Candeska Cikana Community College
    (CCCC), 46
Carnegie Corporation of New York, 200
ceremonies: intertribal, at Haskell, 28; of
    place, 26; at sacred sites, 22
challenges, Hawaiian principles for
    overcoming, 59t, 64–65
change: building commitment to, 151–52;
    conflicts over, 152; education and,
    166; leadership and, 166–71; social
    justice responsibility and, 167–68
change agents, 88, 89; graduate
    programs, 130, 131, 134; social justice,
    134
change, need for, 147
charter schools, Hawaiian, 62
Chief State School Officers (CSSO)
    manual, 187
Chile, 168
Christianity, 18
civil and Native rights movement, 35–36;
    access to higher education, 38
coal, 29
code of conduct, 55
Coffey, Wallace, 21, 22
collaborative leadership style, 165
collaborative learning, 174–75
collective action, self-determination
    and, 193
college entrance rates, 36

College of Muscogee Nation, 39–40
colonial epistemologies, 6
colonization: critical race theory
    on, 121; Indian writers on, 23;
    through Indigenous lens, 182; of
    Indigenous minds, 3; Indigenous
    survival knowledge, 182; individual
    actions and, 135; intergenerational
    impact, 82; lands profaned by, 16;
    power dimensions, 180; redefining
    education on Indigenous terms,
    88; as soul wound, 182, 184; subtle
    experiences of, 133
Comanche people, 17; Medicine Bluffs,
    20–22; tribal leadership, 21
commitment to the whole journey, 59t,
    65–68
communication dynamics, 151; diverse
    views and, 165–66; making parents
    welcome, 172; with parents, 156; tribal
    political representatives, 173
community: advocates for Native
    concerns, 112–13, 131; British
    Columbia, 81; college influence in,
    42–43, 44; curriculum values and,
    161; defining, 7; elder role, 195–96;
    female leadership, 169; historically
    and culturally informed context,
    13–14; holistic model on, 80–81;
    Indian thinking on, 181; Indigenous
    leadership scholars' ties to, 196;
    intergenerational mentors and role
    models, 118, 203; involvement in
    professional development planning
    and training, 189; involvement of,
    171, 172–73; leadership bridge needed,
    196; outreach and involvement, 161;
    principal and, 147, 155; relationship
    building, 150; respect for, 14; role in
    self-determination, 99; role of school,
    172; staffing Native schools, 106
community agency, 88
community-based leadership, 13–14
community leadership: acknowledging
    role and expertise of, 195; basis of
    authority, 196; conversations with
    educational leaders, 8; creation of

teacher education programs, 197–98;
for improving schools, 8
competitiveness as value, 24, 117
complaints, handling, 156
confidence, graduate programs, 132
conscience dialog, 18–19
consensus building, 151; new principal's
role and, 157–58
conversational style, 148
Cook, Captain, 61
counternarrative research, 30
Coyote, 134–35
creation stories, 18
critical race studies, 121, 182
Critical Race Theory (CRT), 121
critical theory, social justice and, 168
Crow tribe, 29
cultural brokers, 113
cultural bureaucrats, 111–12
cultural curriculum integration, 171,
173–75
cultural heritage, deficit model, 161–62
cultural identity: curriculum and,
173–75; Hawaiian principles, 58t,
61–63; intergenerational impact
of colonization, 82; land and,
19; language and, 54; language
revitalization programs and, 23–34;
leadership models and, 73; life force
and, 53; student achievement and,
62–63; teachers as change agents, 88;
Tlingit, 105; tribal colleges and, 37
cultural knowledge, 180–82;
accountability for, 200;
administrators, 113–14; generational
loss of, 19; intergenerational mentors
and role models, 118, 203; non-Native
educators and, 175
cultural knowledge revitalization, 197
culturally responsive education (CRE):
integration and assimilation versus,
4; need for indigenized leadership,
193; NITEP in British Columbia,
100; professional development
programs and, 199; questions raised,
100; self-determination and, 4–5;
skills needed, 99; standards-based

education versus, 147; struggle to
attain, 7; training Native principals,
146
culturally responsive leadership, 161, 162
cultural traditions, impact on leadership,
169–71
culture: CBPD definition of, 184–85;
changes, 161; decisions in culturally
complex society, 120; use of concept,
120–21
culture-based education (CBE), 13,
117–18, 183–84; advocating for, 185;
Indigenous Continuum instrument,
187; Learn-Ed Nations Inventory, 187;
six critical elements, 187
culture-based professional development
(CBPD), 180; described, 183–84;
facilitator role, 185–86; four levels
of relationship, 184–86; learning
communities, 186; "pan-Indian"
training, 189; plan of action, 185;
resources list, 186–89; Tribal Critical
Race Theory and, 183
culture bearers, 118
curriculum, necessary components, 99
Cuyuga, 20

Damien, Father, 72
Dawes Act (1887), 18
decision making: collaboration and
inclusiveness in, 176; data-informed,
166; elders in, 202–203; Native
participation in, 110–11
decolonization, 3; accountability issue,
199–202; building capacity for, 202;
consciousness of goals of, 198; in
education, 84; Indigenous leadership
in higher education, 197; leadership
bridge needed, 196; overview, 195;
process of decolonizing education,
193; state departments of education,
201
deficit model of education, 100, 161–62
degree attainment rates, 36
delegation, art of, 149–50
DeRose, DeDe, 76, 85, 89–90
Diné College, 36, 38–39

Diné-Hopi Cohort Leadership Program
(DHCLP), 142; described, 145–46;
goals, 146; leadership lessons, 148–57;
reasons for joining program, 147;
research findings, 147–48; topics
included, 146. *See also* principals
study (NAU)
distance education, 162
diversity: among future leaders, 167–68;
among Native peoples, 16; among
reservation-based schools, 144;
communication and, 165–66

education: defining, 4; equity in, 198, 199;
future horizon of, 197; Indigenous
systems of, 4; inequalities and
societal attitudes, 193; use of term, 4;
Western view of, 4
educational leadership: career
beginnings, 14; community
beginnings, 14
educational leadership doctoral
programs, 116; creation of, 122;
curriculum, 122–23; educational
outcomes related, 117–20; effective
components, 130–34; implications
of study, 134–36; Indigenous lenses,
120–21; Native American leadership,
120; recommendations for, 136;
research study on, 123–30; themes
facilitating retention, 124–25, 130–31.
See also graduate degrees
educational leadership programs, 194;
contradictions and tensions, 198–99;
in Indigenous communities, 13;
overview, 195; prioritizing localized
Indigenous knowledge, 195–96;
recommendations for, 176–77
educational sovereignty, 5; components
of, 5; first step, 99; lessons about
leadership, 197; localized leadership
and, 13; at local level, 8; overview, 7;
requirements for, 100; resistance and,
19–22; tribal nations' roles, 201
effective schools model, 31n13
elders: as leaders-mentors, 195–96;
Hawai'i, 22–23, 62; and higher

education, 44–45; intergenerational
leadership of, 118, 203; involving
in decision making, 202–203;
outreach and involvement, 161;
respect for expertise, 70; support of
grandparents, 172; tribal member
resources and, 173
Elementary and Secondary Education
Act (ESEA), 114n1, 201
emotional climate in schools, 150
entry plan for principals, 157
epistemologies compared, 6
evidence-based practice, 161, 165
Executive Order 13336 (2004), 179
extracurricular and tribal activities, 172

family: graduate studies and priorities,
129; learning from, 80; support for
graduate studies, 125–26
Family and Child Education Program
(FACE), 174
Family Education Model, 131
fear, uses of, 65
federal educational policies criticized,
99; beneficiary relationship, 111
first-level relationships, 184
First Nations Education Council
(FNEC), 81, 90
First Nations House of Learning, 88
First Nations Longhouse, 88
forced removal, 16, 40
formal education, 4
"fort" Indians, 15
Fort Sill, 20–21
fourth-level relationships, 185
Franklin, Benjamin, 20
Freire, Paulo, 168, 182

geographic place, sense of, 15. *See also*
place, sense of
Gitxsan First Nation, 85, 86–87
goals: Native girls, 169; parents and, 168
Goals 2000, 41–42
government-to-government structure,
200
graduate degrees, 119, 120; advocacy
focus, 127; cohort member support,

125; concerns about, 128–29; confidence, 129–30; creating an indigenized leadership program, 122; deepening comprehension, 127–28; distance education students, 132–33; efficacy and challenges, 132–33; family member support, 125; good fit with program, 126; implications and conclusions, 134–36; mentors and academic persistence, 130–31; retention issues, 124–25, 130–31; support from crucial people, 125–26. *See also* educational leadership doctoral programs; higher education
grandparents, 172
grounded qualitative data analysis theory, 163

Harbuck, LaGaylis, 23–24, 25
hardships and challenges, overcoming, 59t, 64–65
Haskell Indian Nations University, 26–28; AIHEC member, 36; as site of conscience, 28; history, 27
Hatathli, Ned, 41
Hawaiʻi: epistemological structures, 49; Native Hawaiian peoples, 204n7; sacred lands, 22; three legendary journeys summarized, 49, 50
Hawaiian Ethnic Identity (HEI) scale, 49
Hawaiian language revitalization movement, 52–57; commitment to, 67; guiding principles, 58–60t; Hawaiian speakers, 72; history, 64; immersion programs, 64; legacy, 72; making good choices, 69; obstacles, 65; respect for elder expertise, 70
health indicators, Hawaiian, 61–62
hegemonic education systems, 7
higher education: accountability, 202; assimilationist ethic, 35, 133; community-based teacher and leadership preparation programs, 193; degree attainment, 116; equitable partnerships with tribes and schools, 202; history, 35; Indigenous leadership in, 197–98; Indigenous

lens, 135; mainstream values in, 43; opportunities needed, 202; problems with pursuing, 17; Western institutions critiqued, 135. *See also* graduate degrees; tribal colleges and universities (TCUs)
high-stakes exams, 135
history: Hawaiian, 61; tribal patterns of knowledge, 184–85
history education, 41; family history and kinship, 43
holistic learning, Western forms of knowledge compared, 181–82
holistic learning model, 79–81, *80*, 81
holistic relationships, 80–81
honua in Hawaiian culture, 56
hospitality as value, 55
humility as cultural value, 175

identity: leadership and, 23; tribal colleges and, 37
Impact Aid Laws of 1950, 201
inclusion strategies, 117
Indian Control of Indian Policy (1972, Canada), 77, 87
Indian Education Act of 1988, 201
Indian education critiqued, 43
Indian Nations at Risk Task Force Final Report, 41–42, 118
Indian Removal Act, 24. *See also* removal policies
Indian Self-Determination and Education Assistance Act Public Law No. 93-638 (1975), 5, 201; Titles I and II, 10n7
Indigenous epistemologies: as localized knowledge systems, 195; use of term, 6
Indigenous faculty, 100; turnover rates in Southwest, 143–44
Indigenous knowledge: acquisition as process, 170; educational attainment and, 180; epistemological perspectives and leadership, 167; lost or hidden, 37; multilogicality, 181; prioritizing localized, 195–96; recapturing at colleges, 43; salient features, 170–71

Indigenous lens, impact of colonization, 182

Indigenous principles for effective educational leadership summarized, 176

Indigenous Raven, 76

Indigenous ways of knowing (IWOK), 180–81; broad implications, 182; incorporating into public school culture, 185; public education, 185–86; specific purposes of, 183; three forms of knowledge, 180–81. *See also* ways of knowing

Indigenous worldviews, 6; as foundation for children, 57; coming-to-know, 170; confrontations with, 135; epistemological perspectives and leadership, 167; Hawaiian, 54–55; holistic, 170

individualism, 135

industrial model, 105, 107

informal education, 4

intellectual capital, 7

interlibrary loan service, 132–33

International Coalition of Sites of Conscience, 26, 27, 32n14

international indigenous education community, 37

Inventory of Exemplary Hawaiian Leadership Behaviors, 50

Iroquois Confederacy, 17, 20

Jefferson, Thomas, 18, 20, 30n3

Journal of American Indian Education (JAIE), 188

Kamehameha the Great, 52, 63–64; on challenges, 65; commitment to the whole journey, 66–67; guiding principles, *58–60t*; legacy, 71–72; prophecy, 63; recognition in mainstream, 72; respect for mentors, 69–70; respect for spirituality, 68–69

Kansas, 26, 28

Kekūhaupiʻo, 69–70

Kirkness, Verna, 76, 87–89

Kīwlaʻō, 66, 68–69

knowledge: educators as sole proprietors, 104–105; epistemological perspectives, 167, 170; transsystemic, 197

knowledge and skill sets, 164–66

Kumu Honua Mauli Ola Philosophy, 51, 52–57; guiding principles of Indigenous leadership, 57, *58–60t*, 61–72

Lakota people, 131

land: as "empty," 16–17; in British Columbia, 81; cultural identity and, 19; engagement with, 29; homelands of tribes, 19; meaning of, 19; natural resources on, 29; sacred sites, 22; sense of place, 15; TCUs and, 40; tribal efforts to reclaim, 29

land-grant institutions, 44

language: in Hawaiian culture, 54; importance of native tongue, 54; power of, 54

language revitalization programs: British Columbia, 93; cultural identity and, 23–34; Hawaiian, 52–57; research on, 197

language rights legislation, 199

languages: preservation and restoration, 47, 173; word for "leadership," 175

Latino Critical Race Theory, 121

leadership: alumni, 89–90; as "place based," 17; as shared and community-based, 198; behaviors, Hawaiian, 50; collaborative style of, 165; cultural lens for, 72; culturally responsive, 161, 162; in diverse communities, 17; by elders, 195–96; foundations and roles in education, 193–94; Hawaiian guiding principles, 57, 58, *58–60t*, 61–72; Hawaiian perspective, 49, 50–51; identity and, 23; through Indigenous lenses, 120–21; Indigenous principles for effective (summarized), 176; models compared, 72; in Native American paradigm, 120; Native leadership in education, 8, 9; need for, 116; place and, 23; qualities listed,

158; research on, 194; responsive, 153–55; sacred place and, 29; separation of Indigenous lands and, 15–16; seven generation linkages, 28; spirituality and, 198; TCUs, 36–37; ten lessons for principals, 148–57; traditional values, 25; transactional versus transformative, 158; women in roles of, 169
Learn-Ed Nations Inventory, 187
legacy, *60t*, 70–71; British Columbia, 95; leadership skills in next generation, 73
liberation psychology, 180
lifelong learning, 40
listening skills, 151
Locke, John, 16–17

McGregor, Davianna Pomaikaʻi, 22
McKay, Bert, 85
Māmalahoa Kānāwai (Law of the Splintered Paddle), 52
Manifest Destiny, 19, 31n8
Manitoba, 87
Manuelito (Chief), 166
math, science, and technology, 41
matriarchal societies, 17
matrilineal cultures, 169
mauli life force, 53–56
mediator role in administration, 113
Medicine Bluffs, 20–22
medicine wheel, 28
Medicine Wheel teachings, 32n15
memory: as a critical language, 26; collective, of the place, 29
mentors: achievement and career goals, 171–72; elders as, 195–96; gap in mentorship, 118; graduate programs, 130–31; Hawaiian respect for, *60t*, 69–70; positive mentoring, 175; for principals, 153; role models and, 175–76; student achievement related, 118. *See also* role models
micromanaging, 149–50
military service, 35
Mitʾākuyē Oyāśin (all my relations), 131
Mohatt, Jerry, 39

Mohawk, 20
Mother Earth, 18, 29
motivation: of educators, 171; for giving back to the community, 175–76; student, 174; studying, 163
MOWA Choctaw, 24, 31n11
multigenerational educational communities, 41
Muscogee Creek Nation, 39–40

NAIL program. *See* Native American Innovative Leadership (NAIL) program
Nanih Chaha, 24
National Conference of State Legislatures (NCSL), 200
National Indian Brotherhood (Canada), 77
National Indian Education Association (NIEA) Leadership Research Forums, 7–8, 201–202
National Indian School Board Association, 32n13
Native American community, use of term, 204n7
Native American Graves Protection and Repatriation Act (NAGPRA), 19, 22
Native American Innovative Leadership (NAIL) program, 162; background, 164; coursework perspectives, 164; critical theory framework, 168; data analysis, 163; findings, 164; intellectualizing about epistemologies, 170; research methods, 163; skill and knowledge sets, 164–66; study population, 163
Native American Rights Fund (NARF), 187, 200
Native culture, as an artifact, 104
Native Hawaiian peoples, 204n7
Native Indian Teacher Education Program (NITEP), 76–77; alumni leadership, 89–90; as exception, 100; authority to appoint faculty, 87; challenges, 92–94; cochair structure, 90; community-based relationships, 81; culturally responsive education

Native Indian Teacher Education
Program (NITEP) (*continued*)
and, 100; degree granted, 95n3, 96n8;
faculty, 82–83, 87, 88; field centers,
81, 87, 93, 95n7; founding, 77–78;
governance, 81; graduates' levels of
education, *89t*; graduates sharing
experiences, 84; holistic learning
model, 79–81, *80*, 82; indigeneity
addressed, 82; leadership, 86, 87, 90;
logo, 78, *79*; part-time program, 93;
program threads/themes, 83–85;
Raven's significance, 84–85; student
representatives, 92
Native regional corporations (Alaska),
108
Native studies, 41, 43
Navajo Community College (now Diné
College), 36; founding principles,
38–39
Navajo people, 166; Choctaw school
leader, 24–25; first tribal college, 36
Nāwahīokalani'ōpu'u Hawaiian Medium
School, 67–68
New Mexico, 24–25
New Zealand, 64
Nisga'a First Nation, 85
NITEP. *See* Native Indian Teacher
Education Program
No Child Left Behind Act (NCLB):
accountability and teacher
qualifications, 144; anti-Indigenous
practices, 199; as part of Western
paradigm, 184; data-informed
decision making, 166; described,
114n1; guidelines for Indigenous
education, 199; impact of, 199;
industrial model and, 105; need for
steady leadership, 119
nonconfrontational approaches, 117–18
non-Native community, second-level
relationships, 185
non-Native educators: relationship
building by, 195; respect for local
community, 14
nontraditional students, in teacher
education programs, 91

North Dakota, 46
Northern Arizona University (NAU), 142

Office of Indian Education, 162
Oglala Sioux Community College, 39
Oklahoma: Medicine Bluffs, 20–22;
removal policies, 24
Oneida, 20
online class sessions, 128–29
Onondaga, 20
Oppenheim, Opie, 78, *79*
oral history, TCUs, 38
oral tradition, 16; creation stories, 18;
Raven trickster, 78
Oregon, 200
Ouchi, William, management models,
107
ownership of school success, 152–53

Pacific Ocean, 70
parents: attitudes of, 161; community
involvement and, 172; goals and, 168;
participation in language immersion
program, 57; principals and, 156; role
of, 144, 172
participatory action, as methodology,
177
participatory decision making, 111
participatory democracy, 20
patriarchal societies, 17
pedagogical methods, 174
personal agency, 88
personnel issues, principal's focus and,
155, 156
physical behavior, in Hawaiian culture,
55
physical self, 80
Piailug, Mau, *60t*, 71
piko centers, 56
place: contemporary dialogs about,
28–29; engagement with the land,
29; power of, 26–29; traditional
knowledge and, 47; word
"Indigenous" means to be of a, 25. *See
also* sacred place
place, sense of, 15, 19; epistemological
perspectives and leadership, 167;

Hawaii, 22–23; linked to sacred ceremonies, 22; questions to pose, 30; sacred places, 18, 22

political activism, 43. *See also* advocates for Native concerns

political influences and paradigms, 7

Polynesian Triangle, 70

positive mentoring, 175

potlatch, 83, 96n9

power: Indigenous notions of, 7; of place, 26–29

power relations: as asymmetrical, 199; decolonization process and, 84, 196; between state and federal governments, 201; undermining self-determination, 195; unequal, dominant and Indigenous societies, 121

Pratt, Richard H., 18, 19, 26

principals: additional skills needed, 158–59; administrator standards, 145; Alaska Natives, 103; as instructional leaders, 152; community relations, 155; entry plan for, 157; hiring policies, 154–55, 156; knowledge and skills, 146–47; leadership and change, 166–71; leadership lessons, 148–57; leadership qualities, 158; leadership quality and characteristics, 154; listening skills, 25; Navajo high school, 24–25; parents and, 156; reservation schools, 142; settling into new role, 157–59; skills needed, 144–45

principals study (NAU), 142–43; administrator standards, 145; challenges, 144; conditions and issues, 143–44; educational goals, 144–45; parameters, 143; research design and methods, 143; research findings, 147–48; study population, 143. *See also* Diné-Hopi Cohort Leadership Program (DHCLP)

professional development: administrators, 119–20; culture-based, 180, 183–84; higher education programs in, 193;

Indigenously framed, 199; overview, 99–100. *See also* culture-based professional development (CBPD)

public education, 179; as economic tool, 41; assimilation and, 35; British Columbia Aboriginals, 78; Canadian failure of, 77; colonization in, 182; culture-based professional development as bridge, 183; ignorance of tribal governance and self-determination, 13; incorporating Indigenous ways of knowledge into, 185; indigenized education, 182; Indigenous ways of knowing (IWOK), 185–86; mainstream schooling practices critiqued, 184; mainstream values and, 41; role in CBPD model, 186

quincentennial commemoration, 28

Raven, 76, 78, 79, 84–85

Raven and the Sun story, 95

reactive responses, 154

reciprocity, in graduate programs, 122

reclamation and restoration models, 198

relationship building, 164–65

relationship, four levels of, 184–86

religious education, mainstream, 41

religious freedom, protection of, 19, 31nn6, 10

Religious Freedom Restoration Act (1993), 21, 22, 31n10

religious traditions: Medicine Bluffs, 20–21; prohibited, 18

relocation, 47

removal policies, 18; Alabama, 24; forced removal, 16, 40; Iroquois, 20; Oklahoma, 24; TCUs, 40

research: familiarity with localized knowledge, 196; informing leadership knowledge and practice, 131–32; need for, 161; needs in, 99; summarizing current state of, 193–94; tribal colleges and universities, 44–45

reservation-based schools, 142; diversity, 144; poverty barriers to achievement, 145; principals, 142; Southwestern, 143–44
reservations: as base for colleges and universities, 40; establishment of reservation lands, 16; natural resources on, 29
resistance, educational sovereignty and, 19–22
responsive leadership, 153–55
results assurance, 149
rights of tribes established, 21–22
"right things," doing the, 155
rigidity, avoiding, 165
risk taking by principals, 148
road map approach, 146–47
role models, 118; academic success and, 171; mentoring and, 175–76; positive cultural, 175. See also mentors
Ryan, Joan, 76, 85–87

"sacred": acknowledgment of, 18; separation from traditional homelands and, 16
sacred place, 18, 22; curricula, 32n13; leadership and, 29; questions to pose, 30
school governance issues, 144
science, 49
Seattle (Chief), 180
second-level relationships, 185
self-determination: action-oriented leadership, 3; as ongoing struggle, 7; bureaucrats and, 112; collective action and, 193; community role, 99; consciousness of goals of, 198; Euro-American settlers and, 5; through leadership practices and sovereign policies, 9; localized knowledge systems and, 195; localized leadership and, 13; misinterpretation consequences, 199; Native leaders as catalysts, 198; overview, 3, 7; power relations and, 121; tribal education laws, 200–201; use of term, 4–5
self-esteem, 174

self-identity, Western epistemologies, 135
Seneca, 20
sense of place. See place, sense of
Sinte Gleska College/University, 38, 39, 43
sites of conscience, 18–19, 26–27, 28, 32n14
Six Nations, 20
social agency, 5
social change, education and, 166
social class, 5
social identity, boarding schools, 27
social justice responsibility, 167–68
social problems: change agents, 134; Hawaiian, 61–62
social skills, 175
sovereignty: culture defined, 120–21; definition, 5; federal land policies and, 15; power relations and, 121
sovereignty in education: historical process, 3–4; overview, 3
spirituality: colleges and universities, 42; contemporary dialogs about, 28–29; Hawaiian, 52, 59t, 68–69; in Hawaiian culture, 53; historical links to place, 18; Indigenous leadership and, 198; Native studies and, 41
state compacts, 200
state departments of education, 201–202
State Education Agencies, 187
Stein, Wayne, 38
Sterling, Robert, 77
Sto:lo First Nation, 76, 95n1
storytelling, 38, 55
strategic goals, principals and, 149
stress, 154
struggling schools, 155–57
students: as main campus students, 136n3; behavior, 174; relationship building with, 164–65
student success: at colleges, 46; Hawaiian language immersion, 62; improving achievement gaps, 116; inequities, 198; mentorship and role modeling, 118; Native leadership influence on, 117–20; ownership of school success, 152–53; responsibility for learning

and behavior, 153; role models and, 171; tribal member resources and, 173; tribal values related, 174
survival knowledge, 180–81, 182–83
survival, tribal, vision of, 37

teacher education programs: Aboriginal education requirement, 90; British Columbia, 78; community-based relationships, 81; contradictions and tensions, 198–99; emphases needed, 193; ethos of extended family among students, 91; Eurocentric, 100; in Indigenous communities, 13; Indigenous values, 91; interactive learning communities, 83; leadership by students, 90–92; nontraditional students, 91; personal growth, 91–92; pipeline of Native educators, 198; prioritizing localized Indigenous knowledge, 195–96; research on, 194; student retention strategies, 91. *See also* higher education; Native Indian Teacher Education Program (NITEP)
teacher qualifications, NCLB standards, 144
teachers: as sole proprietors of knowledge, 104–105; quality of, 152–53
termination policy, 38
Theory Z, 106–108, *107t*
Theory Z + N, 108–10
third-level relationships, 185
Thompson, Nainoa, 57, 61, 63, 66, 71
Tlingit people, 103, 105
totem poles, 103–104, 105–106
tough issues and doing the right things, 155–57
tradition: Comanche resistance and, 17; education in, 16; historical role of, 16; impact on leadership, 169–71; place and, 47
traditional homelands, 16
traditional knowledge, in Hawaiian culture, 54–55
transactional leadership, 158

transformative leadership, 158
transitions, importance of, 157
transsytemic knowledge, 197
tribal celebrations, 175
tribal college movement: decision making and, 111; founders' vision, 36; reach out to people of tribal communities, 40–41
tribal colleges, use of term, 35
tribal colleges and universities (TCUs): accountability, 45–46; as distinctive, 35; Candeska Cikana Community College, 46; constituencies and leadership, 45–46; defining place-based identity of, 40–42; degrees offered, 44; early definition of mission, 38; economic prosperity modeled by, 42–43; education, 44; faculty and staff characteristics, 44; foundational characteristic, 36; founder challenges, 41–42; funding inequities, 203; governing boards, 46; history, 36, 38; honoring identity of, 46–47; influence in community life, 42; issues listed, 37; leadership, 36–37; leadership of, 203; learned and acquired knowledge, 37; multigenerational educational communities, 41; and other institutions, 47; political activism, 43; presidents, 46; research and scholarship, 44–45; shared governance, 42; social, political, and economic impact, 42–44; spiritual practices, 41, 42; student population, 45; student success, 46; tribal self-governance and, 37, 38; vision and purposes, 37–40; warrior traditions, 46. *See also* Haskell Indian Nations University; higher education
tribal control of education, 5; inclusive conversations, 144
Tribal Critical Race Theory, 121, 124, 182–83; culture-based professional development and, 183
Tribal Education Department National Association (TEDNA), 187

tribal education laws, 200–201
tribal leadership: Comanche, 21; participation in public education, 196; roles in education institutions, 202
tribally chartered colleges, 36
tribally controlled colleges, 36
tribal member resources, student success and, 173
tribal political representatives, 173
tribal schools, 161; public education versus, 179
tribal self-governance, 37, 38
tribal sovereignty: resistance to anti-Indigenous education, 8; tribal colleges and, 36
Turtle Island, 18
Tuscarora, 20

uniting others in a common purpose, *58t*, 63–64
University of British Columbia (UBC), 76; Faculty of Education cuts, 86; institutional changes, 88; Ts"kel graduate program, 88, 89
University of Northern Colorado, 162
urban Indians, 46–47. *See also* public education
U.S. Department of Education, 162

vision: British Columbia, 94; Hawaiian principles, 57, *58t*, 61; uniting others in a common purpose, *58t*, 63–64
voyaging canoes, 50–51; guiding principles, *58–60t*; legacy of, 70–71; modern feats, 63; navigational skills, 68; preparation for, 66; respect for mentors, 69

Washington state, 186
ways of knowing: colleges and universities, 41; curricular integration around, 30; defined, 6; Indigenous knowledge, 170; Native studies, 41, 43.
See also Indigenous ways of knowing (IWOK)
Western education, critique of, 184
Western paradigms versus Indigenous paradigms: administrative frameworks, 109–10; blending of, in NAIL program, 164; children caught in two worlds, 184; colonial power dimensions, 180; deficit model, 161–62; educational institutions and leadership theories, 3; educational models and, 5; educational paradigms compared, 181; education journey and, 4; forms of knowledge compared, 181; harmonious balance between, 177; higher education, 135; Indigenous purpose and methods, 203; intellectualizing process and, 17; leadership paradigms blended, 142; leadership styles compared, 158; mainstream school values, 117–18; nature of education, 8; No Child Left Behind Act, 199; non-Indigenous dispositions of administrators, 198–99; in partnership programs, 195; pedagogy in public education, 179; power of dominant society, 121, 133; professional development grants for Native graduate programs, 200; relative value of each, 121; religious practices, 18; shifting dominance in curricula, 194; social skills, 175; subtle attempts to colonize, 133; use of terms, 9n1; Western schooling as tool of colonization, 184
win/win culture, 150
wōksaṗe, use of term, 35
women in leadership roles, 169
workloads, 154
World Indigenous Nations Higher Education Consortium (WINHEC), 37
worldviews, Indigenous. *See* Indigenous worldviews